ARCHITECTURE POLITIC FORM
edited by Antonio De Rossi

En vain pourtant les Montagnes donnent-elles la facilité de faire de telles observations, si ceux qui les étudient ne savent pas envisager ces grands objets dans leur ensemble, & sous leurs relations les plus étendues. L'unique but de la plupart des Voyageurs qui se disent Naturalistes, c'est de recueillir des curiosités; ils marchent ou plutôt ils rampent, les yeux fixés sur la terre, ramassant çà & là de petits morceaux, sans viser à des observations générales. Ils ressemblent à un Antiquaire qui grateroit la terre à Rome, au milieu du Panthéon ou du Colisée, pour y chercher des fragmens de verre coloré, sans jetter les yeux sur l'architecture de ces superbes édifices. Ce n'est point que je conseille de négliger les observations de détail; je les regarde au contraire, comme l'unique base d'une connoissance solide; mais je voudrais qu'en observant ces détails, on ne perdit jamais de vue les grandes masses & les ensembles; & que la connoissance des grands objets & de leurs rapports fut toujours le but que l'on se proposât en étudiant leurs petites parties.

Horace-Bénédict de Saussure, Discours préliminaire, in Voyages dans les Alpes, précédés d'un essai sur l'histoire naturelle des environs de Genève, 1779

Introduction
The new urban question

Bernardo Secchi

I am deeply convinced that all the urban and metropolitan areas, not only in Europe, in the next decades will have to face three main problems. For as obvious as it may seems, they are of an environmental nature, related to mobility and social inequity. Taken as a whole, they define " the new urban question". Even more obvious is the fact that in each urban and metropolitan area these problems will be tackled in different ways and will have, if that is the case, specific solutions. On the other hand, it is not so obvious to say that every other problem will have to be related to these wider issues, and it is even less obvious that the solution to each one of these issues cannot be found independently from the other two, and that only the metropolitan and urban areas which will achieve this ambitious goal will acquire strength on the international stage. The problems related to mobility and their solutions, which often result in social exclusion and great environmental damage, are in the middle of this stage and have to be dealt with in ways which differ from the past, even the recent one.
1. It is not the first time, at least in western history, that a "urban question" becomes a key node, upon whose solution depend the chances of economic and social development. Take for example the "luxury debate" of the 18th century, that is the controversy about the appropriate setting for the potential or actual capitalist accumulation; the "housing issue" of the mid-19th century, that is the contradictions inherent to the shift from manufacturing to factory production, and the inevitable increase of the proletarian areas in the large industrial city; the *Grossstadt* issue, which is the object of the analysis by Simmel, Beniamin e Kracauer: namely the emerging from the "crowd" within the "im-measureable" space of the metropolis; finally, the birth of an "urban question", based on the "right to the city" and observed by many scholars, in particular by Henry Lefebvre e Michel de Certeau in the Sixties and Seventies. To put it roughly, every single time the structure of an entire economy and society has transformed itself, a urban question has emerged: at the beginning of the industrial revolution, during the shift from manufacturing to factory production, when the Taylorist-Fordist organization of the work gained weight, at the end of the Fordist system and at the beginning of what Bauman calls the liquid society, Beck the society of risk, Rifkon the society of access: a moment in which the growing individualization of society, a deeper awareness of the limited nature of environmental resources, and a growing faith in technological innovation create partially contrasting imaginaries, scenarios, policies and projects.

The "new urban question" defines itself as a chance for reflecting on this aspects and contradictions, and identifies itself with the call for the equal, and universally recognized, rights of citizenship, with the plea for the right to general accessibility as a part of these rights, with the demand for a management of the environmental resources which does not dump an unbearable load on the future generations, incapable of participating to the current decision-making process.
2. The answer to "urban questions" has always entailed the implementation of specific spatial devices, which in turn have called upon the responsibility of specific professionals –*in primis*, although not exclusively, architects and urban planners. It has always been felt that the solution to the problems posed by each "urban question" implied a new spatial organization, in which the features peculiar to the new situation were properly represented: to put it shortly, the bourgeois city, the impressionist metropolis, the modern city, and the fragmented and extended contemporary city. The infrastructures of mobility have been building the framework of these diverse cities and metropolies, interpreting their meanings and ambitions. Meanings and ambitions which in some occasion turned into widely imitated icons: from the great/large *boulevards* and the regularity of the haussmanian urban model to Robert Moses's urban highways; form an idea of hierarchically organized permeability to the pervasive myth of speed.
3. In the second half of the 20th century, an exorbitant price was paid to the myth of velocity. Enormous infrastructures, an increasingly hierarchized invitation to a growing motorization, have ploughed through territories and urban patterns, consequently building barriers hard to overcome, which in turn built *enclaves* coinciding with the settlements of specific social and activity groups. As a consequence, the permeability of the urban territory was sharply reduced, impeding or obstructing the movements of the citizens, their possibility of access to various places, gravely affecting the water flows and their biodiversity. It created areas of increasing congestion at the junctions and the ends, originating a process which only proportioned temporary solutions to the traffic problems, and led to an even worse situation. It is not by chance that today the issue of urban and metropolitan mobility is still a very conflictive one.
4. Every time they tried to deal with issues of mobility they started from the top, adding a big, expensive, and supposedly high-performing infrastructure to the existing network: a highway, a ring road, a subway. At first they were justified by the need to save time in long distance trips, but then they are used

for short and mid-distance trips. The hierarchical structure has always appeared as unavoidable, and has never been tentatively opposed by a isotropic one. We have never started from the bottom, from a detailed observation of the physiology of mobility, the idea of the territory and the city as a spongious body, highly permeable and therefore generally accessible. We have never considered the city as a "porous" body whose permeability must be increased to guarantee the citizens' their right to accessibility. Not even the traffic simulation models, which are in debt with hydraulic analogy, have analyzed in depht the activity of the water in a territory such as a river delta, where an important downflow is obstacled by the slope of the ground and the nature of the soils. A nature which is spongious, atriculated and scarcely hierarchic. We have never pointed out that railways and cars have different functions: the long distance the former, the short ones the latter. By simply juxtaposing them, we lost any chance of improvement.
5. The need for a different energy policy, to reduce CO_2 emissions, to bridge the social gap, to resist in competition in the long term, will possibly lead us to a deeper reflection on the future of our metropolis; to build scenarios instead of predictions; to consider "what would it happen if...", and not only declare what we would abstractly like. To call upon references which diverge from the old ones. To take a critical distance from the idea that the only way to order these territories, which appear chaotic only to the blinded eye, is to build hierarchies, among the different infrastructures, the accessibility of the different places, and among the different subjects, individuals and entities, which have access to it. The studies presented in this volume are a step in this direction.

Antonio De Rossi

Architecture on a GrandeScala

1. Let us immediately clarify a possible misunderstanding. By architecture on a *GrandeScala* we do not mean an architecture of big shapes or big dimensions. The term has nothing to do with bigness either. Nor with the "territory of architecture", or with an expansion of the urban project to a territorial scale. On the contrary, it willingly pursues terminological ambiguity, typical of cartography, between the representation on the small and the *grandeScala*.

We could say that we want to start further upstream, from a conceptual -before than physical- place, in which the definition, denomination and naturalization of the topics is still considered unfinished. A place where the theme is the setting out of the critical field for the scientific debate on the issues. Our point of departure is the following: after a long phase of "creative destruction", which since the Nineties has determined the extension of the processes of physical transformation of the space to the integral scale of the territory, we -not only the architects- long for a return of the urban and territorial project. We also welcome the return of something even more scandalous, after years of theorizations -and sublimations- about the poetics of fragments and urban labyrinths. In the wake of the progressive fading of the spatial categories in the contemporary building and perceptive processes we are looking forward to the project of *shaping the city and the territory*.

From this point of view the signs are many, ranging from the recent international convention *Le Grand Pari de de l'agglomération parisienne* to other stances and moments of debate. In a time where the modern dream of an integral transformation of space seems to have come true once and for all, it is clear that this "need for a shape", which materializes itself in the back-shift towards a reflection on the morphologic sense and meaning of transformations, cannot be completely naive. That is why it is worthy to re-discuss in a critical light some of the lines of investigation -in particular in the Italian and European context- that have dealt with the topic of the physical and morphological project of the contemporary territory.

2. Before analyzing the four topics that have represented an attempt to re-config-ure the issue of urban and territorial transformation, I feel compelled to point out some questions and ambiguities -which I hope might be fruitful- concerning the term *GrandeScala*. The very concept of *grandeScala* has been deliberately excluded from the horizon of theoretical reflection for a long historical period. On the road paved by Walter Benjamin and other 20th Century intellectuals, Carlo Ginzburg and Giovanni Levi took the *jeu d'échelles* as a founding and irreducible factor of a historical research that is theoretically -and politically- re-observed through the lens of micro-history. The rebirth of the term *GrandeScala* cannot leave aside that season of conceptual advances simply because of a revival of the past. The *GrandeScala* that we are dealing with cannot and must not ignore the image of the *jeu d échelles*, the idea of an *inclusive* and *thick scale*. It is the exact opposite of a technocratic vocation: it is a chance to reflect on the eradication and denial of the *ordering value* of the architectural project within a contemporary reality made of reduced, simplifying types of functionalism. It is an ordering value that obvi-ously does not concern only shapes and morphologies, but also the formation and migration of symbols, the economic income, the intertwining histories and geographies, in a whirl of rapid transformations and overlaying physical facts: the language of stones comes into existence.
It is an ordering value that cannot be taken as neutral.
At the same time the term wants to cast some light on an emerging problematic aspect concerning the "*grandeScala*" that, despite being not conceptually detach-

able from the *jeu d échelles*, increasingly needs punctual and specific answers. The architectural history of the 20th Century tried to provide different answers on this issue -at times by means of shortcuts and reductions- along a path that saw the alternation of various monumental styles, new dimensions of modernization, and of debates on *civic centers* and public spaces. From this point of view the image of the *GrandeScala* is meant to bring back on the stage the issue of morphology, its connection to politics, and the need to rethink the geographic dimension in relation to the dialectic between the contemporary acceleration of transformation and the unavoidable process of physical stratification in time. The latter is an element which is everyday more disregarded and consigned to oblivion.

3. Great urban project, landscape, scattered settlement, infrastructural project: it is mainly around these four thematic axes that in the last twenty years the very chance for architecture to affect the physical asset of space has been revolving, at a time when the economic and social changes brought about by the powerful neoliberal season have opened the door to a new era of territorial transformation. It is now possible to retrospectively measure the positivity and the missed opportunities for each of these topics.
The issue of the *urban project*, which started to take shape in the Eighties, has definitely been an extraordinary conceptual instrument to break in that deadlocked situation between plan and individual projects, but it has been especially important to restate the importance of physicality in the transformative process. In this way not only was the project retaking its role of an evaluation tool of the space transformation ideas: it was also becoming one of the funding components of the entire transformation. The limit of that season, especially as far as the Italian experience is concerned, lies in the progressive independence of the physical and composing *côté* of the urban project from the general process. Because of it, it lost most of its initial strength and authority, which resided in its role as a *means*, not only as an *end*. At a time when the urban project was turning into an act of self-sufficient poetic, trivially demanding to realize itself by virtue of its very shapes, in Italy it was losing its innovative impetus, that lied in its "high" dialogic and political potential. This contributed to pave the way to a new, powerful *vague* of the urban project in which the central role assigned to the design of external surfaces and morphologies was directly proportional to the poverty of the intend-

ed urban environment, rather than to the several millions of squared meters built and put on the stage.

Nevertheless, it is around the theme of the *landscape* that many of the expectations of the last decades have revolved, and not only in the architectural dimension. For a long time the landscape essentially represented a new and original perspective, that highlighted the overall data and the connections between things, breaking the traditional disciplinary fences. The landscape-oriented way of looking was the cultural and interpretative answer to a new physical and conceptual dimension, put at stake by the transformations of the contemporary territory. But after the shift from the project *of* landscape to the project *of the* landscape, we witnessed a harsh conflict aimed at assigning the topic to the single disciplines and professional duties and powers. Paradoxically, due to the absence of a critical debate between the different fields, the landscape eventually recreated the umpteenth fence, a fragmented and sector-based vision of space: precisely what it wanted to deny and get over with in the first place. Moreover the focus on the landscape, the programs, and the territorial substratum did not succeed in turning these issues into internal elements of the territorial project; it essentially produced "negative" cards of passive constraints. And landscape planning has rarely managed - from both an interpretative and an operational point of view- to positively confront the settlement transformation that was taking place at the time. As a consequence, the landscape gradually lost its subversive and problematic charge to become a naturalized, appeasing, and often comforting object.

The other main thematic and conceptual focus has been the *extended city* and the *scattered settlements*. In particular for the Italian case, where this topic came in contact with transformation modes which were common to all European countries and with Italian peculiarities as well -such as the key role of incrementalism and individual mobilization in the modification of the territory. This scattered settlements phenomenon has been functioning as an extraordinary descriptive lens to narrate the generation and functioning mechanisms of the territories outside the stable urban spaces. Furthermore, it has showed the existence of a peculiar model of organization of space in the territories of the so-called Third Italy: the Po Plain and the North-East, the Adriatic city and so on, all defined by an economic and social structure rooted in the small and medium family enterprise. The need to understand these mechanisms implies a radical revision of some of the genetic

-and metaphysic- codes of architecture forged in the course of modernity. Unfortunately this analytic refinement of the descriptions rarely managed to turn into a critical and operative knowledge. Politics never really took a planning stance on this question, which is of vital concern not only for the territory, but also for the economic destiny of this country. There is a lingering *laissez-faire*, already over the time limit. At the same time some simplifying readings of the phenomenon are coming back to surface: they reduce it to a mere environmental problem, an issue of building speculation, of extension and expansion of the urban surface starting from an ideal "center" (which one, though?).

The last one to appear was the issue of *infrastructures*. The project of infrastructures was the guiding light for many hopes. It represented the possibility to direct the critical visions of the landscape and of scattered settlements on a very operational issue. That is to say, the infrastructure acts as a *fil rouge*, which, while crisscrossing space and sewing up time, brings about a reflection on the constructed settlements, environment, and landscape, in comprehensive and overall terms. The infrastructure acts as an agent that is not only a *generator,* but also a potential *developer* and *planner* of scattering settlements. Despite the intents made by architecture, the lack of dialog between politics and the operative sectors is a usual problem. Few are the actual achievements. The infrastructural project has gradually got involved in an issue of aesthetization of the infrastructural object.

4. On the other hand, the lack of an actual implementation of these four important thematic and conceptual overtures cannot be adduced *tout court* -as it usually is- to a mere lack of short-circuiting of the planning disciplines with the world of politics and the operational contexts. To maintain this means to assume that there is a correct theoretical core, and that criticism comes from a mere transferring of knowledge to the application field. In line with the epistemological trends of the last decades, the issue should rather be overturned. The lack of implementation of the research lines shows that there is a weak link in the very relationship between theory and practice, and at the same time the absence of a reflection on this critical node shows the heavy epistemological conservatism and politically-based simplifications which define Italian architectural culture.

In spite of this, many of the intuitions and critical interpretations embedded in those four overtures remained valid. Moreover there is still the issue of the physical and morphological project of the territory, given the limits -especially the national ones- of projecting and planning large areas. The depletion of environmental quality and impoverishment of the constructed landscape are widely is a perceived. As for social security, it is also hard to understand which is the objective component and which the induced one. But the gap on the territorial transformations between the citizens and the technical and political world is widening, enough to question and disconcert the right of citizenship itself.

The case of the Turin-Lyon high-speed line in the Susa Valley is paradigmatic, but the examples could be many. As for public opinion, the great projects and transformations of the territory are increasingly leading to the creation of an inextricable maze of relevant critiques and parascientific concerns, between legitimates suspects and conspiracy theories. On the other hand the predominant *modus operandi* is usually rough, camouflaged by an anachronistic technocratism whose main goal is to hide a heavy cultural and projectual deficit. And the theater of the media is blowing on the fire of these increasingly conflictive issues. They all forget -often in bad faith- that one thing is proper information and democratic dissent, and another one is to stage a permanent psychodrama, aimed at creating a climate of everyone against each other that leaves behind only scorched earth, and that is leading to the gradual disappearance of differences, and of any form of civil cohabitation. It also fuels the impossibility to talk about the technical and political value of things, beyond the rhetoric and the pre-packaged images.

Nonetheless, in the last few years there have been important experiences in the opposite direction. The case of the Susa Valley, and the government-appointed TAV Observatory, shows that it is possible to open democratic negotiations seeking the *reconstruction of the points of view* and the creation of a common ground. But the most interesting cases probably concern the middle and large cities, thanks to the experience of the Complex Urban Programs. An important experience, because it could create the intention of a physical transformation and redevelopment of places, starting from the *problems*, destructuring the sectional visions and particular interests, to eventually restructure them through negotiation and dialog.

5. To tackle the issue of the *GrandeScala*, that is the physical and conceptual dimension of territorial transformation, a new way of conceiving the intersection between morphology and politics must be found. We are not going to talk about

decisional processes and *governance*, since it is not part of our duties, powers and capacity. We would rather focus on the connection between *politics* and *shape*; on how the morphological dimension can assist the political dimension in rethinking the transformations of the territory beyond the contemporary deadlock; on how the political dimension can help the morphological one not to behave a self-sufficient and self-referential practice. From this point of view the morphologic dimension can no longer avoid thinking its relationship with the political dimension as a problematic node, which requires thematization and scientific observation. To consider the connection between morphology and politics as just a sequence, and to regard politics as a technique for the implementation of the project of the shape, not affecting the underlying visions of the two words, becomes not only naive and ineffective, but also a guilt. Anyways, it is not only a matter of concreteness and effectiveness: the *GrandeScala*, seen in the particular angle of the *jeu d échelles* as a *thick and comprehensive scale*, is meant to act as a lens to understand the contemporary processes of physical construction of the space in academic and scientific terms.

6. In order to rethink this relationship we must start from the achievements of the recent studies, which constitutes the prerequisites for the frame and the background of this reflection.
First of all the awareness of a building process based, as we said, on a "clash between rationalities and independent and irreconcilable strategies", in which "everyone of them is at the same time limited and absolute: limited because it is built on simplifications and reductions; absolute because it completely controls a portion of space by imposing boundaries".
Secondly, the key role of incrementalism and of an indifferent, "by catalog" planning culture in the urban and territorial transformation processes.
Thirdly, the fragmentation of the decisional processes and the intensifying dispute between the different levels of territorial governance. In the fourth place, the predominance of the argumentative modes in respect to the transformations of rhetoric and metaphorical images, now detached from their original meanings.
Finally, a generalized *laissez-faire* concerning the transformations, that is changing within the Italian context: from a simple growth factor is turning into a limit to economic development.

This is not just the result of a deterioration of the picture, and of the political cultures. It is precisely the new dimension of the transformations, which radically puts at stake the integral structure of the physical space, and especially the very idea of territory as a *generative matrix* of the land fixed capital, causing deep downfalls of the forms of politics. The comparison with the new problems posed by the new transnational forms of the economy is almost too obvious.

This reflects on the difficulty of constructing real and effective forms of metropolitan government in large Italian conurbations. In this case as well, the problem is not simply a lack of a legislative reference that would allow the creation of a metropolitan government. This is a consequence, rather than a cause. The problem lies in the difficulties of conceptualizing new and original projects on a *GrandeScala* in political terms, before starting to manage them; projects that destructure the way in which the relationship between project, politics and territorial planning activity have traditionally been established. The result is often the incapacity to respond to the external challenges, going hand in hand with an increasing local competitiveness in a race to the bottom. This coincides with the "solidification" of administrative borders into physical and project-related borders within neighboring places that should be building alliances instead.

There is a price for all this, every day higher and more blatant; not only in terms of environmental quality, but also of preserving and recreating shared democratic values and economic development. And this is exactly what the *GrandeScala* intends to thematize, starting from the intuition -already verified in the practice- that in this respect the morphological data is not an indifferent and super-structural element, a simple dependent variable of the transformation projects, as it is usually treated. On the contrary, only using the morphological data as a probe and an agent might we try to rewrite in positive terms the relationships between politics and territory.

7. As we said: the morphological data is not indifferent. Before further developing this topic, it is necessary to critically delve, from the perspective of a new positivity and effectiveness in the territorial planning project, into the contemporary causes for the *crisis of the form*. By this term I mean both the transformation of meaning and sense of a few spatial categories traditionally defined, and the dialectic relationship between *forms of politics* and *forms of space*. Given the context, is it still

possible to imagine the project as a place capable of orientating and giving meaning to the single acts of transformation? Is it possible to think of a new, unseen morphologic value of the project? Or maybe – as a consequence of failure of the traditional modus operandi in shaping the transformative phenomena – should we accept as the only viable path the magnification of the fragment and the creation of introflexed places and spaces (in which an internal order, impossible in the outside world, can still be pursued)?

A primary cause for the crisis is definitely *incrementalism*, and the very speed of the transformation process. The incremental construction on the territory undermines any idea of project that holds in its genetic code the fundamental goal of implementing and achieve its own formal design. In the last few years there has been an ongoing debate on this issue, especially in relation to the discussion on the extended city. Both the need to take an open time horizon as a background for the project, and the chance to think in terms of flexibility seem good options to face incrementalism. In this framework, the images of flexibility and permanent metamorphosis have been growing like a sort of myth, and like totalizing, pervasive metaphors. The erasure of the time and physical stratification problems, at the time of building and changing spatial orders, effectively shows how these images and metaphors are founded on simplifications and reductions. At the same time, the debates on flexibility and transformations have rarely questioned from an epistemological point of view the fact that the achievement of the project goals, also in morphological terms, may not coincide with the fulfillment of its formal design. This is a very sensitive issue, linked to some of the ontological categories of the modern project and to the project authorship, seen as a cardinal element of architectonic discipline.

A further factor of crisis is the metamorphosis that, from the early Eighties, radically modified the concept of *public*, and of what today is regarded and defined as *space* and *public good*. It is an immense issue, only addressed here in relation to a particular aspect. The mutated idea of a public undermines the morphological dimension in a very subtle way: it threatens the relationship between use and form, rights and spatial structures, which are generally seen as a given, fixed and stable elements, untouched by the ongoing radical transformations. It is easy to understand the desire not to question this relationship: to modify the idea of public in its physical implications means to imagine -a hard task indeed- the building processes of the territory without these looms, frames and weaves which give sense to the whole, and without the legitimacy of the disciplines -urban planning *in primis*- that deal with spatial projects. Yet it is enough to observe the metamorphosis of the very concept of public space -the public use of a space which is increasingly coming from a private spatial context- to understand the need to rethink this category, from a pre-established *input* to an *output* of the project, which is to be carefully defined every single time.

A third critical factor is the transformation, especially in the last 15-20 years, of the *dimension of "things"*, and the way they *morphologically relate* to each other in space. As far as the notion of dimension is concerned, a self-explanatory example is the metamorphosis of the spaces dedicated to movement and logistics, inside the productive and infrastructural places. As for the relational mode of the different territorial objects, Bernardo Secchi cunningly created the idea of the "right distance", that is the perceptive shift of the ways in which the different functions must relate to each other. A shift determined by the expansion of an idea of *privacy*, safety, distance and separation from polluting activities and so on. This causes a simultaneous process of dilatation and rarefaction of the constructed space, through which the traditional ways to conceive the physical and relational links between the "things" are gradually fading away.

A fourth problematic point is determined by the way in which the project deals with the *economic dimension*. An issue with two sides. On the one hand, on a territorial scale, the always faster variation of fluxes and chances prevents the traditional planning *modus operandi* from giving a morphological background to transformations. To put it simply: there is no time to strengthen, stratify and implement morphologies. This determines an indifference of the ways in which the transformation relates to pre-existent territorial structures, now even theorized by contemporary architectural culture. From the other hand, on a more punctual scale, the considerable surplus generated by the building and real estate market defines an essentially univocal relationship between the economic dimension and morphology. There is no interest in exploring from the perspective of the market a differentiation that regards the construction products but also morphology and the territory, if not in the trivial terms of a localization. Most of all, there is no *feedback* between the final arrangement of the physical and morphological project and the economic dimension of the transformation project; the economic *target* of the intervention unidirectionally predetermines types, forms and technologies, frustrating any chance to work on the assembling phase of the materials on different scales. We can take as an example the missed chances on the modulation of the relationship between private interior space and public urban environment. From this point of view we could almost say that in the last few years the tendency to trivialize has been seen as an actual strategy by the different actors.

A fifth problematic issue is the relationship between morphology and *conformity to the procedure.* The morphological and planning qualities, since they cannot be categorized into parameters and procedures, come from public technicians and decision-makers, increasingly excluded from the processes. Due to their incompatibility with parameters and procedures, they represents a problem rather than a potential value for the technical-administrative process, and are thus replaced by an idea of quality based on the compliance to quantitative data. In a time of incrementalism, the only possible formal quality seems to be that which can be pursued through embellishment and *jolisation.*

A sixth critical aspect is represented by the way in which the *technical and political imaginaries* structure and bring back the issue of territorial transformations. The work of interpretation aimed at the construction of the problems is increasingly infrequent. On the contrary, it is the pre-established images and rhetoric that define the problems. If we think for example of the public imaginary on the "door" (urban door, door to Europe, etc.), now free from every reference to reality, wandering through the mind of politicians, technicians and architects, looking for any chance to turn into a devastating solidified metaphor. From this point of view, a study on the deep metamorphosis of architectonic metaphors in the last decades would really be enlightening. Already an extraordinary instrument of modernity, able to prefigure through epiphanies and short-circuits the city to come, the metaphor seems to be willingly seeking its own trivialization: with the contribution of the media, it is turning into the main place of exchange between the technical, political and civic world. And more. Of primary importance is also the sclerotization of the idea of a physical transformation of space which is essentially based on *ideal types*, and together with other critical views it contributes to the contemporary phenomenon of the gradual *disappearance of scales.* To the problem of environmental quality we could answer with the creation of parks and gardens; to the problem of traffic with ring roads, and roundabouts with a tall streetlight in the center. Very often today it is the by-catalog technical and project solutions that are looking for a problem to be solved, rather than the problems looking for solutions. In this context, the definition of specific morphologies in relation to a particular territory appears as an out-fashioned and superfluous data: the constant reference to the landscape and the differences and identities of the territory do not look like concrete elements, but like a rhetoric as appeasing as the space enhancing techniques.

8. A last element is represented by the crisis which is affecting the edges and the limits of the project, be they profession-related or sector based margins, political or administrative boundaries. Edges and borders increasingly pervaded by the tension caused by the clash between different powers, that are deeply affecting the morphology of objects and territories. A morphology in which the recurrent triviality of the physical results is inversely proportional to the refinement of the reflections on the *governance*, or the energy used by the actors in the conflicts related to the exercise of power. If, as Carlo Olmo said, the issue of the definition of boundaries has represented one of the main places of knowledge -i.e. in the 18th Century- of the modern age, today the boundary -often naturalized and never questioned- represents the utmost manifestation of the contemporary political and morphological crisis.

Nonetheless, after this partial but schematic outlook, it seems that the crisis may not depend entirely on factors external to the project. It might also be a matter of comprehension and conceptualization of the metamorphosis of the overall picture, in which the transformations of the territory are inscribed: the incremental dimension, the complicated regulatory and legislative frame, the *ad libitum* multiplication of the actors involved by the transformative processes, the speed and continuous changes of pace imposed by the economical and political system. Most of the times, as we said, the answer is to project "by catalog", accepting the modes of the processes; occasionally, the choice is to increase the specific weight of the *design* and to intensify the authorial data of the project.

What is nonetheless striking is the existence -observed on a daily basis in ordinary activities - of wide, potentially workable margins. This would imply a radical revision and "weakening" of the will of the project to be first of all a formal prophecy coming true, and of the demiurgic nature of the planner as well. Is it possible to imagine a project aimed at an effective use of space, that starts from the centrality of morphology -thus radically different from the urban planning based on procedures and processes- without pinning its success on a solidification of forms? Is it possible to try to establish a morphology using the form as a means and not only as an end? Is it possible to think of a project that *thematizes* the dimensions of incrementalism and economy, turning them into a *data internal to the project*?

9. To try to redefine this challenging relationship between politics and territory, between the market and the practices through the morphologic project, there are some useful long-term observations on the cultural context of Turin, aimed at establishing a conceptual benchmark. Starting from a cultural *habitus* that -in the wake of Luigi Pareyson's hermeneutic lesson and of Gianni Vattimo's interpretation of Nietzsche and Heidegger- unveils the connection between subject and object in "weak" and anti-metaphysical terms. That affects the way of conceptualizing architecture, seen not as an *object*, but as a practice which concerns the territory in its physical and conceptual entirety in the first place. As Roberto Gabetti wrote in 1983 in his long essay *Progettazione architettonica e ricerca tecnico-scientifica nella costruzione della città*, "all the interventions on the territory can be seen as a product of the building sector." Architectonic planning thus regards all the objects that are "fixed on the territory", both "in the presence of territorial structures (mountains and rivers, cities and roads)" and "in the absence of new structures, in the perspective of a reorganization of the existing ones."
The field of reference of architecture therefore is that of the *constructed environment*, in its concreteness and plot of "canals, roads, railways and houses". For this very reason, architecture "cannot be a qualitative detail, irrelevant to the nature of the production", be it the "small scale of the house" or the "planetary scale of the territory". This *tout court* focus on environment depicts the core of architecture not as a body of rules and precepts, but as a "clinical method", considered as "the strategic orientation of knowledge, aimed at a scientific self-construction towards the individual dimension". A clinical method that is to be applied to the environment as well, since "the relevant specificity not only regards some settled or settling people, but depends on defined physical structures of the territory [...] and their specificities". And before dealing with the transformative project, the focus must be the "micro-structural interpretation of the urban and territorial space",

highlighting the critical and hermeneutic value of the project, confronting a naturalized way of posing -and therefore solving- the problems.

Both the anti-metaphysical and weakening actions on the object to favor a system
of connections dealing with the idea of environment, and the importance of the
clinical method go hand in hand with the intensifying and expanding dialogic value
within the project. That is why we cannot leave aside the political culture of Turin
-from Norberto Bobbio on- that took the importance of the dialogic act and the
building of shared position as the core of its rationale. In this context the architect
is simply an "operator among other operators", and the project loses its meaning
and sense precisely in that interaction and dialog between all the actors, revolving
around the intended transformations. In recent years this have led some other Turin-based interpreters -Carlo Giammarco, Luigi Falco, Gianni Torretta- to compare
the project to a type of "table", a "plot" able not only to prefigure morphological transformations, but also to function as a point of reference *tout court* for the
transformative hypothesis. Therefore the project is seen mainly as the stage and
scenery that allow the different actors to build a common language and images in
order to open a dialog. This highlighting of the dialogic value of the planning activity cannot -willingly or unwillingly- leave aside the "tragic" quality, ontologically
internal to the idea of modern project, which lies in its very *regulatory quality.*

10. Our *idea of a morphological project,* in relation to the transformations of the
physical, and -especially- conceptual territory of the *GrandeScala*, is the one accepting the contextual -morphological and political- conditions we have described
so far, and trying to "internalize" them, turning them into a positive factor and an
active agent in the planning activity. Nevertheless, the long term alignment with
this perspective entails a "weakening" of the traditional epistemological statute
of the project, which is looked at awkwardly in the field of architecture. It means
to reduce that typical quality of "formal prophecy" -characterizing the aforementioned project of modernity-, for which self-fulfillment is the main goal and the
basis of its tension and legitimacy; to increase the strategic and dialogic value of
the project, its instrumental and conceptual nature, aimed at thematizing and defining objectives, scales, dimensions, relational modes. It implies the prevalence of
the *interpretative* on the *constructive* quality. The prevalence of the "trace", in the
words of Carlo Olmo, on "taxonomy". This does not mean to deny the asserting di-

mension of the project, its regulatory quality. On the contrary, it means to change its sign, reducing its self-referential and self-legitimating nature.

At the same time, such a declination of the project-related activities entails a closer focus on the hidden and latent meanings, on the "potentials" to be actualized. An improved visibility, an *openness* that uses the indeterminacy and the pre-political quality of metaphorical images, following a line of research already envisaged by Giuseppe Dematteis through the idea of a "poetic geography". The effects of this unveiling and opening process can be very concrete as well. Apart from the unsolved functional and environmental problems, most of the criticality of the contemporary territorial project is determined by the very reductionist and sectional way in which the problems are *constructed*: a deconstruction of the apparent problems, and rewriting of the questions -referring once again to the key role of the *jeu d échelles*- that can have a fall-out effect also on the economic dimension of the project.

11. This aspect of the project-related activities conceptualizes the overcoming of incrementalism and its prohibitive costs (economical, functional, environmental, political), insomuch as it does not relate the issue to an external political rationality; this in turn would be able to legitimate an inherent rationality of forms -the dream of most architects-, to which all the actors must adequate. To try to contrast it, one must accept and internalize the rationale, the dust-like and temporally-open quality, with the goal of re-planning them into a project-process of a superior order, and into a different "cadre d'ensemble".

This planning approach deals in analogous terms with the relationship between the economic and morphologic dimension, but with a double meaning. In the light of the ever faster variation of chances and fluxes, the perspective of the *GrandeScala* represents the possibility to provide the local systems with a "background", to *morphologically infra-structure* them in order to improve their duration against a horizon in which, as Giuseppe Dematteis wrote, "to design the territory means to represent diversity, in terms of possible local answers to global changes". Moreover, the relationship between economy and territorial morphology, never taken into account, must be thematized as an internal element of the designing activity. Apart from its connection with this planning vision, the point is its economic value, put at stake by morphology. This means that we should evaluate not only the negative costs, but also the positive economic external effects, determined by the different urban and territorial morphologic patterns.

12. This particular view, fueled by both the late local theorizations and the valuable epistemological contributions, regards the project as a type of "negotiation table" and a "plot", through which the initial transformative hypothesis can be built. It is the planning configuration that, through the creation of a common language which has a morphologic nature as well, allows the different positions to "condense", thus becoming pronounceable, modifiable, and convergent. In this picture, the morphological project is not only the end: it is also the *means* through which the transformation can take place.

This aspect of the project regards the building of a territorial morphology as the setting out of looms, frames, weaves and structures. In order to do so, it uses the individual materials found *in* and *on* the ground, its goal being not the imposition of further shapes on space, but the *emergence of figures creating meaning* from existing processes and elements.

In this approach to the project, key is the operation of *recognition*, *reorganization* and *representation*, in which determinants -as theorized by Roberto Gabetti and Aimaro Isola- are the acts of "replacement-revival", "comment-expansion", "contiguity-continuity". It is an idea of territorial project based on the *centrality of morphology*. It is a form whose beauty and legitimacy do not spring from a mere "structural" quality. Its value is measured in its capacity to hold things in tension, fostering knowledge, and therefore action. It is a form which does not freeze things; on the contrary, it is a *tendency towards*, ontologically focusing not on *objects*, but on the way in which their *relationships* are structured.

Of vital importance is the attempt to shift from an idea of project basically seen as the prescription of quantities and qualities of the transformations, according to non-negotiable rationalities -guaranteed by the experts according to compliance criteria- towards a *culture of argumentation*, able to determine places of living much before it plans the spatial and productive organization according to regulated procedures. To do so, the project must be able to radically affect the technical and political *imaginaries*: by denaturalizing the well-established manners to analyze the topics -the pre-packaged, by-catalog solutions, rather than the solutions depending upon the problems; using the shifts of meaning as departure points for the project work. From this point of view, in the contemporary society, where the analysis of the phenomena is a redundant and meticulous process, never colliding with the times and facts of politics, the first duty of the project -if observed as an instrument of knowledge- is to try to rewrite the apparently given reality, stepping away from the critical resetting of the project-related themes.

The project for an architecture of the *GrandeScala* also holds as a prerogative the reflection on time; on the interweaving, contemporary long-term transformations; on the possibility for space to comprehend different temporal dimensions and historical in-depths, that take the civilizing and cultural processes into account. It is on this aspect that the match of a radical action towards a truly contemporary analysis of the right of citizenship is played. A project which has an inner *eco-sustainable* nature, because it deals with an idea of transformation that envisages the maximization of the existent through its proper interpretation, geographical and environmental in the first place. Even if most of the times it tends to be left apart, the shape and the territorial patterns are all but indifferent to energy and sustainability issues. And the idea of a project of territorial transformation, able to regard as materials of the project not only the building features *on the ground*, but their *very substratum*, can really represent a turning point with the way in which the physical modification of space is seen. In this way the traditional founding system of values of architecture is radically transformed.

This ensemble of reflections shows that the issue of architecture on a *GrandeScala*, with its dialogic *jeu d échelles* between the morphologic dimension and the political horizon, is quite an original one -despite it stems from a crossing of pre-existing objects, phenomena and perspectives. The optic of the *GrandeScala* brings to light an absence and a deficiency, and the subsequent need to take an important action on these crucial nodes, in between pedagogy and politics.

Alessandro Armando
Giovanni Durbiano

The values of others

27

Turin. Residential area of Dora Park, photo, Alessandro Cane

Alessandro Armando
and Giovanni Durbiano

The values of others

I. Operational context
Specificity of a project-related research – definition of the scale – preliminary architecture and discursive practices – consensual processes – cultural debts and political milieu – the ordinary as a paradigm.

1. Despite being incomplete, scarcely cumulative and methodologically not coordinated, the research experiences studying the geomorphology of the territory that are contained in this volume can be seen as the expression of a specific conceptual consistency. Be they studies for large plans or transformative guidelines, readings of geographical schedules or drawings of infrastructures, this planning research move within a concrete field of work. A work in which the repetition of some issues relative to the legitimacy of the mandate of the intellectual technician, the functions of the design in the decision-making process, and the relation between architectural figures and political projects define an operating horizon that is sufficiently defined so as to be conceptualized.
What holds together the diverse lines of research concerning architecture on the *GrandeScala* -conducted by different groups in different times- is not a cultural identity, but an often implicit questioning of epistemological borders. An approach stemming from the acknowledgment of the past failures and contradictions, that measures itself with the systems of material productions of territorial and spatial transformation, that from the experience of its limits derives its own consistency, defining its own specific autonomy. The causes of this relative specificity are essentially of an empirical order.
2. First of all it is a matter of scale. The research studies address a need of housing quality that cannot be theorized in advance. As a consequence, the topics that

are dealt with concern a normative, social and physical framework that cannot be previously defined in the operational mandate. To delimit the scale of intervention (where "scale" does not mean the geometrical dimension, but the order of the issues to be covered) is part of the planning problem that must be tackled. The absence of set of rules formalizing the definition of the project-related problems and the limits of the work to do (which on the contrary allow the professional ethics to be effective), constantly deflects the research activity towards a multitude of different levels to be acted upon. In other words, the project-related research creates its own scale of references: it defines the topics, identifies the instruments, chooses the designated actors, and establishes the physical boundaries of transformation through a peculiar development of the clients' mandate. The specificity of this research is primarily caused by the impossibility to predetermine the structure of the scale of intervention, and as a consequence, to define it in the course of the research.

3. Another peculiar feature of these experiences lies in the temporal phase of the process in which they are inescapably carved. As a matter of facts, this project-related research situates itself in a well-defined condition of suspension: in between political choice (determined by the dialog between the actors and the powers involved) and its implementation (determined by technical criteria of data conformity). Therefore it is above any translation in terms of the building industry, and above the sirens' enchanting call of architectural languages. This condition of "preliminary" architecture, even if it is seen as a limit because of its partiality, constitutes a privileged point of view to assess the legitimacy and the argumentative potential of the project outside the rigid structures defined by technical duties and powers and political choices. The construction of the scale of intervention is complemented by the definition of the dialog with the actors involved, and

especially of the discursive practices through which to empirically organize the argumentation.

4. In parallel to the first two features, there is a third element granting some degree of specificity to this research: the difficulty to measure the effectiveness of a project on the level of its material realization. This condition, which in the perspective of a traditional planner represents the maximum frustration, can be overturned in prerogative if observed from a wider perspective. The legal constraints on building actually imply an effort of prefiguration that leads the way to the final result through a multiplicity of plans, in which the final form of a single product is not the only possibility. The work on the definition of the topics, the intervention program, the organization of the debates to be held, and the choice of the architectural figures to be discussed does not aim at a single outcome, but it is open to a variety of possible results. Thus the effectiveness of this work is not exclusively measured by the level of authorship of the final product -which is still the main concern of the traditional planner-, but on its ability to trigger open processes involving different areas and the highest possible consensus.

5. Planning the scale of intervention, defining the horizon and the argumentative practices, measuring the effectiveness of the consensus: -apparently- nothing new on this front. One must object that this pertains to the field of the planning practices, that is to say to a knowledge defining the rules and the diagrams -and not the shapes and the design- of the territory. Yet this is not true, because the instrument through which the planning research is held is the architectural figure indeed: the old and timeless drawn shape, but with different goals from the present ones. The project of the shape in its traditional form presents itself as a prescriptive statement -more or less credible- in the context of a present truth unveiling a possible future. On the other hand, in this particular operational condition the drawing loses its assertive function, in favor of an essentially interpretative one. The habit of laying the issues on the political table, dialoguing with the often contradictory expressions of will of the different actors, and the combining function of any democratic process governing a physical transformation have brought about a specific planning attitude in which the result of the drawing keeps being verified on the basis of its capacity to order, orient and translate the different interactive purposes. It is the very legitimation of the project that, by this practice, changes its nature. If the drawing constitutes the strategic instrument to define a common plan, the project loses its function of revealing pre-existent realities and their

future projections, and acquires a primarily dialogic value. A value that lies in the ability to understand and restructure in the shape of the drawing the topics that are being expressed in different languages, be they numbers, norms, moral or political issues.
6. These considerations on the changing statute of the project and, subsequently, of the social mandate of the planner are not the result of an experience which can be circumscribed to the research practices presented in this volume. The specific analysis on the role of the planner as an intellectual technician, seen as an "operator, part of a teamwork" by the building industry is rooted in Turin's architectonic culture [Gabetti 1983] and represents a referential context that is vital for our studies. The lack of a hierarchical recognition of the planner in the decision-making process -which is propaedeutic to a physical transformation-, is related to the competence required of an architect by a certain political culture. Turin's architectural culture, in opposition to other Italian schools started in the Fifties, did not find an implicit reference in the political culture of the Italian Communist Party, which have historically presented itself to the intellectuals the alternative to the government [Durbiano 2000]. As a consequence, it did not establish its own formal models relating on the basis of (or waiting for) a radical social and political transformation, which could make these models real as fragments of a future order. Despite sharing some of the topics of that research line (subject to the crisis of the Modern Project in its ethic premises even more than its aesthetic ones), the *milieu* of Turin experience is permeated by a political culture drawing from both social Catholicism and the liberal-democratic model. A political culture that implies a notion of democratic dialectic revolving around the paradigm of pluralism and the merciless evaluation tool of the individuals. Therefore revolving around an idea of the "social" not as an object that is meaningful on its own, but as a set of mobile interrelations within constantly changing patterns. Within this dialectic -and the formal rules governing it-, the project has acquired a contractual quality, and a relational and strategical statute of knowledge. While this concept is generally accepted on a methodological basis, the results are not. The analysis of this specific working experience (primarily in the department, where it first took shape, but also in places such as Turin's Urban Center or some local professional realities, where it has branched out) allows to define some issues whose boundaries cannot be entirely superposed to a generic local planning attitude.
7. What is the meaning of this peculiarity? The filter through which this cultural basis has been reinterpreted into original forms is of a partly material and partly political

nature. First of all the context in which they have been produced is given by a place in which the job is carried out by an institutional plurality, and not by single individuals. In such a diverse context, the teamwork hinders the linguistic syntheses that reproduce by-catalog solutions; on the contrary, it favors a synthetic-analytical process in which the discussion prevails on the thematization of the problems and the definition of the solutions, in order to identify a common argumentation. The formalization of the topics, required by any collective work, has fostered a use of the architectural figure not in the authorial sense; it is rather an expression of a cognitive tension aimed at evaluating the effectiveness and relevance of the design in its social interactions. This difference in the shaping process of the project-related choices between an individual author and an "institutionally collective" one measures itself also with the function attributed to the work of architecture. Such is the case of the best local professional activities, aiming at being unique and perfect (i.e. see the emblematic value of works such as the Bottega d'Erasmo in Turin, or the Residenziale ovest in Ivrea by Gabetti & Isola, but also Derossi's Berlin tower, or the Casa dell'obelisco by Jaretti and Luzi, or Ranieri's Noviziato delle Suore della Carità, both in Turin), whereas the departmental works' function is to identify a common reproducible mode. It is mainly a political difference: low key rather than virtuosity, focus on the good practices rather than on the complete but unrepeatable instances, search for an inferable rationality rather than for the ineffability of poetics. This mirrors a new, considerate attitude towards a dimension of the project as a social practice, a technical-intellectual action properly projected within an operational political horizon. Even the social mandate of the architect is overturned: in the first case the implicit interlocutor is the debate on the language of architecture, held on the comparison of *exempla*, reproduced in series by the current practices; on the other hand the principle of ordinariness is seen as a shared and social measure within the department, free of hierarchical mediation between high and low, model and copy. Once defined the internal operational context of the specific practice dealing with the relation between form and politics, it is possible to formulate a few hypotheses on the great transformative potential related to this experience.

II. The blurred boundaries of a practice
Practices and exempla – (language) practice as argumentation – (project) practice as organization – clinical corrections – possible deviations on the clinical method – organization of the decision-making process.

1. Far from reducing the relationship between the authenticity of the individual authors and the conventionality of the collective ones to a matter of inter-generational struggle, we have to admit that, being the operational conditions radically different, it is necessary to critically reconsider some of the tutelary modes that have been imposed by the authority of the former on the praxis and the method of the latter.

Meanwhile, the calls for "modesty" related to the project, and for a "clinical", "micro-physical" attention to a neat and circumscribed observation could have generated distorted visions of the *episteme* in the research applied to the territory, thus overshadowing the real reason for these calls. This in turn could gradually dismantle the role of the academic planner, which tends to be regarded as effectual, rather than *authentic*. The reasons for this are of a different nature and origin, but they can be briefly outlined as follows. In the first place the individualizing dimension of the research –which Roberto Gabetti will conceptualize in the "clinical method"– historically situates itself in an operational context whose primary goal is the critique of the standardization of a (socioeconomic and political) paradigm. A paradigm that has been generalizing and imposing de facto a direct bind between the organization of industrial production and the territorial management and governance, thus leading to an irreversible crisis. Meanwhile both the "praxis" of the production of projects (in terms of increased productivity and diversification of the tools of design), and the modes of distribution and organization of the decision-making powers on the territory have been radically changing. As a result, the traditional separation between technical, economical, and political roles is redesigned on the basis of geographies that are far away from the "Aristotelian" divisions between science, technique and art. Furthermore the organization of architecture as scientific research carried out through the *practice* of the project saw the transformation of the very object of that action. It has moved from a strategy of "making", meant as a mediation within the productive series, to a strategy of "acting" that is more *communicative* than polytechnic, aimed at building decisions before than territories. In this case as well, the causes are presumably rooted in history, but in the last thirty years the shapes of institutions have changed. From the one hand the local authorities have acquired powers of direct action on the orientation guidelines for the territory; from the other they had the possibility to *unconditionally exercise* them, *free from the terms and conditions* of the productive organization, like it systematically happened until the end of the Seventies. In line with this argumentative attempt, we aspire at retracing some of the founding ideas of the project-related research on the *GrandeScala*, which have been deeply influencing our research line from the beginning.

In Turin, the choice of designating the project as the founding medium of scientific research (the equation "planning research=scientific research" actually appeared in a 1984 paper by the team working with Gabetti and Isola) has essentially meant the need to establish the anti-theoretical consistence of its work. Hence the resulting idea of architecture as a *practice* based on the ordinary, the context, the "modesty" of the architect-researcher, guaranteed and balanced by the *exemplum* of individuality and authenticity of the work of the architect-authors, at least those who are close on a cultural level. On the other hand Gabetti declared that "the planning activity can be internal to a process of scientific research, but not *tout court*" [Gabetti 1983]. Although he cunningly stops here, he evokes the irreducibility of a *quid* which is not "practical" but authentic and unutterable (thus external to a reflection on "the architectonic planning and technical scientific research").

2. In this context, the ways in which the "practice" is metodologically organized never refer to the horizon of the language studies, although they have deeply affected phylosophy by suggesting a "pragmatic turn" [Apel 1973] of knowledge from its epistemic bases. When trying to detect the general aspects of these discussions, the key role of the language and the *argumentative practicesstands* out a mile. In Germany the "practical philosophy" started in the Sixties has left a deep mark on a debate that often took the shape of a juxtaposition between Neo-Aristotelian "contextualist" (such as Bubner, disciple of Gadamer), and post-Kantian "universalist", such as Jürgen Habermas e Karl Otto Apel. The second stance revolved around linguistic communication and its out of context and out of perspective potential, openly opposed to the untranslatable and unique (clinical?) nature of the truth, of hermeneutic origin. From the point of view of this "pragmatic" philosophers, the language studies of Anglo-Saxon influence have opened new perspectives on the construction of meaning, and on the inter-subjective – thus not "authentic"– value of truth. The "discovery" of the linguistic medium therefore provided new ways out from the juxtaposition of apodictic paradigms, that until then seemed to envisage absolute visions of the world: it was the "linguistic turn" [Rorty 1967].

The studies on language, in between semiotics and linguistics, from the Seventies have also included some reflections on architecture. Contrary to what happened in philosophical debates, the focus on linguistics for architecture meant a season of abstractions, both in Italy [Koenig 1964; Eco 1967; De Fusco 1967 e 2003; Garroni 1970; Lenza 1975] and on an international level [Eisenman 1971 e 1973, Gandelsonas 1973 e 1979], paving the way to the postmodern suggestions of Deconstructionism [Wigley 1989; Derrida 1990; Tschumi 1995; Eisenman 1998; Somol 1999]: in all these cases the approach to the project and the visions of architecture is all but "pragmatic" [Armando 2008].

3. On the other hand, Turin's architecture culture and the experiences constituting its background have little to do with the language studies, apart from few, partial exceptions [Brusasco and Torretta 1971] that did not have consequences. Nonetheless it could be only an apparent distance: Turin's *milieu* of research was definitely not interested in the connections between Deconstructionism in philisophy and in architecture. On the contrary, the working hypotheses on the table were of a pragmatist nature, and their premises could be reconciled -even unexpectedly- with the philosophy of language.

Between the end of the Seventies and the beginning of the Eighties, Gabetti proposed some definitions that pointed out the need of an encounter between philosophical though and project practice, in relation to the epistemology of architecture. In the acts of a seminar on research of 1984, he stated that "the Enlightenment can be [...] brought back to the original ground of the encyclopedists, where the proximity between philosophy and praxis was of great importance and influence, with all the exquisite examples from the field of production.This revival of the Enlightenment does not seem as remote, since I believe the debate on the issue is still a major one".

One year earlier Gabetti had explained his epistemic reflection on the project more in details, through the definition of a *clinical method* first used by the French philosopher Gilles-Gaston Granger: "Borrowing the term from medicine, we will call *clinical* method the strategic orientation of knowledge aiming at a scientific organization towards individuality" [Granger 1980, cit. in Gabetti 1983]. In this way Gabetti is critically addressing those experiences that had been extending the criteria of factory organization to urban and territorial organization (of which Turin's forma *urbis* is a self explanatory evidence). Nevertheless, instead of considering the connections between the logic of industrial production and the rationality of the project as a degeneration – or as a "reduction to a mere technical work" of architecture [Tafuri 1969]– Gabetti highlighted their key role as the basis for "the proximity between philosophy and practice", science and technique, architecture and production. It is actually the development of industrial production that allowed to expand corporate organization of production to the building sector: the logic of prototypes, the organization of the building site, the reduction of the minimal tolerance of the components, the management of the times of realization of the works, and the prevention of accidents [Gabetti 1977]. The critique is rather addressed to the "architects and urban planners [that] had the chance to definitely leave aside the individual and his history" [Gabetti 1983]. It is not a matter of an hostile foresight of a "Capital Plan" that has crushed the promises of progress in the name of profit; it is rather the degeneration of a technical rationality, in the reductionist forms of Taylorism, which has duly imposed unsuccessful strategies, causing the crisis of the same economic productive system from where it came. Therefore the organization of the production and of the rationality of the project of architecture have to restate their necessary interdependence; on the other hand, it is necessary to re-examine the objectifying and sectional limits of the *scientific organization* of work, and its degeneration along a deterministic path. In this way the pragmatic strategy is safeguarded; the organizational structure of production -according to an approach that ultimately merged physics and mathematics with the "human and philosophical" sciences [Gabetti 1984]– entails a ratio that is not far from the experiences of Taylorism revisited in a *clinical* light.

4. But who is Gilles-Gaston Granger, and why does Gabetti quotes him to express his key stance? From the one hand, the proximity of views with Granger is blatantly close to the proposal of expanding the meaning of "rationality" through the definition of a "strategy", holding together the necessary "representation of the circumstances and modes of a system of symbols and the "spirit that ought to pervade that decision". That is to say, he addresses the need for an "organization of the production, that can be extended to the simplest levels of organization", to the implicit condition that architecture planning is "left a little aside" with respect to the method (*Ibidem*).

Nevertheless, Gabetti's interpretation seems to stretch considerably Granger's position on at least four classes of questions, (whose sources heve been extracted from, respectively, an essay on language by the same Granger of 1992, from *Qu'est-ce que la philosophie* by Gilles Deleuze and Felix Guattari of 1995, and from a study on Granger by Gianni Paganini, published in the *Storia della filosofia* by Mario Dal Pra, of 1998).

In the first place Granger is an epistemologist and a philosoper of the language –author of the most authoritative translation of Ludwig Wittgenstein's *Tractatus Logico-Philosophicus* in France. From the Sixties, he situates himslef in the track of Jean Cavaillés's program for a "philosophy of concept", as opposed to the "philosophies of consciousness". From Wittgenstein's philosophy, Granger takes back the constructive value of the "linguistic game", described in the *Philosophical Investigations:* "By means of the indefinite plurality of the "linguistic games", the philosophical description –which is not a scientific explanation– leads us to detect the rules of a "philosophical grammar" in every example of use" [Granger 2003]. Hence the anti-subjectivist idea of an ""interventionist ego", that "creates its own rules of the game of knowledge", actually "building" the object; in Granger's view, this construction is precisely a "job", not a free permanent gift from an impenetrable supernatural nature" [Granger 1967, in Paganini 1998]. This is also the basis for a formalist epistemology, essential to understand Granger's idea of "strategy".

Secondly, Granger is known for his "philosophy of stile", which is not only what is quoted by Gabetti himself ("In retrospect, we can definitely describe style as a strategy"), but also the principle of transformation of the experience into information, structure or model [Granger 1968 and 1988], according to constructivist, thus conventional, procedures.

In the third place, the overturning of Husserl's perspective is one of Granger's cornerstones, to the point that he defines phenomenology as "the illustrious metamorphosis of a dying ideology"; an "ideology", that of Husserl, accused of "implementing the return to things through transcendental subjectivity, but that in the end interpreted science as a "remedy to the natural alienation of the individual"" [Granger 1956, in Paganini 1998].

Lastly, Granger sees the "clinical practice" as essentially aimed at including the individual dimension -the reality of subjects- in a scientific knowledge which, being formalist and conventional, cannot find any other way to actualize itself. That is to say, every science needs to be *practiced* to call itself such. In Granger's perspective then, History cannot be regarded as a science: "If the notion of individual can be introduced into science only through the mediation of a practice, History presents itself as a "clinic with no practice""[*Ibidem*]. He maintains that "History would defy classification among the sciences, "to the extent that its goal is not to elaborate models to manipulate reality, but to "rebuild those very same realities, necessarily experienced as individual". [...] For Granger, the most blatant example of this ambiguity was the very school of the *Annales*: the historicist [...] seemed to him as a "speculative clinician", willing to reach the individual, but "only with the look, without ever touching it" " [Granger 1959, cit. in Paganini 1998]. From this position it seems hard to recognize the central role assigned by Gabetti to History: a fundamental *clinical* data for the project.

5. Seen in perspective, Gabetti's stances seem to focus more on a unequivocal way out from the late-idealist dichotomies between the architect-poet and the "mere technical work". This does not mean to abandon the Husserlian notion of authenticity, meant as a horizon of meaning for knowledge: "Not only the human operations of an artistic or humanistic nature need science; they satisfy their very nature along the path leading to a rational ideal of human life: in the horizon of "scientificity"" [Paci, in Gabetti 1984].

Until that point, the core problem was still tied to the effects of its action, in a coherently-defined framework, so as to "produce positive results and authentic solutions " [Gabetti 1983]: the "practice". On the other hand, once the guarantee of an "authentic" subject is lost (for lack of a mandate, rather than authority in itself), the architecture project could be marginalized even more: not only as knowledge aiming at "organizing the production", but also, out of necessity, knowledge oriented to *organizing the decision;* not only "practice" as the science of making, but also pragmatic as the science of talking, translating into figures, acting "inter-subjectively" in an uncertain context of fragmented decisions.

III. The planner as a translator.
Intellectual technician, turin "secular" area – rationality of the production and rationality of the project – new local decision-makers – infrastructural project as linear model, guidelines instead of prescriptions, figures of concordance and connection – extension of the practice of drawing – from the expert to the translator – tasks of the translator – inter-semiotic translation.

1. The image of the "intellectual-technician" is the core of Gabetti's views on the role of the project and on the epistemological foundation of scientific research in architecture. The meaning he attaches to this definition is double: on the one hand, it is inscribed in the history of Italian intellectuals, starting from the second of the sixth collections of Gramsci's *Prison Notebooks*, dedicated to *The intellectuals and the organization of culture* (1949). In this sense, the category of the technician-intellectual is used by Gabetti to narrate the evolution of productive organization, in general and in the field of the building industry, from the beginning of fascism on: "If the technician-engineers have been the actors of the "scientific management", the [...] industrial engineer, and occasionally the architects, have been the protagonists of the construction planning, : all technician-intellectuals –or intellectual-technicians– that redistributed their new roles between fascist corporations, avant-garde magazines, and current professional practice" [Gabetti 1977]. From another point of view, the image of the "intellectual-technician" is used to project into the future the aforementioned possibility of a connection between science, technique and art: "I would like their initiatives to be more and more interconnected, so that the quality of things becomes a suitable common ground to bring the opposite banks closer: the journey might be going towards a re-foundation of our disoriented and fragmented activity, towards authentic and shared meanings..." [Gabetti 1990].

Against the background of Gabetti's intellectual technician, in between the historical acknowledgment of an unsuccessful cultural project and the wish for an "authentic" restructuring of theoretical, practical ans poetic knowledge, stand the interpretations of the "secular" philosophers from Turin such as Nicola Abbagnano, Norberto Bobbio, and Ludovico Geymonat, but also Enzo Paci, Giulio Preti and Remo Cantoni. In this diverse contexts, in the first two decades after the war the main features of a philosophical and political program emerged; a program of a liberal-democratic type, that will come critically close to Marx both by getting close to Anglo-Saxon pragmatism [Preti 1956], and by welcoming the filter of existentialism and phenomenology (see Paci, and the creation of "aut-aut" magazine in 1951). It is in this *milieu* that an analysis on the basis of a humanized scientific research was carried on – even by means of a research on the method [Geymonat 1953]– far from the scholar-like syntheses of a theological, ideological or scientistic origin.

2. In the volume *Architettura, Industria, Piemonte* (1977) Gabetti analyzed the fracture and the limits that had progressively dismantled the paradigms of a highly Taylorist production structure. A structure in which the intellectual technicians had been developing a specialist function aimed at a clear separation of competences: "The revival of the debate on the intellectual work in the building and planning sector can focus the discussion with more clarity on the key node: the type of mediation provided by the intellectual work for the production needs of the building industry and territory management" [Gabetti 1977]. This "key node" will eventually relate to the reflections on the method, but in 1977 points out two conditions defining the *praxisof* the project: the centrality of productive rationality in defining the scientific consistency of the project, and the structural (but not *causal*) relationship between the industry and the shape of the territory.

Against the "false dichotomies between architecture and the building industry, ordinary production and exceptions" stands the pragmatic approach of the intellectual technician, providing a "type of mediation" to the "production needs". The orders of complexity deriving from this task concern the capacity to answer to radically different conditions in the factory, and, as a consequence, in the building industry and territory management. It is a matter of tackling a real discontinuity, a "crisis, that not even the prophets of society and politics thought would burst before the early Seventies" [*Ibidem*]. Gabetti's answer to the crisis of the paradigms and the economic structures will be naturally oriented towards "individuality", fueled by the suspect towards the systematization and the "recipes", but with the stable goal of a better organization of a *perspicuous horizon* of knowledge, able to penetrate contradictions in a *clinical* and authentic way. In this way the goal of an effect on the reality of the planning action seems harder to achieve, but its points of reference remain the same: the other intellectual technicians, the production systems, the clients. Most of all it does not include the public decision-making scene, whose rationality and possibility of movement always seem subordinate to the industry: "The failure of a programming of the economy, the local, regional, and territorial interventions, and the growing gap between North and South can have, as we saw, political roots, but they had a direct -not mediated- connection with what can be defined -in a restrictive, "corporate" way- as "organization of the work" " [*Ibidem*]. In Gabetti's views, the rationalization of the production sector in Italy should have "contained territorial planning within itself" [*ibidem*], exactly because the power of local authorities seemed closely tied to the bureaucratic-administrative sphere more than to the initiatives of construction and management of the territory: it is the production sector to guide, and govern de facto, the transformation of places.

3. The entire background of *Architettura, Industria, Piemonte* supposes a representation of the dynamics of the relationship between power, productive forms and territorial transformation that enters a "system" crisis, from which it can only emerge if transfigured. Thirty years later that representation shows all its changes, in the first place in the shape of political institutions: by reorganizing the delegations of local governance, which have transformed the Regions in the main political subjects related to the territory with the Bassanini Law in 1997, the Constitutional Law of 1999 and the Constitutional Reform of 2001; but also the different features of the Provinces and the Municipalities, after the institution of direct election of the President of the Province (L. 81, 25/03/1993) and the Mayor, by virtue of the new normative system consolidated into the Single Text on the Organization of the Local Authorities (D. Lgs. 267/2000). In addition to this, the Calderoli draft law addressed to the Council of Ministers on September 11, 2008 would aim at ensuring that the Provinces have independence in the fields of income and expenses, through the power of instituting taxes, co-ownerships and equalizing funds, and at the same time planning the future transformation of seven provinces (among which Turin) into *metropolitan cities*. From the end of the Nineties local authorities have gradually taken over the area of the territorial transformation, to an extent and degree that were unknown until that moment.

4. In Piedmont the processes of physical transformation on a vast scale –in *primis* those concerning the High Speed Line and the crossing of the Susa Valley– have highlighted the "scalar" fractures between the decision making and the exercise of power (of action, but also of veto), and the impossibility to govern the processes from above –maybe by virtue of a tight connection between the political and the industrial sectors. On the other hand, all the other proposals of transformation of the physical space surrounding Turin metropolitan area in the last twenty years have held the project for an infrastructure as a guideline. This was mainly caused by the specific consistency of the infrastructures as *manufactured products*, which can be planned according to lines of productive organization: from studies on the viability and "impact", to the executive documents and building sites. Nevertheless, the

contradiction between the processes oriented to the "organization of the work" and the many *ground* resistances (of a political or technical-administrative nature, regarding interests and claims) has virtually never been overcome by technical rationality, or efficiency (and this is undeniable also with respect to some works, such as the subway and the underground railway link). If this is blatant for the case of the High Speed Line [Bobbio and Dansero 2008], more big projects of transformation had to gradually adequate to the new strategies of creation of consensus: through the representation of the future states of the physical space they had to make the implementation possible, by will and not by law.

The case of Corso Marche is paradigmatic in this sense: the preliminary project was published on "Il giornale dell'architettura [no.73, April 2009], in conjunction with the public presentation publicized by the Province of Turin -the promoter together with some of the Municipalities, that signed an agreement protocol in 2005. The production of the project of course have also provided for the drafting of variance zoning plans, which every Municipality have interpreted as non-binding guidelines within its own instruments of urban planning. The outcome of this process, also in its formal aspects, can be observed in the terms of a great concerted operation, whose results are mainly communicative (the choice of a magazine for the "official" publishing is a symptom), and not prescriptive.

More in general, in the absence of great, prevailing vectors that guide the strategic framework of the transformations - like it happened in part until the mid-Eighties, because of the weight of the big industry- the need for an agreed, common *figure* as a gravitational center for the various actors is taking shape. All the actors have a share of conditioning power, as the authority to oppose the building sites: such is the case of the "Venaus uprising" against the High Speed. The cross-reference conditions between the coordination boards and the setting up of municipal urban plannings are, however, under the constant influence of the micro-physical processes intervening when the real-estate agents, the building industry and the soil market interact with the decision-making sphere. As a consequence, between the design of a territorial scale and the implementing actions (instruments and executive plans) there is always a shift that can appear contradictory, if not conflictual. This happens because the big territory projects, when they manage to unify in a single pattern the expectations and the balances of the subjects governing the different parts of the territory, act in advance and on the basis of a circumstantial rationality with respect to the economic and financial, but also social, aspects of the processes. In this scenario, the city no longer seems "the product of the industrial products" [Guiducci 1957, in Gabetti 1977], the result of the forms of organization of production; it is rather the *place* where the unifying figures superpose: the institutional "boards", the economic actors and public opinions -the case of Corso Marche-, and the delimitation of the (administrative, property, and sectoral) borders. In other words, the physical shape of the territory seems more affected by circumstances in which the divergences between the decision-makers and the owners of economic resources manage to lead to partial agreements than by latent dynamics, ascribable to some kind of technical or economic rationality.

5. In the light of these changes in the mechanisms of physical transformation, Gabetti's conclusions of 1977 ought to be revisited, at least in respect to the form of knowledge that can be conveyed through the architecture project. In Gabetti's view the pervasiveness of the factory system, even at the decision-making level, is to be organized according to "clinical" mediation practices; despite its crisis, it is not being questioned. Therefore the project can find a solution to the "constant self-reproduction of the industrial buildings" [*Ibidem*], or try to curb the "abdication of the administrations in favor of company policies" [Gabetti 1983]. What really seems discriminatory is the opposite of an abdication: the unprecedented availability of political power to local administrative actors, which in contexts of economic production act on the basis of the chance, rather than the need. In this sense the profile of the "intellectual-technician" seems to be radically transformed by the breaking in of the decision-making dimension in its own operational context. The knowledge of architecture can no longer be structured according to the *praxis* of drawing as an "instrument for organizing the work, guiding and monitoring the "tasks" assigned to the construction workers, the engineer, and the workshop technician" [Brusantin 1978, in Gabetti 1983]; nor can it be legitimated on the basis of an "authentic" authorial interpretation, acting *clinically* "even at the simplest levels of rationalization" (*Ibidem*). Before being able to structure the project in detail until its realization in the building sites, the architect is expected to *translate into a form* the diverse problems and intentions; their spatial result is mainly undetermined, and their actual influence on the physical assets, which are generated by the process itself, is generally indeterminable.

6. According to this close examination, the type of "planner-expert" (the intellectual technician in Gabetti's words) seems more and more detached from the profile of a

"planner-translator", called to act in the aforementioned contexts. The experienced planner actually receives a mandate that is guaranteed *before* he acts: as an intellectual who is *organic* to an asset holding most of the political and economical instruments of transformation. For this reason the final representations of this asset do not concern the creation of open balances between the decision-makers, but the "clinical closure" of hypotheses based on stable values and criteria. The planner acts in compliance with a statute (the professional order and its ethics) and a role, formally codified within a system of procedures, assignments, responsibilities and signatures. As an "expert", he/she guarantees the *conformity* between the programs and their implementations, acting within a field of knowledge and responsibilities whose legitimation is not object of negotiation.

On the contrary, the hypothesis of a "planner-translator" entails a deformation of the professional role towards an increased capacity of producing hypotheses of *potential* conformity, or "figures" within uncertain scenarios; on the other hand his/her (technical and authorial) mandate becomes less recognizable. It is by trying to extend his/her own boundaries of legitimation that the planner as a translator can create connections of meaning, unifying fields that are separated by different sectoral and specialized knowledge, and by forms of conflict (of powers, interests, values).

The epistemic difference between these two types lies in the key role of the argumentation and decision-making phases, which characterize the "planner-translator". The metaphor of the translator is useful to highlight the deconstructive and representational function of the project in the decision-making phase, where the different stances are structured according to argumentative patterns. In this case the "translations" of the project should govern both the sphere of the political competence (the *powers*), and that of the technical competence (the *knowledge*). The reference to the aforementioned constructive and conventional function of language is now clear, with respect to both the studies of the "pragmatic" philosophers like Habermas and Apel, and the different interpretations surrounding Granger's ideas. Given a context in which "nobody has the exclusive of the common medium, which is rather to be shared inter-subjectively" [Habermas 2002], the drawing of a future state of the physical shape provides an instrument to ground the knowledge and the powers; this in turn is able to mirror the coexistence of two different representations that might be untranslatable in the sphere of verbal argumentation. This is made possible by the conventional force of the symbols of drawing [Granger 1980], whose substantiality is to be considered as completely *external* to a disciplinary system of values, and therefore as a *sign of definition*. Only if the project is capable of becoming *other* will it be possible to use it in figural terms, extensively structuring its values and conflicts through a representation of physical transformation.

If the primary goal of a project is still the *agreement* of the parties -and not the fulfillment of objective, not even "authentic" values-, it is nonetheless necessary to establish a set of conditions by which the project can be used a s a "common medium" in an argumentative context.

7. In a text of 1921 titled *The task of the translator*, a young Walter Benjamin highlights a series of problematic nodes regarding translation and the specificity of the role of the literary translator. Despite its slightly old-fashioned universalist aspirations, this essay provides a clearer definition of the role of the planner as a translator, so different from the architect as an author.

Benjamin sees as structurally limited the possibility of conveying into a different language the essence of the source. For this reason he regards "translatability" as an inner property of the text, in a way anticipating Popper's *falsifiability* of scientific theories: "Translatability is essentially inherent to some texts. This does not mean that their translation is vital *for* the works themselves; it means that a specific meaning, inherent to the original texts, manifests itself in their translatability" [Benjamin 1955]. In an analogous way, it could be maintained that it is the very *drawing of the decisions* that makes the involved subjects falsifiable (that is, more or less translatable into project figures).

In Benjamin's views, the translatability of a text thus becomes the primary criterion of its *quality*: a successful translation is a "supreme confirmation" of the vitality and the *survival skills* (and the reproducibility) of the original text, of their proximity to the "real language, the truth, the doctrine" (*Ibidem*). In this light it is well worh mentioning the "task of the translator", which Benjamin thinks is to be "interpreted as a task per se, clearly distinct from that of the poet". Tranlsation appears as an ambivalent "proper form": on the one hand it is contingent and meant to last only a limited time, on the other it fulfills the primary goal of "reedeming in one's language the pure language that is contained in another one, or setting it free from the prison of the text through translation". In this sense, the "pure language" acquires a universalist quality, which should be meant as a unique (conventional) chance for a "mutual understanding", wished for by philosophers like Habermas by means of the shared use of the linguistic (and figural) medium.

It is no coincidence that Benjamin warns: "The primary mistake of the translator is to stick to the contingent stadium of his language, instead of letting it be violently shaken and upset by the foreign language". For the "planner-translator" as well, the capacity of being upset by the "foreign languages" (of sectoral rationalities and contradictory intentionalities) seems to be an essential principle for the quality of the project, given the specificity of a role that is always contingent –in relation to the position and the available "languages"–, aimed at representing values and criteria that are not its own.

8. In 1985 Jacques Derrida brings back to the debate Benjamin's issue of translatability in *Des Tours de Babel*, and cites a taxonomy by Roman Jackobson [*On Translation*, 1959] that gives a definition of the relationship of mutual translatability between verbal language and project figures. Jakobson actually discerns between *intralinguistic* translations (those interpreting linguistic signs by means of other linguistic signs from the same language), *interlinguistic* translations (what is normally meant for translation from a language into another), and *intersemiotic* translations, or *transmutations* (those interpreting the linguistic signs of a language *by means of a non-linguistic system of signs* [Jakobson 1963].

If it is true that the architecture project, when the conditions for its *immediate* development are guaranteed until the final phases, presents itself as a mainly figural instrument for the representation of multiple intentionalities, then it could also fit under Jakobson's category of *intersemiotic translation*; along and after Derrida's deconstruction, from that category it could recapture the constructive value of the project as an instrument of mediation in the decision-making process.

IV. Politics and form
Short-circuit between ideology and language – necessary future and states of possibilities – political culture and programmatic project identity – fragmentation and democratization of urban space: the conventional role of the figure – recognizing the values in the deliberative arena.

1. The function of the planner as a translator is now a fact, along with his/her chance of acquiring a political value; this is partly due to the changing historical coinditions.

Italian architecture culture has been holding a deeply ambivalent relationship with the dimension of proper political action –or at least its most original part has, building its own legitimation from a radical crisis of the cultural conventions created by the Modern Movement. Through the implicit acknowledgment of a "primacy of politics", seen in essentially ideological terms (thus as a conflict between opposing lines), architectural culture has exercised its political mandate juxtaposing its representations to those of the dominant power. This activity, only possible within the exclusive register of architectural writing, has entailed the exaltation of authorial originality and the subsequent devaluation of the planner's competence to satisfy a social demand of housing quality according to empiric bases. Symbolically in parallel to the research that pervaded the literary debate throughout the so-called "period of commitment", the best examples of this culture are those that managed to give the floor to meanings that represented a critical alternative to a homogeneous and dominant condition. Therefore the Gallaratese, the Zen, the Civic Center of Pieve or Modena's cemetery are first of all code messages, addressed to the narrow community of competent readers, in "mental search of a leak, a weak link in the impenetrable fortress holding us captive" [Calvino 1967]. In this context the "toughness" of architectural writing is not an option (or a mistake, as it is trivially seen), but a problematic necessary condition: "Then what I, and others, will write shall have a metal soul, like the thin steel file hidden in the loaf of bread" [Fortini 1962]. Architecture cannot benefit from an environment that is independent from the artistic-literary one, as it was first pointed out in those years [Burger 1974]. The priority of the political ideology and representational function of architecture therefore seems to acquire solidity in a game of mutual legitimation, that leaves aside the contents of the immediate and specific demand for life quality. The values are previously defined (by politics), and architecture can only represent them (through language). Plurality and fragmentation are features of the languages (that are in fact different: one for every author), but the values are not defined through a common construction, that might be potentially plural and fragmented. Upon the conclusion of his *storia dell'architettura italiana*, Tafuri defines an operational framework that is entirely contained within the representational function of authorial languages. As a consequence, he only recognizes a role of the architect that refers to an "other from the self", rooted in the present social and political action.

2. Unless the political models are radically transformed, this correspondence between ideology and languages is hard to overcome. This provides a good reason to use a distinct periodization, derived from a political historiography, in order to mark a turning point in an otherwise stagnant relationship between politics and form. It is with the end of the short century that Italy experiences a season of reconceptualization of the political praxis and its goals. In *Cittadinanza* [1990], Salvatore Veca defines the limits of a normative theory based on the value of pluralism, in which the principle of citizenship establishes a tension between the "being" and the "must be" of political action; this is turn is inspired by the mainstream theories of modern, still unachieved, emancipation: Liberalism and Socialism. Times are ready (they already were twenty years ago for technical elaboration, but maybe not for practical action), to finally reconsider a pragmatic model of politics, able to award a social mandate to the planner, which is not limited to a mere representational function: it focuses on the combinatorial configuration of the values entailed by the mediation of the figure. Veca identifies two models of political actions that are associated to two distinct temporal perspectives. The first model coincides with the ideological message, which consists in the definition of the goals in the long run. In this sense politics is seen as a permanent shift between the present contingency and the future goals, according to a model that isolates politics from everyday life and pins it to a horizon that transcends present reality.

If we move from an idea of politics as discourse to one of politics as a measure (that is to the dimension of action, where the project is seen as a medium of agreement), this horizon is turned upside down. Rationality in this sense is limited. It allows for a closer look on the contingent dynamics, and acts in the logic of the present; a present defined by the maze of ties and chances in which it structures itself The reasons to act are not generated by an authentic interpretation of the ultimate goals of society; they are to be found in the very dynamics of the present. In this case, Veca warns, "the fundamental category is that of possibility, whereas in the case of ideology it is necessity". If the mandate of the architect is no longer to represent a future state of the world seen as necessary, and it is replaced by the socially shared construction of states of possibility, even the traditional relationship between politics and form changes sign.

3. In facts, the pragmatic model needs new forms of relationship between technical and political cultures. A relationship built on an identity that transcends ideologies,

organic interpretations and scatological visions, that lies on the cultural background of a shared reading of society, and on the definition of shared codes and symbolic universes. In this context, the role of the intellectual-specialist (the architect-translator), who has the abilities to govern his potential fields of expertise, comes to the forefront. This figure has been historically marginalized by Italian political culture, whose main concern has been to subordinate the technical cultures to the "primacy of politics", that is outside the contents. It has relegated the concrete programs, thus the project, to the background or to an instrumental dimension. In the contemporary Italian political system the convergence on a culturally based, programmatic axis of project-related identity not only did not succeed; it has also been partly overwhelmed and replaced by an identity of ethical values, which has been so pervasive as to permeate almost the entire space of the raison d'être of political parties [Biasco 2007].

In order to overcome the short-circuit of ideology-representation, it is vital to measure ourselves on this programmatic project-related identity. An identity built on the calculable definition of the social sectors affected by the costs and benefits of public action, and on the link between the interests at stake and the different, opposing stances on the issue. "Starting from goals that can be achieved in the context of the existing economic and productive organization, focused on social organization and the well-being of the community, and not on "politics"" [ibidem]. These ingredients are the product of a positivist culture in a broad sense, and of a pragmatic action that today can be historically considered as globally accepted (take the exceptional mediatic example of Barack Obama's politics). Nevertheless, in the Italian case this phenomenon is only present in some local administrative experiences (not the traditional "red regions", nor the more recent "green municipalities" of the Lega Nord, or the colorless ones of the small centers governed by the civic lists [Diamanti 2003]).

4. If observed through the lens of territorial transformation, the effectiveness of a fully paradigmatic political model seems of utter importance. The loss of an image of the city as composed of homogeneous and discrete parts, the prevailing metamorphosis affecting the single objects and buildings, the exponential growth of the subjects and the institutions that have legal, economic and political resources to change small portion of the physical space: all these phenomena are intrinsically connected to the democratization process of the city and the territory. But they also

contribute to shattering from within the univocality of the physical image through which the city has expressed itself until a few decades ago – take for example the omology of Turin and the "factory city" [De Rossi and Durbiano 2006]. This fragmentation of the collective space in many subsets of collective space, which is specular to the hyper-fragmentation of the actors and their imaginary, produces a superposition of functions and quantities, signs and symbols, that requires distinct forms of control and governance. It also requires new forms of interpretations of the role of the planner. Once it was possible to recognize a substantial unity of the social and political context for the technical and intellectual work (like the planning of Turin on the basis of the production paradigm, as described by Gabetti in *Architettura Industria Piemonte* of 1977). On the other hand, we are now witnessing the co-presence and the *mise en scène* of intentionality, and of self-representations that seem to be lacking predefined points of reference and stable connections with what is recognized as public space (like the Turin of the Olympic Passion, addressed by Cristina Bianchetti (2008). The metamorphosis is not only physical and socio-political: it takes place in the conceptualization of the instruments of work and its ethical rationale. In the city of standardization, the project aims at unveiling exemplary fragments, legitimated by the critical interpretation of the author (i.e. the Bottega). On the contrary, in the contemporary city inhabited by multitudes of minorities looking for a territory to build in their own image, the planning political commitment cannot but aim at building connections, common places for formal universes and social expectations. Thus the ability of the "planner-translator" is to choose and organize the figures for the mediation. Figures that allow the translatability of the fragmented powers and knowledge, on the basis of shared conventions. If in the time of standardization the answer was the authenticity of the fragment, in the time of fragmentation the goal is to scan the standardizing potential of the figure.

5. Nevertheless, this model has some limits. The role of the figure as an instrument of mediation and agreement can be successful only if it is inscribed in a political practice that fully acknowledges the extent of the boundaries of the democratic arena. Habermas identifies two traditional models of politics: the liberal one and the republican one. They differ in terms of their approach to the democratic process. While in the liberal model politics is aimed at aggregating and imposing private social interests on the state machinery, in the republican one it aims at

both intermediating and socializing. If in the first case the planner plays the part of an intellectual and technical mediator between the interested authority and the different contradictory private interests, in the second model the planner shares and internalizes the values of the different actors: he has a primarily authorial function. Habermas also suggests the political notion of "deliberative democracy", characterized by the idea that an arena dealing with problems of overall social relevance can be generated from within the political public sphere. Inside this arena each theory has a local, not a global value. No point of view can be considered superior to the others, in any way. Their prominence and relevance depend on the reasons for their adoption. In this way politics cannot be placed at the top, nor can it be "an ordering model" of society; it just becomes one of the many systems of action [Habermas 1998].

In the perspective of a deliberative democracy, the project cannot be legitimated by the values that lie outside the arena (that is, in the planner's mind), but only by the capacity to effectively relate to the program; it cannot be legitimated by an a priori conception of the architectural values (meant as a system coherent with the plan of interpretation), but by the sharing of the figures of mediation. Politics and form thus find a new possible point of reference, and the figure finds a non self-referential role.

V. Style in the time of convention
Quality as fidelity to the given values or balance between the agreed values – the planner as a substitute – style and social demand for the project – architecture quality as a legislative structure and values in conflict.

1. Is it enough to build the arena, recognize the values at stake, and translate them into a shared figure? Is this all the relationship between the project and the political sphere? Or are there essential elements of authorial subjectivity inherent in architectural writing, regardless of the work-group, the argumentative function, and the relevance of the political contents of any physical transformation? In other words: can the planner's fidelity to values that are genuinely and intimately experienced be weakened, to the point of being nullified? Can the planner-translator nullify the planner-author? In order to answer this question it might be useful to reconsider the cornerstone of the authorial conception of architecture: the principle of quality.

The meaning of the expression "architectural quality" is established in relation to the distinct social categories that use it. Architectural quality as completeness and control of the forms of the spaces; as conformity to a set of prescriptive rules, or to an imaginary that shoulg give internal coherence to the solutions related to a specific value... But in the context of a value judgment, these distinct meanings attributed to the term "quality" can be divided into two groups. If by quality we mean an intrinsic and hidden quality to be reached an unveiled through a mainly authorial process, then the evaluation tool will be authenticity. Authenticity towards the pre-established values, towards the truth owned by the author. If, on the contrary, by quality we mean the intersection point between the types of argumentation that the different actors put on the decision-making table, then the truths multiply and the evaluation tool can only depend upon the degree of balance achieved: the agreement between the parties. The more high and complex is the balance of the convention between the different truths, and the internal cohesion between figure and shared values, the higher will architectural quality be.

In this sense the relationship between the two perspectives is determined by the degree of relevance of the public good that is the object of the project, thus by the degree of socialization of the problem addressed by architecture. The more the problem is private (the design of a chair, of an isolated villa, of a urban brand in need of a signature...), the more will the first perspective prevail; the more the problem is public (architecture on a GrandeScala), the more will the second perspective be preferred. And also: the more direct the relationship between the architect and the client is, the more the project will have a merely representative function. The more will the relationship be mediated by a series of intermediate (political, institutional, technical) levels, the more the project's goal will be mediation. A solution of continuity between the two ideas of quality does not exist; while the first one is an individual practice, the second is a social one. As a consequence, the issue can be tackled through an analysis centered on the political values of the form, that is our main focus.

2. But this difference is not enough. In the shift from the model to reality, things get further confused. According to the model, the first step of a planning political action is the definition of the decision-makers and the rules of sharing of the corresponding interests and values. A conventional approach to the

project actually entails an intelligible argumentative dynamic, and a transparent decision-making process. The interests and values that are brought in the arena are chosen and selected on the basis of criteria defined by the rules of democratic (deliberative) politics; in this way they are legitimated, and therefore respectable. On the contrary, it is far from obvious that the decision-makers should respect their mandate to act in the interest of the represented subject in the concrete practice of urban and territorial transformation (it is well known how the urban-planning, environmental, and administrative techniques often answer to their own criteria of relevance, regardless of their actual objective). As it is far from obvious that the actors involved know how to work out the interests and needs that they ought to convey in the form of values.

This common condition of anonymity of the client, opacity of the debate and indeterminacy of the actors in the decision-making arena creates an emptiness of content that is used by the planner as space of maneuvering. In the absence of transparency and clarity of contents, the architect compensates with a charge of undue (but often required) responsibility. From here the star system is just one step away. Instead of interpreting the question the planner literally incorporates it, presenting itself as the vehicle for the solution. Architects instead of architectures. The conjure instead of the observation and the translation (to the delight of those -journalists or councilors- that in this way would be able to reduce a complex physical transformation into an immediately recognizable, thus communicable, sign).

3. Beyond its media-related consequences, this responsibility "in substitution" taken by the architect is a fact that shifts once again the plan of the legitimation of the planner from the level of convention to the authorial one.

Therefore the osmotic relationship between subjective elaboration and social practice comes back to the front —as it always will. In other words, there is always the problem of style. An issue intimately related to the consistency of the limits of the architect-author: the extensible limits of the "elastic cage" within which the subject experiences the world. As a limit, rather than as an advantage.

The literary critic Gianfranco Contini has defined style as "the way in which an author experiences things". That is, the way in which an author organizes his interpretative tools in the face of the complex reality he is observing. If observed in this light, style in architecture is meant to understand the personal hierarchy of values of an author, but not the values expressed by a social system. If the horizon of the political dimension is what can be said, then on a political level style it is what cannot.

When analyzed from within, that is by composing and studying the shaping process within the planner's mind, the project-related action cannot but clash with the indescribable inner life of the artist. Here the epoché stands as the guardian of the impenetrability of the inner and external worlds to any deterministic interpretive key. That is to say: we are not able to investigate, we are not able to know.

But instead of looking from an internal perspective, if we observe the project from the outside, internalizing the perspective of the user who formulates a project question, the mist dissipates revealing silhouettes of arguments, interests... and behind them the subjects who proposed them. From this specific point of view, and with this relative clarity, architectural writing too can be the object of a critical discourse. Even the most unintelligible sign of adherence to pre-established and subjective values (like another acute angle by Zaha Hadid or a shift of a plan by Eisenman) can be analyzed and evaluated according to a specific judgment of aesthetic quality.

Architectural writing, if we observe its results in terms of project demand, measures itself with the social conventions expressed by architectural quality.

4. There is a warning: to situate the observatory outside the center of the formation of architectural writing implies the realistic acknowledgment of the specific localization of any notion of aesthetic quality, and even more when this is architectural quality. Quality in architecture is not an objective requisite, but an historical, anthropological product that legitimates itself on the grounds of contextually determined forces. The authoritative nature of this idea of quality depends on the fact that it is essentially a legislative structure. And as such, it interprets the needs of the dominant classes and cultures (and the present coexistence of a kaleidoscopic plurality of conventions of quality is just the inevitable consequence of the fragmentation of the social bodies and the imaginaries, which pervades the contemporary urban condition).

In this perspective that does not absolutize the aesthetic value, nor does it entirely subordinate it to values that are perceived as ethically superior, the consistency of urban quality is defined by a normative aspect (regarding the coding system) that is related to the authority of the creators of that system (of conflicting powers). According to this pragmatic conception – that brings authority closer to the side of the users (and greater responsibility to the cultural industry) – the aesthetic value and social convention establish an historically determined relationship. The values proposed by the decision makers, the figures establishing the possible mediations, and the drawings that represent them in symbolic terms are relative and contextual. And the project originates from dialog and conflict.

Bibliography

APEL, K. O., 1973, *Transformation der Philosophie*, Francoforte, Suhrkamp; part. It. trans. 1977, Comunità e comunicazione, Torino, Rosenberg & Sellier

ARMANDO, A., 2008, *La soglia dell'arte. Peter Eisenman, Robert Smithson e il problema dell'autore dopo le nuove avanguardie*, Torino, Edizioni SEB 27

BAZZANELLA, L. [e altri], 2006, *Progetto, Storie e Teorie*, Torino, Celid (1984)

BENJAMIN, W., 1962, *Il compito del traduttore*, in Angelus Novus, Torino, Einaudi (1923)

BIANCHETTI, C., 2008, *Urbanistica e sfera pubblica*, Roma, Donzelli

BIASCO, S., 2006, *La sinistra postcomunista e gli intellettuali*, in "Italianieuropei" n. 4

BOBBIO, L., DANSERO, E., 2008, *La TAV e la valle di Susa. Geografie in competizione*, Torino, Allemandi

BÜRGER, P., 1990, *Teoria dell'avanguardia*, Torino, Bollati Boringhieri (1974)

CALVINO, I., 1967, *Il conte di Montecristo*, in Ti con zero, Torino, Einaudi

DAL PRA, M., PAGANINI, L., 1998, *Storia della filosofia, vol. XI, La seconda metà del Novecento*, Padova, Vallardi

DE ROSSI, A., DURBIANO, G., 2006, *Torino 1980- 2011. L'immagine fisica della città*, Torino, Allemandi

DIAMANTI, I., 2003 *Bianco, rosso, verde... e azzurro. Mappe e colori dell'Italia politica*, Bologna, Il Mulino

DURBIANO, G., 2000, *I Nuovi Maestri. Architetti tra politica e cultura nell'Italia del dopoguerra*, Venezia, Marsilio

FORTINI, F., 1962, *Astuti come colombe*, in "Menabò", n.5

GABETTI, R., 1977, *Architettura Industria Piemonte negli ultimi cinquant'anni*, Torino, Cassa di Risparmio di Torino

GABETTI, R., 1983, *Progettazione architettonica e ricerca tecnico-scientifica nella costruzione della città*, in GABETTI, R., MUSSO, E., OLMO, C., ROGGERO, M. F., Storia e progetto, vol. 6, Milano, Franco Angeli

GABETTI, R., 1990, *Sapere enciclopedico e sapere politecnico*, in "Atti e Rassegna tecnica della Società Ingegneri e Architetti in Torino", nn. 6-7

GEYMONAT, L., 1953, *Saggi di filosofia neorazionalistica*, Torino, Einaudi

GRANGER, G. G., (1992), *Le langage dans la philosophie d'aujourd'hui*, in FLØISTAD, G. (edited by), 2005, Language, Meaning, Interpretation, Dordrecht, NL e Norwell, USA (2003), Kluwer Academic Publishers

HABERMAS, J., 1998, *L'inclusione dell'altro. Studi di teoria e politica*, Milano, Feltrinelli (1996)

HABERMAS, J., 2002, *Il futuro della natura umana*, Einaudi, Torino

JAKOBSON, R., 1966, *Saggi di linguistica generale*, Milano, Feltrinelli (1963)

OLMO, C., 1980, *La città industriale*, Torino, Einaudi

PRETI, G., 1957, *Praxis ed empirismo*, Torino, Einaudi; 2007, Milano, Bruno Mondadori

RELLA, F., 2004, *Pensare per figure. Freud, Platone, Kafka, il postumano*, Roma, Fazi

TAFURI, M., 1969, *Per una critica dell'ideologia architettonica*, in "Contropiano", n. 1

TAFURI, M., 1986, *Storia dell'architetturta italiana, 1945-1985*, Torino, Einaudi

VECA, S., 1990, *Cittadinanza. Riflessioni filosofiche sull'idea di emancipazione*, Milano, Feltrinelli

Liliana Bazzanella
Carlo Giammarco

For an architecture of the territory
Project, actors, processes

59

Liliana Bazzanella
and Carlo Giammarco

For an architecture of the territory
Project, actors, processes

To design morphology, the physical form of the space as an environment and
a landscape to live in, means to imagine the *architecture of the territory*, in the
labyrinthine scenario of contemporary transformations and towards the horizons
of a variety of landscapes, expressions of the cultural, physical, environmental
peculiarities of our society. To imagine the architecture of the territory means also to
focus the attention on some key words pronounced by the culture of sustainability:
low soil consumption and attention to the features of the different soils, mobility
with a low environmental impact, human resources, re-use of the existent, social
sharing of the transformations, extended right to the landscape and to good living
conditions.

Therefore it means to open the culture of architecture, in a more radical approach
than the past, to new paths of ethical responsibility and social utility, and to new
directions that are consistent with the new awareness –the interdependence of
even tiny actions and their global effects on the territory, the awareness of the
limits of the development and the finite nature of many non renewable resources –,
alongside the strategy of the "durable development" [Brundtland 1987], which are
nonetheless experiencing a hard time in global and local policies.

The slogan *GrandeScala* refers to the dilated dimensions of a new complexity
of processes, meeting in the project of architecture of the territory, the physical
space of living, the points of view and the cultures of the many actors and
decision-makers, and the gazes and the contaminations of many competences and
projects. These in turn are already walking along paths that are marked by words
fueled by new, extended abilities and sensibility in respect to the limited world
in which we live (geographers, climatologists, pedologists, agronomists, hydro-
geologists...).

So how much can the dimension of the project on the *GrandeScala* be extended? Which dimension of the *GrandeScala* is effective to put into practice the parallel use of the terms architecture-territory in the context of the transformation of the living space?

Which is the appropriate spatial discipline for a trans-disciplinary scientific community, aiming at improving the quality of the living environments in the context of architectures of the territory able to open trans-scale debates on different levels, to question a vision that too often is only directed to the episodic forms of the constructed land?

The contemporary perception brought about by the satellite view might enable more adventurous juxtapositions with the planetary geographical scale –on which the environmental consumption of the soil and the risk of an environmental collapse are measured, and the still indistinct movement of innovative and uncertain projects on the global, regional and local scale is evaluated. This could also enable the identification of complex figures generated by the connection between the constructed land and the natural landscape, the cultivated fields and the abandoned ones, and the open spaces within the fabric of the urban expansion.

The need for a renewed focus to the form and the quality of the "spaces in negative" and their contexts might be back on the stage, in order to imagine the architecture of living on a global scale?

Leaving aside abstraction, we could pragmatically agree on a project on the *GrandeScala*, that is *geographically variable,* keeping in mind the opportunities and the chances for experimenting that appear on the operative scene.

It is essential to address once again the problem of disciplinary cultures, and of knowledge through the project: to cross the *GrandeScala* –geographical, social, economic, and political– with the words of architecture, exploring the spaces that are being created, measuring the meaning of the old terms (sedimented by their culture) and new terms (often mint through the contamination of knowledge and the instances of contemporary society) in relation to the design of the territory.

On several occasions of reflection and debate on the topics of the *GrandeScala*, Bernardo Secchi maintained that if we concentrate on the effectiveness of the urban and territorial projects, the scales of the plans and projects cannot coincide with the administrative and institutional scales. He also underlined the emergence of a new European urban geography that forces us to think on an increasingly wider scale [Secchi 1999 e 2002].

Three cases as examples. The large European metropolitan region, the North-Western Metropolitan Area under formation; meant not as an agglomeration of cities (Brussels, The Hague, Amsterdam, Antwerp, Cologne...) but as a territory, a big "inhabited park" whose architecture could be the morphological and social result of a planning approach on the *GrandeScala*, and its necessarily innovative instruments, actors and processes.

In the case of the *métropole lilloise,* which is a laboratory of the project on the *GrandeScala,* throughout the years a system of political, economic, and cultural actors has been taking shape, trying to produce a strategic consistence around a common metropolitan project of *mutation sans croissance* [Mons et al. 2009].

In a recent national study titled *Infrastrutture della mobilità e ambiente insediativo della conurbazione torinese,* to which participated a research unit of the DiPrADI, of Turin Polytechnic University, there have been several attempts to structure the morphologies of the *GrandeScala* in the dimension of the metropolitan mutation, and to interpret possible scenarios of future transformations. These transformations are in fact evoking new frameworks (both in terms of *governance* and of the appropriate instruments for the ongoing processes) that, in the words of Cesare Macchi Cassia, will open the door to "the democratic value represented by the collective control of our environmental future".

The list of cases and topics is still long, if we include the material presented to the convention *Trasmettere città sostenibili,* within the recent XXIII UIA World Congress, held in Turin in 2008.

There is a field of research and experimenting to be explored, thinking about "what to do" in the reality of the multifaceted processes in act, in the context of the announced revolution of the "durable development". The design of the territory can measure itself both as a tool for research, applying its potential of figurative exploration and the cultural references of architecture to new problems and terrains of transformations, and as an object of research, through "field-tests" and theoretical reflection. The goal is to define possible innovative proceedings, and to experiment new project-related roles to be presented and generalized by the operational and decision-making processes governing the transformations of the inhabited land.

This planning research is at the same time an experimental application of the project to the contemporary territory and to emergent problems, and an innovative reflection on the project and its paths and proceedings.

In the "Post-City Age" [Webber 1968], an expression also used by Rem Koolhaas, the dimension of academic research has finally the possibility to participate in the design of the morphology on a vast scale, in critical places and critical moments of the decision-making process regarding the construction of places: situations in which the morphological research of the project is usually peripheral, and the reasons of form are poorly argumented.

Nonetheless, the debate on the increasing territorial scale in the field of architecture is not a new one. We could resort to a critical discussion on the long run, but we prefer quoting Vittorio Gregotti, that in *Il territorio dell'architettura,* of 1966 was talking about *figures* of the territory and disciplinary tradition of architecture; about the landscape –the material of the project– as a general picture of life, and the approach to the *GrandeScala*, essential for the maitrise of the landscape on a regional scale.

We are not so much thinking about an expansion of the project-related disciplines of architecture towards a new scale; rather, we are talking in terms of a different dimension of the project, related to original geographies and new ways of living in the territory.

Our society is marked by imperfect forms of democracy, tinged with authoritarian and oligarchic degenerations, deep inequalities, mazes between institutional powers that are defined on the territory and economic and financial powers that are now transnational, but also with calls to universal values to be confirmed, everyone's right to reason on the future. In such a scenario, the issue of the intervention on the *GrandeScala* marking the territory could mean the negation of the social and cultural values of reference, and the irreversible erasure of the social and cultural material. On the other hand, if we reflects on the possibilities and potential of a more structured approach for the construction of new territorial geographies and of a *modus operandi* that is closer to the individuals and their aspirations, we can work on projects on the *GrandeScala*: they mark the territory by parts, in a perspective of systematization of different landscapes, in which the ordinary, the excellencies, and the memory interweave to define shared identities.

We must learn to read the connections between the open, cultivated and natural spaces on the one hand, and the constructed land on the other, through complex and original parameters. This would transfuse with new meaning the traditional concepts of city and countryside, center and outskirts, which appear outdated also in the light of the new geographies: the critical ones of the scattered settlements and the immaterial ones of the computer networks.

These multiple perspectives to be structured do not fit in the traditional gaze of the urban project and planning. Stefano Boeri suggests an *eclectic atlas* of the contemporary territory as an instrument to establish connections between the elements and the objects forming the territory, the words we use to "define and create representations of the territory, and the symbolic images we create to associate the objects and the words" [Boeri 2007].

A few operational tests on a large scale have opened the vocabulary of architecture to new meanings and new integrations, suggested by the architecture of the territory.

It is interesting to mention the recent presidential consultation on *Le Grand Paris*, in which 10 important international architectural firms were invited to suggest alternative visions on the long-term future of Paris, keeping two essential parameters in mind: the Kyoto guidelines on ecosustainability and the urban reintegration of the *banlieues*.

Some words of a new vocabulary have acquired an experimental value also in the field of the planning research, started in the Eighties by a group of researcher of the school of Turin: it focused on the trans-scale dimension, questioning from a local point of view the issues that have involved mainly public actors of the territory. Many researchers from a number of disciplines regarding the emergent local dimension have been appointed to record, by means of case studies, general phenomena related to the complex dimension of the contemporary transformations in Europe. In this way they have been building a genre of planning research, that on behalf of different subjects (local authorities, Ministries, CNR, public-private societies...) has been applied to emergent topics and problems of urban and territorial transformations in relation to/dealing with the redevelopment of the outskirts, alteration of the industrial empty spaces, the extended city and the scattered settlements, environment and constructed landscape, forms of the public space and urban centrality, architecture of the infrastructure and forms of settlement.

Among the cognitive instruments used to analyze these topics of architecture of the territory, the most common have been the tools of formal exploration and figurative investigation of the project, and a few innovative experimental paths to explore the real processes of transformations. The goal is to improve the current practices of management and production of the city and the territory; in the perspective, to quote Roberto Gabetti, of "architecture as a necessary value for the transformation of places".

For years, during these research on behalf of external Bodies, carried out by the Department of Planning and Industrial Design of Turin Polytechnic University, the words of architecture have been playing with the actors and processes operating and deciding the transformations: opening project issues before they are dealt with from an operational point of view, and interpreting the latent demands for research through dialog and field comparison, rather than by providing particular answers to particular needs.

The role and contribution of the planning research on the urban and territorial scale has been analyzed through the dialog with the urban plans, the intervention programs, and the (local, regional, national) public policies of settlement. At times this has originated unusual contaminations between sectional actors and knowledge, as shown by the study *Forme insediative ambiente infrastrutture*, published by Marsilio between 2002 and 2004 in three volumes: *Atlante, Manuale and Esperienze*.

There have also been attempts to utter words related to the architecture of the territory in the context of the European space of research, in relation to politics of research that are often not very open to architecture and its research strategies, hybridizing elements of the fields of architecture and art into projects of enhancement of memories and territorial heritage (UE – Cultura 2000, *Arch/Art Progetto di spazi sensoriali in contesti territoriali*. Casi studio in Italia Francia Belgio, 2004).

In the several different case studies, the working lines have been constantly aimed at setting up "sketches" of the overall planning vision, within the spatial dimension opened by the experimenting activity and at any step of the process of territorial transformation, dialoging with the different actors involved around the decision-making and operational boards. And together with the sketches, we were setting up a morphological lexicon that is apt to communicate, to be shared in the different operational situations. A lexicon that is often constituted of metaphors (the urban door, but also the door of a territory, the parts of a valley corridor, the threshold, the limit...) through which they have been trying to tackle the question of the specialized languages and the difficulty to communicate between actors with different roles and cultural backgrounds.

The words of morphology and of the evoked imaginaries could and should have introduced themselves into the processes, and enter the toolboxes of the decision-makers, actors and operators: like a fil rouge, useful during the negotiation of the operational interests, in the technical offices, in the building-sites... But this has rarely happened.

Often the relationships that are not easily built between form, politics and institutions are not enough if they do not involve the -even tiny- connections with society, and those with the economic and productive system, with the building industry in its many facets.

In this context of attention to the effectiveness of the processes, which are also assessed in relation to the material results, we have been questioning the role of the technical competences and the social responsibility of architecture, along a curved path that have touched and experienced many of the conceptual and operational instruments identified in the last decades. Two threads, in particular, held together our operational thinking: on the one hand *the use of the practice* of the morphological planning configurations on different scales and with different ends –starting from the recurrent use of the overall project for a large area, and from the simulation of alternatives; on the other hand, the reflections on the *modes of representation and communication* of the planning proposals.

We have also produced manuals of good practices on various scales, to suggest "consistent solutions" and to exemplify in negative: suggestions for the ordinary professional practice and instruments to foster a more extensive knowledge of the territory, which is surely more effective when it is built on the encounter between technicians, politics and citizens –as for the case of the *Manuale di indirizzi per il comune di Chiomonte* edited within the project Interreg CulturAlp [2005].

We have explored the effectiveness of guidelines that are expression of the goals of the decision-maker/controller and, at the same time, a point of reference for the operators and the designers, in order to promote an *in itinere* debate among the different actors. A debate that is made more structured by following the suggestions of the project drafts, and by producing *check lists* of project-related focus areas, also meant as qualitative assessment criteria.

Some preliminary planning explorations have been carried out –like in the cases shown in *Progettare il programma* [1998]– in order to interpret and convey into guidelines the programs of public administrations as the basis for competitions regarding the design, the assignment of a project, the competitive tenders.

And yet, on several occasions, the project images have gone hand in hand with the decision-making process, simulating scenarios that, through the interaction with the actors involved, represented the effects on the quality of urban landscapes of politics, project potentials, actions posed on the contractual, decision-making table; with the support of advanced technologies of simulation and communication, managed by the LAQ-TIP (Laboratorio di alta qualità –Progetti territoriali integrati del Politecnico di Torino).

If today's challenge for research and intervention, in the context of the connections between form and politics, is to rethink the important creative project dimension that can read the possible form of the metropolitan and regional dimension of transformation, then the operational path that can be traced (starting from the experiences of the DiPrADI group of Turin Polytechnic University) is to focus on the field experimentation of some basic issues. That is to say, to find out which and how many disciplines, politics, decision-making systems, actors, and processes are referred to a project of architecture of the territory that aims at acquiring public responsibility on a scenario that is marked by problems such as soil consumption, the shared value of sustainability, the strategies of durable development in general; to find out which new ideas can be experimented to design the landscape of the living environment, the shape of the empty and constructed land, within the territorial image of a "urban development without growth", structuring the elements of the morphological culture alongside those of the ecologic culture for the interventions that concern the cross-scale agglomeration territory-city-buildings, consistently to the logic of the *GrandeScala*...

However the question "who designs the territory dealing with places instead of spaces", proposed by Giuseppe Dematteis in the Nineties, is still an important issue in the cultural and operational debates; both in the debate between the decision-makers and the operators involved in the policies and processes of organization and transformation of the contemporary territory, and between the academic training institutions.

In the post-urban territory which is the result of the settlement process of the last decades (extended city, *ville éparpillée*, urban sprawl and the likes: a collection of oxymorons depending on the latitude of the language), we are experiencing the loss of the value attributed to the identitary features of the territory in favor of the urgences and the chances of economic growth: they often bring about "not the development of the places but the development in the places" [Becattini 2002], seen as spaces to be occupied even to the detriment of the socially established local identities.

Therefore we are assisting to a deficit in the planning and direction of the processes that gives free hand to summations of sector-based projects; on the other hand, it is the actual demand of a new, necessary creativity able to interpret the "statute" of the territory and to revive through transformation the shared value of a common social heritage.

Some of these urgencies are being debated both by universities and by the institutions of territorial governance. We wonder whether there is a consolidated scientific corpus regarding the project for the contemporary territory, on which to base the formative criteria of the figure of territorial planner, seen as a type of "individual or institutional conductor", in the words of Alberto Magnaghi.

It might be very useful to set up an explicit platform to discuss the experiences and the new formative projects carried out by the different Universities in this direction. While thinking about the new professional figures to be trained, the connection with innovative practices of territorial governance is of central importance, and from this point of view the scenario is not encouraging. On the other hand, we can agree with Magnaghi that it is of vital importance to support the creation of a scientific statute, since this would produce an integrated, multiscale and multidisciplinary approach towards a project of architecture of the territory that is finally able to social and institutional integration.

In this way it is essential to develop, around the table of territorial governance, decision-making cultures and integration processes that might foster the "producers of territory" (builders, farmers, traders, financiers, industrialists etc.) to redefine the respective interest concerning the projects of enhancement of the territory as a common good; with the knowledge, to cite Magnaghi again, that the protection of the territorial architecture, and the "positive transformation of the patrimonial assets into durable and sustainable forms require an active citizenship that combines expert and contextual knowledge" in the form of concertation and participatory democracy.

A positive sign of the relation form-politics can be seen in the research path that, passing also through studies regarding a portion of regional territory, the Susa Valley, for the territorial plan of the Region, led to the recent developments of the Piano Paesaggistico Regionale (PPR) of the Region Piedmont, that are dealt with elsewhere in this volume. Thanks to a wide range of competences they have developed materials that talk about morphology and architecture on the *GrandeScala*, both by identifying the territorial contexts –elements of the "implicit project" [Dematteis 2002]– and in the proposal of guidelines for the practices and the interventions, and in the organization of the transformations. Even if the result of the decision-making path is still unknown, and we are far from an effective operational verification, this search for the PPR constitutes an innovative experience that can contribute to a reflection that is necessary for a shared rewriting of the vocabulary of architecture in the dimension of the project, opening new geographies and new ways of living in the contemporary territory.

Architecture on the *GrandeScala*, territory as a value and a social inheritance, sustainability as extensive and inter-scalar focus: these are maybe the keywords of one of the strategic research lines on which the multidisciplinary scientific resources can be focused on, to contribute to innovate politics, creativity and processes in the context of the transformations of the stratified mosaic of the landscape of living.

Bibliography

BAZZANELLA, L. et al., Periferia torinese. Progetti per la modificazione, Torino, Celid

BAZZANELLA, L., CALLEGARI, G., CROTTI, M., DE ROSSI, A., 2005, *Metodologie per il recupero degli spazi pubblici negli insediamenti storici - Progetto Cultura Conoscenza e miglioramento dei centri storici e dei paesaggi culturali nel territorio alpino*, Regione Piemonte, Savigliano, L'Artistica Editrice

BAZZANELLA, L., GIAMMARCO, C.. (edited by), 1986, *Progettare le periferie*, Torino, Celid

BECATTINI, G., 2002, *Miti e paradossi del mondo contemporaneo*, Roma, Donzelli

BOERI, S., MULTIPLICITY.LAB, 2007, *Milano: cronache dell'abitare*, Bruno Mondadori, Milano

DE ROSSI, A. et al., (edited by), 2000, *Linee nel paesaggio. Esplorazioni nei territori della trasformazione*, Torino, UTET

DEMATTEIS, G., 2002, *Progetto implicito. Il contributo della geografia umana alle scienze del territorio*, Milano, Franco Angeli

DEMATTEIS, G., LANZA, C., 2006, *Spazio geografico e spazio economico*, in Conti, S., DEMATTEIS, G., LANZA, C., NANO, F., *Geografia dell'economia mondiale*, UTET

GIAMMARCO, C., BAZZANELLA, L., DE ROSSI, A., 1998, *Progettare il programma. Contributi della ricerca progettuale nella trasformazione dei paesaggi urbani*, Torino, Celid

GIAMMARCO, C., ISOLA, A., 1993, *Disegnare le periferie*, Roma, NIS

GREGOTTI, V., 1966, *Il territorio dell'architettura*, Milano, Feltrinelli (2008)

ISOLA, A. et al., 2002, *In.fra Forme insediative e infrastrutture. Ricerche coordinate da Aimaro Isola in 12 scuole di architettura. Atlante*, Venezia, Marsilio

ISOLA, A. et al., 2004, *In.fra Forme insediative, ambiente e infrastrutture. Ricerche coordinate da Aimaro Isola e Liliana Bazzanella in 11 scuole di architettura. Esperienze*, Venezia, Marsilio

ISOLA, A., et al., 2002, *In.fra Forme insediative e infrastrutture. Ricerche coordinate da Aimaro Isola in 12 scuole di architettura. Manuale*, Venezia, Marsilio

MAGNAGHI, A., 2000, *Il progetto locale*, Torino, Bollati Boringhieri

PARIS, D., MONS, D., COLLECTIF, 2009, *Lille métropole - Laboratoire du renouveau urbain*, Marsiglia, Parenthèses, 2009

RIGAMONTI, R. (edited by), 1997, *Ricerche per una architettura dei luoghi*, Torino, Celid

SECCHI B., 1999, *"Città moderna, città contemporanea e loro futuri"*, in Dematteis G. et al., I futuri della città. Tesi a confronto, Angeli, Milano.

SECCHI, B. et al., *La città europea del XXI secolo. Lezioni di storia urbana*, Skira, Milano 2002

UNITED NATIONS WORLD COMMISSION ON ENVIRONMENT AND DEVELOPMENT, 1987, *Bruntland Report*, ONU

WEBBER, M., 1968, The *Post-City* Age, in "Daedalus", n. 97

Regione Piemonte, *Piano Paesaggistico Regionale* (D.G.R. n. 53-11975 del 04 agosto 2009): www.regione.piemonte.it/sit/argomenti/pianifica/paesaggio/ppr.htm

Progetto *Le Grand Paris*: www.legrandparis.culture.gouv.fr

Area metropolitana di Lille: www.lillemetropole.fr

Gustavo Ambrosini
Mauro Berta

Territorial figures

Morphological devices to shape the urban form

73

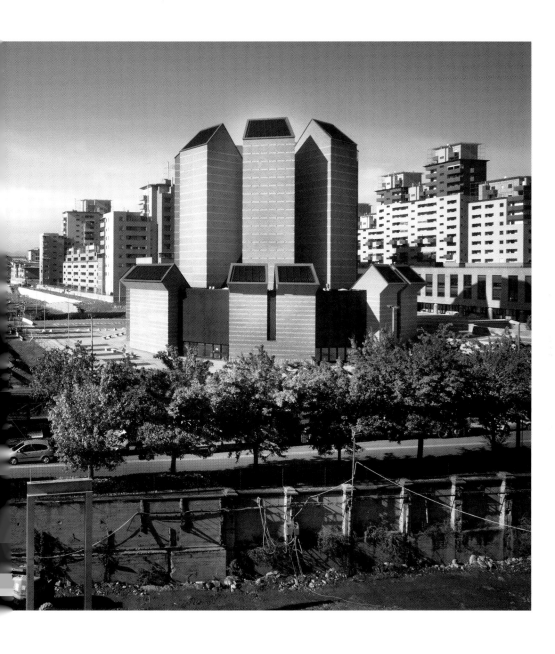

Turin. Spine 3, the scenery of the former Teksid with the parish of the Holy Face, photo, Alessandro Cane

Gustavo Ambrosini
and Mauro Berta

Territorial figures
Morphological devices
to shape the urban form

I. The reasons of form

"The project as a flag". In the Mid-Eighties, on the southern outskirts of Turin, the members of the Nichelino District Committee were reclaiming with these words the implementation of a service plan, drafted by the Municipality following the guidelines of Turin Polytechnic University, trying to prevent it from falling into the indeterminacy and oblivion of the "standards". Oddly enough, these words succeeded in forcing the new public administration to re-examine and take into consideration the initial project. These words were enlightened by the awareness that the form of those services was at the same time a requisite and a consequence of a concerted political action; an action that took into account the plurality of interests and expectations, unveiling their nature of a collective good of vital importance within the decision-making process.

This example points out one of the most important topics in the context of urban planning: the relationship between the political dimension of the city and the material substance of urban places. That is to say, the ways in which the public city actually translates itself into specific places and definite shapes, which is normally the result of conflicting views between administrative choices and implementation opportunities, need of self-representation and shared symbols, collective and private interests. To investigate the mutual connections between (urban) *form* and *politics* requires a double, apparently contradictory effort. It is a matter of defining a field of investigation centered on the connections between the two terms, in order to demolish any instance of alleged self-sufficiency, and any outdated epistemological fence. To be able to do so, it is essential to explore the two terms separately, in the context of the specific disciplines, so as to evaluate the features and instruments that could be useful to answer to the constantly changing conditions. Within the disciplinary field of architecture, it is essential to question the mechanisms that shape the practice of urban design, meant as an "artistic practice" that confronts itself –and, by this means, builds its own legitimacy– with the empirical conditions, the form of things and the reason of that form. [Gregotti 1993].

In spite of its brevity, this essay is aimed at contributing to the analysis of this practice, observing it from an angle that has been gradually acquiring scientific solidity within a narrow cultural *milieu* and in a definite time-span: Turin architecture scene and the field defined by the specific stances that have been gaining weight during the last thirty years. Our goal is to identify some key nodes, able to guide possible further discussions.

Our objective is to highlight the methodological features through which some of the strategies of form were developed within the urban project. This does not mean to give unlimited "trust" to design, regarded as a self-sufficient field of action. To take the *GrandeScala* as an interpretative point of view means to look at the project as a modeling of the problems, rather than as a merely technical solution; an instrument aimed at acknowledging the different interests and their negotiation; a point of condensation of the different uses of public and private places, wishes and commitments; an "exchange between a plurality of actors, values, interests and competences" [Bianchetti 2008]. A "return" tension towards the physical data must be held as a point of reference, as an essential horizon of responsibility that bases its disciplinary relevance on its ability to question the morphological scale of the territorial transformations.

The point of departure is a widely shared concept: one of the main features of Turin architecture scene is the originality of a continuous complementary relationship between the theoretical production, in the context of an academic intellectual *elite*, and a sound intellectual pragmatism, of strong polytechnic derivation, deeply rooted in the school of Turin [Gabetti 1990]. An approach that has always taken into consideration the concrete experience of the real or planned transformations, the building sites, and the proposed and implemented forms; not as a mere verification of previous theoretical approaches, but as a real place of methodological construction of the project. This in turn has been regarded as a chance to dialog and interact with the many economic, social, and political realities that constitute the city and its territory [Gabetti 1965].

This approach is based on the awareness of the complex, heterogeneous Turin cultural line, that only on occasions managed to promote its own cultural "institutional" immediacy [Olmo 1992], to the point that too often it has been presented as a tradition "with no teachers or institutions". On the other hand, the background thesis is that it is possible to detect some lines of continuity that enable to mark out a clearly defined position; this in turn would be the result of a line of research on the diverse morphology of settlement of the contemporary city and territory. This is not meant to recreate a *posteriori* the scientific value of a research path; it is rather an attempt to focus on some meaningful aspects of an approach that grounds its own originality and visibility on the programmatic denial of a strict and peremptory codification, and at the same time on the development of a capacity of adaptation and communication with the operational contexts.

II. Urban form between project and theory
These experiences have been developed in the cultural context surrounding the figures of Roberto Gabetti and Aimaro Isola at the beginning of the Eighties. The point of reference is a planning methodology (and a figurative heritage) that, without mixing roles and personal biographies, presents some common traits both in the trial projects carried out by a research group of the Faculty of Architecture in Turin, and in the diverse professional experiences of Gabetti and Isola.
It is a line of project research that definitely leaves aside some of the most significant experiences of the second post-war period, which took morphology and urban form as a primary operational research area in the field of architecture. The

differences and nuances of these experiences have always been highlighted by members of Turin cultural scene.

First of all, within the process of construction of urban forms, and the working class neighborhoods. At the beginning of the Eighties the last area-plans for working-class neighborhoods, drafted according to the Law 167 of 1972, marked the end of a season: the construction of the public city. They also marked the decline of the idea of reinventing the spatial form of the city, started forty years before with the policy of the INA Casa districts. This topic would require an extensive analysis, but this essay is only aimed at pointing out how a few Turin-based examples have entailed a radical questioning of the current composition instruments.

In the case of the Falchera district, built between 1950 and 1956 following the project by Astengo, Molli-Boffa, Passanti, Renacco and Rizzotti, the reference to the process of "deformation" of the internal courtyard structure of the "cascina", was only an excuse to borrow planimetric forms on the model of analogous districts in Scandinavia. It is true that the different residential areas of three-story houses placed in form of a U, like "open wings" around the green areas, have created an intricate pattern that is hard to situate (the well-known "derailed train", as defined by Mollino). Nevertheless, they have also created an effective balance by alternating buildings and green areas, and have given a new meaning to the morphological rules contained in the handbooks of the "Piano incremento occupazione operaia" edited by INA Casa, which suggested creating "private spaces" and "closed, intimate volumes" [id. 1950]. But the explicit clash was mainly on the level of the style features of the buildings, as for the case of the "anti-modern" linguistic challenges proposed by Passanti.

The loneliness of the Falchera district, outside the city, could be seen as a programmatic fragment of that "Po Valley production chain" projected towards Milan, which conveyed the image of the ABRR plan, developed by the group led by Astengo in the immediate post-war period [Astengo et al. 1947]. On the contrary, the isolation of the Vallette district, built between 1954 and 1962, seems to favor an implicit plan of social segregation [Pace 2001]. Of the three projects presented by the appointed groups (respectively coordinated by Levi Montalcini, Renacco e Cavallari Murat), the winner was Renacco's proposal. It was subsequently reformulated more than once, yet keeping the structure of intricate road patterns that spread out from the service center, branching out to "four minimal units of neighborhood". These are not tied to any precise morphological principle, and along the many structure of an organic and functionalist derivation they leave space to the part realized by Cavallari Murat, Gabetti and Isola, and Ranieri: this in turn partly reproduces their initial project, through a continuity of tall and low buildings interconnected by roofs and porches, to form an original sequence of green court-yards. As such, it reflects the clash between the study on morphological continuity and the open space on the one hand, and the compositional juxtaposition "high buildings – low buildings" on the other, which will turn into the standardizing linguistic code of the second seven-year period of INA casa, and of the subse-quent area plans of the law 167 of 1962. Also this principle has been stigmatized by Mollino, who took part to the planning of a district along Corso Sebastopoli (1957-1960), and denounced the distortion of the initial idea as the "moral failure of the project". By the Mid-Seventies the so-called "new" Falchera district surrounded the original core with a disturbing sequence of fences and towers that were no longer regulating the soil, but indifferently punctuating the land. These unworka-ble physical results are the symbol of the end of a season of experimental models of construction of space.

Secondly, in the same years the theories of urban form took a radical shift away from their debut, within the movement of Italian Neorationalism. That is to say, away from that *corpus* of studies on urban morphology that have been influencing for more than twenty years –although with radically different results– an important part of the Italian architecture culture, to the point that abroad it is regarded as a veritable "school" [Moudon 1994]. A school that, contrary to other experiences such as the English tradition of Conzen and Whitehand, or the "school of Versail-les" of Panerai and Castex, has grounded its planning methodology on the reco-very of a tight and indissoluble relationship, "operating" [Muratori, 1960] in the historical substance of the city and the territory.

The biggest difference between the Turin experience and this cultural model – which developed between the Sixties and the Seventies around the Faculties of Venice, Milan and Rome– is precisely their distance. A distance essentially created on ordinary topics, a fact that further highlights the difference between the distin-ct approaches.

What they have in common is the vision of history as a field for a planning action; on the other hand, this makes the heterogeneity between the respective operational attitudes even more visible. The setting is the international debate that in the Mid-Thirties was already trying to reintroduce the study of architecture as a new active instrument for constructing a planning methodology [Pagano, Daniel 1936]; it presented its features as parameters to re-interpret in a critical light the differences between the housing models of the consolidated city and those of the *existenz minimum*, and to measure their real implications on the construction of urban fabrics [Samonà 1935; 1959]; it identified an "environmental pre-existence", from which to borrow linguistic and syntactic material in order to develop a modern, genuinely independent language [Rogers 1955]. The connection to the historical dimension was in part built on a new season of studies regarding architecture, cities, and architects, such as the Turin-based studies conducted by Cavallari Murat, Passanti and Gabetti.

There is a neat separation with the approach envisaging an overall re-founding of the planning activity in rational and "logical" terms [Grassi 1967], as a sequence of necessary and sufficient moves to neutralize individualism that derive any action from the analytic framework, which on the contrary led to a breaking point in this very approach. The reason was its incapacity to accompany a thorough knowledge of the historical fabrics and their evolutions with a proactive model, if not by means of a necessary "reductionism" that depicted the city as the "assembling and organizing of few permanent and immutable elements." [Solà Morales 1984]. This methodological scenario did not succeed in Turin; on the contrary, the research was focused on "the creation of an always renewing connection with things, objects, and cities [...]", rejecting the "quicker and more effective" tendency to "replace everything with the Symbol: total, abstract, and immaterial. An entirely mental and para-scientific symbol" [Gabetti, Isola 1965]. It was not by coincidence that the distance from the results of the aforementioned research and their own cultural paradigms was highlighted by the sharp contrast between the uncertain and ironical *ready-made* expressed on the one hand by Gabetti and Isola in "Architettura/Conoscenza", and on the other the severe austerity of the 1981-82 "Strada novissima", presented by Aldo Rossi for Architettura/Idea at the XVI Milan Triennial Exhibition [Gabetti, Isola 1981].

The crisis of Neorationalism was overcome in Turin by means of a sharp shift on the conceptual level, that was still revolving around the same idea of necessary relationship with history. A history that in this case had turned into the ideal partner for an intellectual, ironic dialog, rich in references and new proposals. In the slightly ironic words of Manfredo Tafuri [1986] when talking about the first experiences of Gabetti and Isola, it was a *flirt* that did not consider the use of evocative images and references as a snobbish disengagement (the "withdrawal" of Banham's famous article [1959]). It rather regarded it as the very foundation of a balanced dialog between project and history, almost an elective affinity: "Either we have a relationship with History, be it an engagement or a fragile affair, or we have no relations with History, and can follow a path of a repertoire of form or get stuck in the absolute, astral "classical world"" [Gabetti, Isola 1971].

Especially in a moment when the project was expanding on the territory to become urban or landscape project: take for instance the planning and research experiences that during the Eighties were disseminated through the Department and some professional studies. That is to say, when the topic of the *GrandeScala* started to gain weight: a new dimension of the architectural debate that is obviously conceptual before than physical; that confronts itself not only with the extension of the project to the scale of the city and the territory, but particularly with the multiplication of the actors involved, the topics and the contradictions, materialized by different chances of transformation.

A dimension that has essentially shaped itself on a few, important recurrent topics: the big urban project, the indeterminate spaces of the scattered settlements, the recovery of the wide, empty urban spaces created by the contraction of the industry and, lastly, the road infrastructures seen as a morphological device [Isola et al., 2002 (a) e (b); 2004]. Privileged grounds to develop variable and complementary strategies and instruments, on whose background lied the issue of the *landscape*, far from the attempts of disciplinary acquisition and from merely normative deviations; on the contrary, it was an active tool for both the continuous reinterpretation of the territory and the construction of a continuity of the space, experienced "from the intimate to the polis" [Isola, 1999]. In that case the interpretation of the project as a "trace" or an "experience" –usual ideas in the views of Gabetti and Isola–, and the definition of a "narrative" dimension of architecture [Derossi 2001] constituted the formal pretext and the trigger device of a rewriting process of the city and the territory. As a consequence, the territory was investigated, represented, dismounted in its constitutive elements, then turned into a single bearing, a foothold for architecture in order to become architecture. The relationship was one of mutual and symmetrical interchange between nature and artifice, whose legitimacy was out of doubt: "[…] like agriculture, the building industry can and must change nature" [Gabetti, Isola 1977].

Turin peculiar scene did not only spring from the specific eccentric condition of its approach to the proper "schools"[Olmo 1998], nor from the relative isolation that its culture has always experienced and, in a way, cultivated; also Carlo Mollino underlined its apathy in the face of the innovative drive of Modernity with its definition of "city of the quicksand" [Mollino 1934], subsequently borrowed by Ettore Lavazza.

If one of the lines of research seems to have (almost) withstood to the cyclic upturning that has repeatedly crossed the debate on architecture of the last thirty years, it is because it was apparently "weaker" (the reference to Vattimo is not accidental) in respect to more assertive approaches. It did not reclaim independence of its disciplinary statute, it did not present itself as a method that could be coded: "Utopia, synthetic vision, aprioristic approach, will, program, scheme, methodology: big obstacles that have been avoided, and nothing else" [Gabetti, Isola 1977]. Because it was tied to an idea of experience influenced by Pareyson's view, a continuous and progressive construction of its modus operandi that was always restating its own legitimacy. Because it was the result of an approach to the project that regarded it as a polytechnic practice, a strategic action the enabled a cumulative process and questioning of the results, on the basis of viable observations. The "corpus" constituted by the works of Gabetti and Isola is paradigmatic in this sense.

III. Figures
Even if it is impossible to find transferable taxonomies in order to investigate on the many trial projects regarding the morphological scale, we can try to retrace some of the mechanisms of formation of the figures that are used by the designed morphologies to shape what used to be called urban design (now urban landscape, urbanized territory, landscape *tout court*). Due to the brevity of this essay, we

are going to refer to just a few project cases; they have not been chosen for being paradigmatic, but because they are significantly situated within the debate on the forms of the urban project, which developed in Italy in the Mid-Eighties. Therefore they are not models, but rather clues to help us deciphering strategies of form. *Urban mending.* The state of the progress of the Mission Banlieues 89, set up in France in 1983, was illustrated by 200 projects for the redevelopment of the urban outskirts, which in 1986 opened the International Convention *Progettare le periferie*, held in Turin. It was an important step in the setting of a debate on the quality of urban environments, in a historical moment in which the unsolved problems of the city as a whole, and the worsening conditions of the more remote outskirts were highlighting the "social need" for organizing, defining and signifying the space. Turin witnessed an intense season of research, that saw the school of architecture collaborating, thanks to conventions and research contracts, with the public subjects that acted as the main actors governing the transformations – Region, municipal administrations, IACP, Department of Public Works and so on. The goal was to experiment theories and operational methodologies for the redevelopment of the outskirts [Bazzanella, Giammarco 1986; Rigamonti 1997]

The pilot project for the services of the "Castello di Nichelino" district, realized by the research group of the Polytechnics (coordinated by Gabetti with L. Bazzanella, L. Falco, C. Giammarco, S. Giriodi, A. Isola, L. Mamino, and R. Rigamonti) and mentioned at the beginning of this essay, anticipated and sketched out some of the features of this line of investigation: a large avenue crosses transversely the "great empty meadow", randomly surrounded by the fences and residential towers of the Area Plan for the working-class neighborhoods. Standing against the background of the mountain arch, it connects three different parts –a core of service crafts, a park, and a large plateau of educational, socio-cultural, and commercial services. A strategy aiming at "mending" the heterogeneous results of distinct and casual instances that could not be qualified, and "aggregating" elements whose nature of public space, meant to host social and shared activities, was explicitly declared through "speaking" architectural forms. The shape of the long "porch" seems to be an evocative icon for all this, as a supporting element for a system of spaces that is provided with a figurative independence, relatively detached from the forms gravitating around it: the representation of a collective space, the "solidification" of the idea of a path.

This could be accomplished only by creating a balance between: the stability of the dispositive and typological requirements of the collective spaces; the stability of the building technologies and the rules of composition of the architectural elements; the programmatic flexibility provided by the projected forms to a process of ongoing redefinition of the needs of the services. The different strategies for a new mode of intervention on the shape of the city –exemplified by the concept of pilot-project– were based on the dialog with the operations that were closer to fixed architectural solutions (take for example the emblematic comparison between the project for the Nichelino district, presented by Gabetti, and the plan for the Corassori Area, presented by Gregotti, on the occasion of the 1984 INU Convention, held in Stresa). The debate on the shape of the city revolved around the need for the so-called "third generation plans" to take into consideration the physical features of the city and the territory, since they represented the overcoming of the artificial juxtaposition "city of the Plan – city by parts".

The same Gregotti, when commenting on the Nichelino district in the issue no. 82 of "Urbanistica", talked about "some elements of nostalgia for the big works of neoclassical and eclectic derivation, that rather than imposing their presence as a global reference" often emerge in the form of fragments; he noted how what had been usually regarded as residual parts –columns and porches– was coming right to the front, defining the overall figure and charging it with meaning [Gregotti 1986].

Morphology as a typological innovation. "Architecture as modification": the double issue of "Casabella" magazine published in the January of 1984 represented a moment of fundamental synthesis for the debate on the urban project in Europe, and clearly defined the boundaries of the field of action of the project. A project that must be meant as an "modification", that is to say a "rewriting of the constitutive rules of the morphological and functional asset, of the economical and social role of a part of the territory" [Gregotti 1993], in a city (and a territory) that must be meant as the stratification of historical material to be studied and interpreted. The "changing conditions" described by Bernardo Secchi's article [1984] addresses the need to abandon the stability of universalist topics such as the types, which mirrors an holistic idea of society, to "observe the meaning of the single architectural objects within the systems of connections of every single urban part". Among the different levels of a possible "strategy of modification" highlighted by Croset e Brandolini, the editors of that issue, the most revealing one seems to be the modification of the system of connections between the object and its context of placement, from a physical and perceptive point of view, and the mechanisms of modification of these connections.

In a rich gallery of projects – such as the re-qualification of Murcia old mills by Navarro Baldeweg, Consuegra's Plaza de la Encarnacion in Sevilla, Lauro's plan for Venice, the Klösterli area in Berna designed by Tesar, Eisenman's Ohio State University–, Gabetti and Isola presented their project for the completion of a block in Turin historic center.

The text attached by the authors, "The sketch of a project", despite its apparently humorist narrative style actually establishes the definite cultural, economical, technical, and political boundaries of an operation that discards the hypothesis of "disguising, camouflaging [...] and dissimulating while following the road lines". The result would be to "find one's direction in a maze of narrow passages, embedded between the buildings. Dark public spaces, shadowy private places: uninhabitable present and future living spaces". In other words, to walk along new paths that use –even unconsciously– devices from other contexts. For example the tectonic *device* of emptying the residential block by "turning" its facade in order to let in the sunlight creates a spatial articulation from the simplicity of the section: the volumes are compressed at the angles, and vertically follow the line of the facade while assuming the shape of a pyramid with the sides inclined inward. A sequence of terraced steps facing a street/courtyard, a collective protected space, is situated on the first level to cover a pre-existent warehouse.

This overturned the idea of pure conservation, seen as the "transformation into a museum", which was pervading the debate on the re-qualification of the historic city centers: it played with the relationship between tradition and innovation in a new key. This strategy also denied the uniqueness of the building to "reveal the existent under a new light through the project, modifying it by creating subtle systems of contrasts and differences" [Gregotti 1984]. In this way it explored and demolished the limits of the notion of typology, until it dissolved the topic of the constructed object into a necessary reformulation of the urban morphology.

Landscape as openness and inclusion. The XVII Milan Triennial Exhibition of 1987, titled "The imagined cities: new projects for nine cities" cast some light on the issue of reusing and giving back a meaning and a role to the parts of a rapidly changing city; interweaving the path of a curious traveler, willing to capture the key aspects of the urban form and architecture of the nine proposed cities, through the projects developed by the invited architects on the most urgent issues.

Five Turin citizens (Derossi, Jaretti, De Ferrari, Roggero, Gabetti) and three international hosts (Kleihues, Bohigas, Navarro Baldeweg) coordinated the planning groups that were redesigning the area occupied by the large abandoned industrial settlements in the north-western part of the city, around the Dora River. The preliminary dossier, edited by Derossi, explicitly pointed out the issue of the "decentralization" as a necessary prefiguration of new life scenarios for the future of cities, signaling two possible path to be followed. The first one is the "polycentric" vision, that reminds once again to the city as a –sometimes implicit– unitary system, within which to operate in search of a proper form to give stability and durability. The second path is the abolition of the notion of structure, so that the urban facts can become events, no longer pursuing their own legitimation by creating a system; as a consequence, the action becomes the "metaphor of an attitude towards the project that focuses on the "eventual" quality of the city" [Derossi 1988].

The project developed by the research group of Turin Polytechnic University (the same that presented the project for the Nichelino district) seemed to escape from the limits of field between these two polarities (in which many of the different proposal were situated). It did not refrain from the idea of relating the project to a system, but this very system was situating itself in a more abstract and conceptual order that brought the inclusive scale of the landscape mark back to (this part of) the city. A bastion modeled in a variety of ways, made of grassy slopes covering the different activities to be located, surrounding the winding line of the river like a frame, like the symbol of a natural approach to be revived. Its goal was not to mend the tear produced in the city by the shift to the scale of the big industry, but to rebuild a continuity of fluxes revolving around the new park of the Dora River, as shown in the picture.

It was a process of invention of the landscape, which had little to do with the idea of *mimesis*; it rather referred to the strategies used by Gabetti and Isola in some projects to define a few morphological devices on the *GrandeScala*, in order to hypothesize the future transformations of a place in a peculiar, yet not fixed manner: drawings of form taking into account the processual quality of action.

Such is the case of the project for the Centro Direzionale in Candiolo (1973), where the principle of settlement of the big green ring is based on few rules: section-geometry-scale. They generate a tension between absoluteness and imperativeness of the gesture on the one hand, and the ability to control and harmonize the perceptive qualities of the landscape on the other. The planimetric sketch shows the main road patterns and the two rings on a territorial scale: the garden of the Palazzina di Caccia di Stupinigi and the one of the proposed intervention. It enables the comprehension not of the idea of mimesis, but of the innovative charge of the geometries (here the rings) that create references on more than one scale: from the *mise en scene* of the principle of distribution of the activities, to the visual interconnections between the peculiarities of the vegetation and the geography of the site (up to the arch of the Alps).

Or the case of the project for the competition regarding the Bicocca area in Milan (1985), in which the rediscovery/reinvention of the territorial fabric of the Roman *aggeratio* became the structuring framework for the morphology of the buildings, and for the public and collective paths. Given the impossibility to interpret the symbols of the past in a literal way, their use as explicit pretexts has almost stigmatized the ineffectiveness of cheap, direct transpositions from History (mocking the excessively deductive approaches to urban structures). At the same time it has moved the reference to an abstract and figurative plan, that comprehends the distinct scales of the project.

There are three conceptual figures, located on different –and at times complementary– plans, crossing in a non linear way most of the planning research experiences that have been developed in a specific cultural context in the last twenty years: the "mending" as densification and physical-relational aggregation by partial instances of continuity; the typological reinvention as a structural component of the morphological pattern of a part of the territory; an open attitude to the landscape, seen as a category able to establish a different conceptual order on the interweaving scales, between nature and artifice.

Figures that, time after time, have constituted case studies of possible planning devices for the different geographical contexts: not rules, but pretexts for a mechanism of construction of the form that does not reinvent the human being in the physical world; it rather regards it as a resource from which to draw material, in order to spread the proper forms of *civitas* across different places. "Strong Images" against the indifferent space, able to "adjectivize" and give figurative centrality to the structure of the collective space, the systems of urban green, the traces of memory [Giammarco 1986]. It is on the level of the image that the relationship with the tradition and stratification of a place has been operating, through a process in which "the maze of "conscious and unconscious" relations, memories and objects structures itself, expressing itself in dramatic "narration images"" [Vitale 1987]; these condensate the maze of knowledge and experiences into an always temporary idea.

An attitude that is not far from the mechanisms of transposition in architectural terms of elements that belong to a variety of heterogeneous fields, like in the works by Carlo Mollino. Mechanisms that, as Bruno Reich recently pointed out, act as analogies: an analogical thinking that is radically different from the intention to reorganize the discipline on the basis of the specificity of the "analogous architecture", which reminds of Rossi. On the contrary, it crosses the boundaries of the pure architecture to draw from a wider universe of references. Mechanisms that "deny the linearity of the planning process, referring to a process the acts by means of "generative metaphors", quoting repertoires and situations that are "stored in the memory"" [Reichlin 2006].

As illustrated by many of Umberto Eco's works, it is the use of the metaphor that highlights its knowledge value: the substitution of a literal term by a figurative term entails a condition of alienation that requires an interpretative surplus, and fosters our reflection on the analogies and differences between things. In this sense the ideas coming from the fields of geography represent an essential contribution. Giuseppe Dematteis, while describing the notion of metaphorical mediation in the Humanities as a "useful imprecision" leading us to a better understanding of the features of the world, talks of a necessary metaphorical effectiveness of the categories and models of geographical description: "metaphors are like open conceptual images, enabling the representation of some aspects that are still poorly defined from a theoretical point of view, in order to produce a better definition of the same" [Dematteis 1995].

These planning strategies envisage specific devices of form acting as figures-metaphors, so as to "introduce in the circuits of the exchange of communication a few conceptual images that, despite holding concrete object and things as literary references, entail potential inter-subjective relationships; these in turn are able to introduce in the discourse new meanings and their related intentions, expectations, and implicit projects" [Id.].

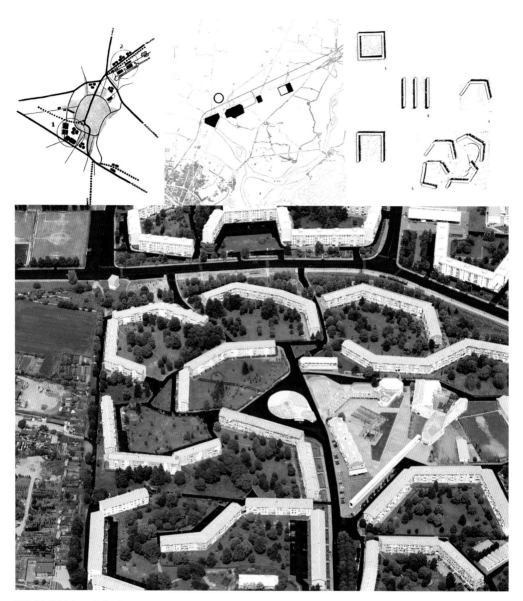

950-56. "Falchera" district.
Above from the left. Sketch of the urban plan, attached to the Regional Plan: the two industrial-residential settlements of Falchera and Mirafiori are visible, on the northern and southern edge of the city (Metron, 1954, 52-53). The big industrial-residential complexes in the Stura-Settimo strip (Metron, 1954, 52-53). Composition schemes about the open blocks at Falchera. (Metron, 1954, 52-53).
Below. Aerial view of the district at present (graphic processing).

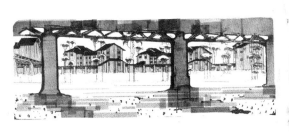
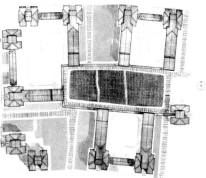

1958-78. INA houses at "Le Vallette" district.
Above from the left. Perspective view, with the elevated pedestrian way (Isola private archive). Plan of lot "G", designed by R. Gabetti, A. Isola, A. Cavallari Murat and G. Raineri.
Below. Aerial view of the district at present (graphic processing).

Above on the left. 1973: general model of the project for the "Castello" district, Nichelino (Turin). Architects: R. Gabetti coordinator, L. Bazzanella, L. Falco, C. Giammarco, S. Giriodi, A. Isola, L. Mamino, R. Rigamonti (DIPRADI archive, Turin Polytechnic).
Above on the right. 1980-83: drawings for the Block 13 project, in the ancient Turin city centre, Via S. Agostino. Architects: R. Gabetti, A. Isola, G. Drocco (Isola private archive).

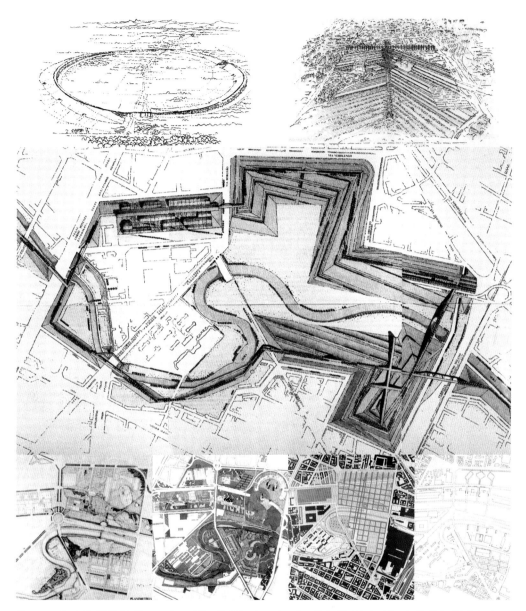

Above on the left. 1973: bird's eye view of the Fiat Headquarter, Candiolo (Turin). Architects: R. Gabetti, A. Isola, G. Drocco, L. Re (Isola private archive).

Above on the right. 1985-1988: perspective sketch of the Bicocca district, Milan. Architects: R. Gabetti, A. Isola and others (Isola private archive).

Pages 92-93. 1987: urban renovation projects for the industrial areas on the Dora Riparia river, Turin. R. Gabetti (in the center); below: M. F. Roggero, S. Jaretti, J. P. Kleihues, J. N. Baldeweg, O. Bohigas, G. De Ferrari, P. Derossi.

With no intention of presenting them as univocal values, these strategies can be found in many studies and experimental projects on the transformation of contemporary territories, on behalf of territorial entities and public actors: a plurality of experiences carried out by the research group of the Department of Planning of the Faculty of Architecture (that in recent years has been attracting new generations of academics), addressing problems and dimensions that are never the same, from topical urban transformations to large regional projects. Strategies that are different in their form, but hold a tension that unifies —at times in an implicit, "behind the gaze" way— three key aspects for the people operating and living on the territory: the design of the public space, the spatial organization of the activities, and the quality of the architecture of the different places. This is a point of departure for the discipline, that creates a precise methodological specificity: the need to work on the morphological figures on the urban and territorial scale as a strategy of form (of settlements, open spaces and infrastructures), required to give weight and relevance to the design on the *GrandeScala*.

Bibliography
"Controspazio" n. 4-5 October-November 1977
ASTENGO, G., BIANCO, M., RENACCO, N., RIZZOTTI, A., 1974, *Piano Regionale Piemontese*, in: "Metron", n.14
BANHAM, R., 1959, *The Italian retreat from Modern Architecture*, in: "The Architectural Review", n. 747
BAZZANELLA, L., GIAMMARCO, C.. (edited by), 1986, *Progettare le periferie*, Torino, Celid
BIANCHETTI, C., 2008, *Urbanistica e sfera pubblica*, Roma Donzelli, 2008
CELLINI, F., D'AMATO, C., 1985, *Gabetti e Isola. Progetti e architetture 1950-1985*, Milano, Electa
DEMATTEIS, G., 1995, *Progetto implicito*, Milano, Franco Angeli
DEROSSI, P. (edited by), 1988, *Progettare nella città*, Torino, Allemandi
DEROSSI, P., 2001, *Pietro Derossi. Per un'architettura narrativa. Architetture e progetti 1959-2000*, Milano, Skira
GABETTI, R., 1965, *La situazione architettonica di Torino dal dopoguerra ad oggi 1945-1965*, in: DEZZI BARDESCHI, M., VINCA MASINI, L., (edited by), *Prima triennale itinerante d'architettura italiana contemporanea*, Firenze, Centro Proposte
GABETTI, R., 1971, *Introduzione*, in OLMO, C. M., *Politica e forma*, Firenze, Valsecchi
GABETTI, R., 1990, *Sapere enciclopedico e sapere politecnico*, in: "Atti e Rassegna Tecnica della Società degli Ingegneri e degli Architetti in Torino", Nuova Serie, A. 44, n. 6-7, June-July
GABETTI, R., 1992, *Variabili e costanti della cultura architettonica torinese: dal 1945 ad oggi, con un passaggio al futuro*, in: OLMO, C., (edited by), *Cantieri e disegni. Architetture e piani per Torino. 1945-1990*, Torino, Allemandi
GABETTI, R., ISOLA, A., 1965, *Tipologia e manualistica*, in "Atti e Rassegna Tecnica della Società degli Ingegneri e degli Architetti in Torino", n. 4, April 1965
GABETTI, R., ISOLA, A., 1977, *Sulla schiena del drago*, in: "Controspazio", n. 4-5, IX year, 1977
GABETTI, R., ISOLA, A., 1981, *Architettura/Conoscenza*, Catalogo della mostra omonima, XVI Triennale di Milano, December 15, 1981- January 31, 1982, Firenze, Alinari
GIAMMARCO, C., 1984, *Pensiero debole e immagini forti*, in: BAZZANELLA, L. et al., *Periferia torinese. Progetti per la modificazione*, Torino, Celid
GREGOTTI, V., 1984, *Modificazione*, in: "Casabella" *Architettura come modificazione*, monographic issue, n. 498/499, January-February
GREGOTTI, V., 1986, *Nichelino: la riqualificazione della periferia*, in: "Urbanistica", n. 82, February
GREGOTTI, V., 1993, *La città visibile*, Torino, Einaudi
GUERRA, A., MORRESI, M., 1996, *Gabetti e Isola*, Milano, Electa
ISOLA, A., 1999, *Necessità di architectura*, in: DE ROSSI, A. et al., (edited by), *Linee nel paesaggio. Esplorazioni nei territori della trasformazione*, Torino, UTET
ISOLA, A. et al., 2002 (a), *In.fra Forme insediative e infrastrutture. Ricerche coordinate da Aimaro Isola in 12 scuole di architettura. Atlante*, Venezia, Marsilio
ISOLA, A., et al., 2002 (b), *In.fra Forme insediative e infrastrutture. Ricerche coordinate da Aimaro Isola in 12 scuole di architettura. Manuale*, Venezia, Marsilio
ISOLA, A. et al., 2004, *In.fra Forme insediative, ambiente e infrastrutture. Ricerche coordinate da Aimaro Isola e Liliana Bazzanella in 11 scuole di architettura. Esperienze*, Venezia, Marsilio
MOLLINO, C., 1934, *Architettura di Torino. Le sabbie mobili*, in: "L'Italia letteraria ", n. 45, November 19
MOUDON, A. V., 1994, *Getting to know the built landscape*, in: FRANCK, K. A., SCHNEEKLOTH, L. H., *Ordering Space: Types in Architecture and Design*, New York, Van Nostrand Reinhold
MURATORI, S., 1960, *Studi per una operante storia urbana di Venezia*, Roma, Istituto Poligrafico dello Stato, Libreria dello Stato

OLMO, C., 1992, *Un'architettura antiretorica*, in: OLMO, C., (edited by), *Cantieri e disegni. Architetture e piani per Torino. 1945-1990*, Torino, Allemandi

OLMO, C., 1993, *Gabetti e Isola: architetture*, Torino, Allemandi

PAGANO, G., DANIEL, G., 1936, *Architettura rurale italiana*, "Quaderni della Triennale", Milano, Hoepli

PACE, S., 2001, *Oltre Falchera. L'Ina-Casa a Torino e dintorni*, in DI BIAGI, P., *La grande ricostruzione. Il piano Ina-Casa e l'Italia degli anni '50*, Roma, Donzelli

PACE, S. (edited by), 2006, *Carlo Mollino architetto*, Milano, Electa

REICHLIN, B., 2006, *Carlo Mollino nelle costruzioni e negli scritti*, in CALLEGARI, G., DE ROSSI, A., PACE, S. (edited by), 2006, *Paesaggi in verticale. Storia, progetto e valorizzazione del territorio alpino*, Venezia, Marsilio

RIGAMONTI, R. (edited by), 1997, *Ricerche per una architettura dei luoghi*, Torino, Celid

ROGERS, E. N., 1955, *Le preesistenze ambientali e i temi pratici contemporanei*, in: "Casabella-Continuità", n. 204, 1955

S.A., 1950, *Piano incremento occupazione operaia – Case per lavoratori. Suggerimenti esempi e norme per la progettazione urbanistica. Progetti tipo*, vol. 2, Roma, Tipografia M. Danesi

SAMONÀ, G., 1935, *La casa popolare degli anni '30*, Napoli, Epsa Politecnica Editrice (edited by MANIERI, M. E., Venezia, Marsilio, 1982)

SAMONÀ, G., 1959, *L' urbanistica e l' avvenire della città negli stati europei*, Bari, Laterza

SECCHI, B., 1984, *Le condizioni sono cambiate*, in: "Casabella" *Architettura come modificazione*, monographic issue, n. 498/499, January-February

SOLÀ MORALES (DE), I., 1984, *"Tendenza": neorazionalismo e figurazione*, in: "A.D. Architectural Design", vol. 54, nn. 5-6, 1984.

TAFURI, M., 1986, *Storia dell'architettura italiana, 1945-1985*, Torino, Einaudi

VITALE, D., 1987, *Gabetti e Isola*, in: VITALE, D. (edited by), *Il Quinto. Progetto per il Quinto Palazzo Uffici della Snam a San Donato Milanese*, Milano, Snam

Ndt: The Ina-Casa plan was the social housing plan for the whole Italian territory, set up in the second post-war period.

Ndt: The typical Piedmontese farmhouse.

Ndt: plan for the development of factory work

Ndt: Gianni Vattimo, important Italian contemporary philosopher. According to Vattimo there are no indisputable grounds, and the weak thought is an attitude of Postmodernity which accepts the burden of "error" and all that is historical and human.

Ndt: Istituto Autonomo Case Popolari (Indipendent Insitute for Social Housing)

Davide Rolfo

The illusory triviality of summation

The illusory triviality of summation

Turin. 3 ex factory Teksid, photo, Alessandro Cane

Davide Rolfo

The illusory triviality of summation

I. Substrata

In his short-story *Lo spazio inutile,* Ermanno Bencivenga narrates about a man "who did not need much space": bothered by the unused space, the protagonist concentrates on the essential, the one that he needs for his everyday life, to go to work, erasing from his mind everything that is not immediately useful; in the long run the useless space, offended, starts to withdraw, to flee, generating in human beings a mysterious feeling of relief. The story ends as follows: "Today our man has definitely won his battle. The only space he has left is the one occupied by his body. Of course there is no space left to move, but who cares? Move to go where? And why?" [Bencivenga 1995].

Some of the processes with more ancient origins today seem to be significantly evident. These processes are external to the field of architectural knowledge, but the assessment of their result is an ineluctable premise to try to understand the form that is being assumed by the territory; this in turn has an effect on the very processes, following a circular path –definitely not within a deterministic mechanism in terms of a "vulgar Marxism", but in a mediated, unstructured fashion. The studies on the territorial morphology represent a privileged observation point for comparing the interconnections between the forms of the urbs and the civitas, between *cityscape* and *mindscape*, allowing for a vision able to isolate us from the naive, sometimes too explicit peculiarities of the single urban and building issues. The consequences of this situation can be many and unpredictable. As an example let us think of the effects of living in the scattered "megalopoli padana": it is "likely that also the visual perception of the generation that today is 20 or 30 is completely different from that of their fathers or older brothers" [Belpoliti 2001]. Some of the elements that constitute this complex narration can be delineated as follows.

With the crisis of representativeness generated by the decay and the disappearance of the macro-organizations (typically: mass parties, trade unions, the big industry, some aspects of the welfare state), the actors of both the social and the territorial scene no longer seem to be expecting "visions" or guidelines from their own representatives: they only expect solutions to specific individual cases. From a strictly democratic point of view, the vote of opinion is replaced by the vote "oriented towards the outputs [...], based, if only apparently, on the concept of *do ut des*" [Bobbio 1984]. In a similar way, as far as the form of the territory is concerned, in a process of "global hunt for privileges that end up neutralizing each other" [Firpo 2001], the massive and generalized use of individual solutions seems to question the very concept of a "shared space" (in the broadest sense: in our perspective even the project for a railway line can be structured as an "individual solution").

At the same time, in an only apparently paradoxical manner, the actors with the right to intervene (category including both the represented and the representative subjects) multiply: the increase in the examples of representativeness is further fragmenting the demands and the expectations, lessening the chance for a shared narration. In the context of the building of a city, the process of course is not new, and it is widely documented from several points of view [for instance: Gabetti, Olmo 1989; Zucconi 1989; Romano 1993], but in the age of pluralistic democracy it appears, or is represented, as always less manageable.

The fall of most of the filters allowing to represent and portray the demand, together with the multiplication of the "interested parties/legal beneficiaries" of the transformations, almost inevitably brings about a fragmentation and a weakening not only of the political and technical imaginary, but also of the formal ones; the phenomenon is still a *topos* for the complaints of the intellectual class "in the time of its technical reproducibility" and it has already been highlighted, although within a general literary context and from a "non progressive" perspective –i.e. by Aldous Huxley, quoted by Walter Benjamin [Benjamin 1966]. A class –or maybe a number of groups connected by sporadic and fortuitous links [Bauman 2002]– in which the stakeholders and the decision makers usually become one. The result of a-scientific bourgeoisie that is only by far related to its XIX century equivalent [Nipperdey 1994], it is now producing technical and formal systems of ideas that turn out to be extremely shallow. Even in this case, the process self-increasing. The housing, settlement and formal models are usually regarded as established, and therefore they are not subject to being questioned; rather, they are generally reproduced. Such a flattening strengthens the tendency to ask "questions that are structured like answers" [Secchi 2000]. This reasoning is of a general nature: it applies to politicians, technicians, and economic operators, and is inserted into a weak institutional framework, in which the equation "public operator = setting up and monitoring of the plan / private operator = initiative" is no longer valid from the Sixties onwards [Crosta 1984]. The disorientation and the fragmentation of the approach to the problems of the territory is no longer an "individual" fact, but an institutional stance.

In the context of the great dichotomy –both consolidated and theoretic– between the decision-making processes that refer to the rational model and those that refer to the incremental one [Howlett, Ramesh 2003], such an approach would make the decision making practices shift closer to the second modality. The incremental model, being based on a sequence of partial balances, revolves around the "try and error" approach. As far as the topics of the architectural debate are concerned, once the decisions produced according to this modality are translated onto the physical reality of the territory, they seem to reveal the path lying behind them in a transparent manner. Furthermore, from an abstract perspective, the incremental decision-making model is in itself a process guided by the offer, and strongly conditioned by the decisions made in the past; once again, the physical crystallization of the decision-making processes in the "scattered city" seems to invariably confirm these features. The accumulation of building and infrastructural objects takes place by addition, by means of "simple" processes [Munarin, Tosi 2001]. The resulting

erosion affects not only the physical territory, but also the capital accumulation, through the production of brutal forms of settlement that do not respond to economic criteria –in its etymological sense of good management [Camagni, Gibelli, Rigamonti 2002]. We could underline how an evaluation of this kind, with respect to the analysis of a phenomenon (but not to the methodologies of intervention) is blatantly influenced by a neo-reformist interpretation, as it is effectively summarized by Bianchetti [Bianchetti 2003]. Even admitting that we are observing a modality of territorial management that respond to a "pure" neo-liberal philosophy, a model in which the planning is only a means to assign a value to the land and escapes any strategic definition, nonetheless it seems that the decision makers (in a broad sense) do not comprehend the *limited nature* of the territory and its available resources, the *non-reversibility* of most choices, the impossibility to consider the strategic moves as *indefinitely repeatable*; the recent events regarding the Susa Valley are paradigmatic in this respect.
André Corboz saw that some parts of the territorial program, the ones "that are dealt with in a brutal and improper manner, are still incomplete" [Corboz 1985]: we wonder if the continuous, incremental accumulation of signs might lead us not only to a difficulty in interpreting the "texts", and to consequently act upon them, but also to the impossibility of writing other texts and, ultimately, to a paralysis.

II. The "School of Turin"
The trajectory "urban project – territorial project – landscape project" (as described by Antonio De Rossi elsewhere in this text), setting in motion a type of neutralization of the bearer of knowledge, in a few decades seems to have led to a shift in Italian architectural research: from the design of the urban structure to the expression of opinions on the ornamental aspects (as shown by the multitude of competitions of ideas where the theme is urban furniture). The overall features of the vaguely defined "School of Turin" (this very definition would probably be rejected by many of those who are considered members of the school) enables a definitely peculiar look on this sequence: not being outraged [Gregotti 1990a], not emphasizing the value of the tiny observation [Viganò 1999], but also free from a self-satisfied cynicism [Desideri, Ilardi 1997].
Turin architectural scene, characterized by its "almost avant-gards" [Gabetti 1965, 1990], is defined by an ancient awareness of the distance between abstract models that are hard to reach in their integrity: the ancient, baroque design

of the territory, always unfinished and dependent upon the fortunes of a Casa Savoia with a very relative weight on the European scene; the more recent results of a Taylorist system that, despite being very advanced with respect to the rest of Italy, is not even comparable with its overseas prototype [Gabetti 1977]; on a more general scale, in the post war period the divergence between the Anglo-Saxon and northern European politics of territorial organization and the national ones, governed by a general *laissez faire*. Irony –at times disenchanted–, attention to popular architectures even in marginal contexts (as in the case of Mollino, Gabetti, Comoli, Mamino), history (Passanti) and philology (Cavallari Murat) aimed at operativeness: all these factors are involved in the definition of a –strict– heterodoxy that is discreet, accurate, and flexible.

The well-documented interest for the international scene and its cultural and technical icons is tempered by different factors: the consideration of the local, even tiny, provincial, and poor peculiarities, from the perspective of both the place and the building habits; the "gentle and ironic" approach to tradition; the permanence of the figure of the "architect-scholar"; the focus on the building yard and the practices of the "job", pervaded with a technical pragmatism that at times looks slightly suspicious [Croset 1990].

This attitude of a part of the local architectural culture can be clearly traced at least until the Eighties (when the scene becomes further fragmented): it concerns an *elite* that is, at least formally, jealous of its own cultural and professional independence, in between the "Fiat monoculture" on the one hand, and the rigid "organic" intellectual on the other. The contacts with these two sectors –and their "bases"– will be invariably aristocratically punctual [Papuzzi, in Bobbio 2002], and the perimeter of that very *elite* will be gently, though firmly monitored.

Some of the best professional successes of this veritable "manner of doing" that rejects the principle of authority are buildings that, on different scales, "do not want to be buildings": almost free from the "ideological" identification of the formal figure, they are integrated in the landscape in a way that is not yet mimetic (Gabetti, Isola, Re, *Centro residenziale Olivetti*, Ivrea 1969-74), and they take as a stronghold the processes of natural colonization (Gabetti, Isola, Varaldo, *Uffici giudiziari*, Alba, 1982-87) or the progressive human adaptation (Luzi, Besso Cordero, Ville urbane, Torino, 1980-86). Therefore they bring back the temporal dimension, with all the "inaccuracies", the changes and the adjustments of the case.

Since we are dealing with an attitude, a behavior abstracted from the scale of application, it is possible to summarize the distance between this attitude and others, which have nonetheless contributed to the identity of Italian architecture, comparing (as an example) the two stances on the dimensions of the living space. On the one hand Vittorio Gregotti's harsh words: "The block of flats, the small buildings, the suburban detached house, which still stubbornly shows a meager sense of the private property, of possession as a value, are *Kitsch* typologies in terms of the relationship between behavior and object" [Gregotti 1990b]; on the other hand, Elio Luzi talks with a voltairean sense of humor of the chances of personalizing the *Ville urbane*, paraphrasing one of the cornerstone of the Enlightenment: "I may disapprove your concrete dwarfs, but I will defend until death your right to use them".

III. Hidden Strategies

The above-mentioned cultural attitude holds in mind, though in an implicit and (voluntarily?) not systematized manner, how the issue of the form of the territory comes *before* its application to architecture; as a consequence, it enables an analysis of the territory based on the observation of rules and situations that are seen as resources, elements whose strength and contradictions can be used from time to time. This also works in the intentionally provocative case of dealing with planning criteria [Falco 1999], criticizing their merely bureaucratic aspect while shifting the focus on their importance as a "tool": an instrument to be used to achieve other goals, which refrain from the slavish respect of the rules.
The distance from a reductionist attitude is clearly stated: "Today we do not aim to extract for observation even a single phenomenon of the architectural question (dealing with the tiny object and the large settlement), nor to explain it in a scholarly fashion. It is useful to analyze and discuss a phenomenon only to the point where the connections with other phenomena are created and destroyed; other systems, places, and times, according to a view that is radically opposed to the positivist method. Instead of stating absolute truths, we make provisional suggestions" [Gabetti 1971].
Free from coercive or thaumaturgical pretensions, the instances on the table are considered as elements to be translated in a dialogic process, in which the very bearer of architectural competences, besides representing a necessarily aware critical look, acts as an "interpreter" [Bauman 1992], an "intermediary adviser"

inter pares. A "patient game" [Tosoni 1992] is created with these elements, and with the subjects who represent and bear them.

A typical instrument of the argumentative manner to practice this "game" (through which to write the drama, in the words of Gordon Cullen) is building project-related representations. This would immediately and clearly highlight how the summation of different results, if combined in a different way, can generate very distinct outcomes. Secondly, like in every strategy, and especially in the games based on a strategic approach (chess, pool), it would point out how some moves end up inhibiting others: 2 plus 2 is not always 4, and once you have 4 (or 3 or 5) you cannot always go back to 2 plus 2.

Typically, along the research path followed by the Department of Architectural Planning and Industrial Design of Turin Polytechnic University (DiPrADI), but also by the Turin Metropolitan Urban Center, related to the Department by scientific and biographical proximity, the means through which the creation of these "project-drawings" is accomplished are those of the architectural meta-project: from the scenarios to the manuals, from the reflections on the role of the processes and the programs to the setting up of practices on different scales. Other essays that are collected in this volume describe some application cases, more or less recent, whose apparent heterogeneity can be explained by the mainly operational nature of the research of the "School of Turin", its attitude and its evolution. Regardless of the scale of reasoning (from micro-urban redevelopment to the territorial assets to a regional scale), the overall goal is to identify some stances, some guidelines to rapidly and flexibly rebuild the city and the territory through time, free from the traditional coercive rules. The drawings and the planning sketches, keeping the *construction* and *substruction* on the same level, and analyzing their actual and potential connections, structure themselves as answers: they model the suggestions of the context, whose peculiarities are always regarded as the result of relational connections rather than of individual features. Inoculating in the territorial processes the physical representations and the possible solutions made of punctual problems, and with the support of the images, the goal is to open a debate on these issues using mutually understandable languages: in Secchi's words, before the questions are structured as answers.

From a political point of view it might be useful to eliminate the nodes that could generate disagreements, at the risk of presenting marginal agreements as successes [Healey 2003] and getting caught in the logic of neutralization of the above-mentioned bearer of competences. On the other hand, the described process deals at the same time with the stakeholders and the decision makers, properly highlighting the contradictions; it is aimed at a "return from the window" of a wide perspective, detached from the established incremental logic, within a more general idea of public interest.

Bibliography
BAUMAN, Z., 1992, *La decadenza degli intellettuali. Da legislatori a interpreti*, Torino Bollati Boringhieri (*Legislators and Interpreters. On modernity, post-modernity and intellectuals*, 1987)
BAUMAN, Z., 2002, *Modernità liquida*, Roma-Bari, Laterza (*Liquid Modernity*, 2000)
BELPOLITI, M., 2001, *Padania, la città più grande del mondo*, in "La Stampa", 6 marzo
BENCIVENGA, E., 1995, *Giocare per forza. Critica della società del divertimento*, Milano, Mondadori
BENJAMIN, W., *1966, L'opera d'arte nell'epoca della sua riproducibilità tecnica*, Torino, Einaudi (*Das Kunstverk in Zeitalter seiner tecnhnischen Reproduziebarkeit*, "Zeitschrift für Sozialforschung", 1936, Frankfurt am Main, Suhrkamp Verlag, 1955); in the footnote 21 of the italian edition Benjamin refers to the french edition of the A. Huxley's writing *Beyond the Mexique Bay. A Traveller's Journal*, London, 1934
BIANCHETTI, C., 2003, *Abitare la città contemporanea*, Milano, Skira
BIANCHETTI, C., 2008, *Urbanistica e sfera pubblica*, Roma Donzelli
BOBBIO, N., 1984, *Il futuro della democrazia*, Torino, Einaudi (*Il futuro della democrazia*, in "Nuova civiltà delle macchine" n. II, summer 1984)
BOBBIO, N., 2002, *Trent'anni di storia della cultura a Torino (1920-1950)*, Torino, Einaudi(the reference is to the *Introduzione* by A. PAPUZZI, not present in the original version: Torino, CRT, 1977)
CAMAGNI, R., GIBELLI, M. C., RIGAMONTI, P., 2002, *I costi collettivi della città dispersa*, Firenze, Alinea
CORBOZ, A., 1985, *Il territorio come palinsesto*, in "Casabella" n. 516, september (*Le territoire come palimpseste*, in "Diogène" n. 121, january-march 1983)
CROSET, P.-A., 1990, *Architetture in Piemonte 1980-1989*, in *Architettura degli anni '80 in Piemonte*, Milano, Electa

CROSTA, P. L., 1984, *La progettazione sociale del piano. Territorio, società e stato nel capitalismo maturo*, Milano, Franco Angeli

DESIDERI, P., ILARDI, M. (a cura di edited by), 1997, *Attraversamenti. I nuovi territori dello spazio pubblico*, Genova, costa & nolan

FALCO, L., 1999, *L'indice di edificabilità. Un attrezzo dell'urbanista*, Utet, Torino

FIRPO, L., 2001, *Cultura e politica*, in "La Stampa", 20 March, 20 (the article is a foreseeing of the posthumous publishing on "Pensiero mazziniano", 2001, of the essay *Cultura e politica*, 1979).

GABETTI, R., 1965, *La situazione architettonica di Torino dal dopoguerra ad oggi. 1945-1965*, in *Prima Triennale Itinerante d'architettura italiana*, Firenze, Centro Proposte

GABETTI, R., 1971, *Introduzione*, in OLMO, C. M., *Politica e forma*, Firenze, Valsecchi

GABETTI, R., 1977, *Architettura Industria Piemonte negli ultimi cinquant'anni*, Torino, Cassa di Risparmio di Torino

GABETTI, R., 1992, *Variabili e costanti della cultura architettonica torinese: dal 1945 ad oggi, con un passaggio al futuro*, in: OLMO, C., (edited by), *Cantieri e disegni. Architetture e piani per Torino. 1945-1990*, Torino, Allemandi

GABETTI, R., OLMO, C., 1989, *Alle radici dell'architettura contemporanea. Il cantiere building yard e la parola*, Torino, Einaudi

GREGOTTI, V., 1990a, *Tipologie atopiche*, in "Casabella", n. 568

GREGOTTI, V., 1990b, *Kitsch e architettura*, in G. DORFLES, *Il Kitsch. Antologia del cattivo gusto*, Milano, Mazzotta

HEALEY, P., 2003, *Città e istituzioni. Piani collaborativi in società frammentate*, Bari, Dedalo (*Collaborative planning. Shaping Places in Fragmented Societies*, Macmillan Press, London 1997)

HOWLETT, M., RAMESH, M., 2003, *Come studiare le politiche pubbliche*, Bologna, Il Mulino (*Studying Public Policy. Policy Cycles and Policy Subsystems*, Toronto, Oxford University Press, 1995)

MUNARIN, S., TOSI, M. C., 2001, *Tracce di città. Esplorazioni di un territorio abitato: l'area veneta*, Milano, Franco Angeli

NIPPERDEY, T., 1994, *Come la borghesia ha inventato il moderno*, Roma, Donzelli (*Wie das Bürgertum die Moderne fand*, Berlin, Wolf Jobst Siedler Verlag, 1988)

OLMO, C., 1992, *Un'architettura antiretorica*, in: OLMO, C., (edited by), *Cantieri e disegni. Architetture e piani per Torino. 1945-1990*, Torino, Allemandi

ROMANO, M., 1993, *L'estetica della città europea. Forme e immagini*, Torino, Einaudi

SECCHI, B., 2000, *Prima lezione di urbanistica urban planning*, Roma-Bari, Laterza

TOSONI, P., 1992, *Il gioco paziente. Biagio Garzena e la teoria dei modelli per la progettazione*, Torino, Celid

VIGANÒ, P., 1999, *La città elementare*, Milano, Skira

ZUCCONI, G., 1989, *La città contesa. Dagli ingegneri sanitari agli urbanisti (1855-1942)*, Milano, Jaca Book

Paolo Antonelli

Economy and form in the GrandeScala Project

Economy and form in the *GrandeScala* Project

Turin. Porta Susa station, photo, Alessandro Cane

Paolo Antonelli

Economy and form
in the *GrandeScala* Project

Within ordinary building and planning practices for urban and territorial purposes, the traditional economic doctrine has been extended so as to acquire all-encompassing features, thus becoming a sort of film wrapping up the reality. Virtually everything has been given a commercial value, resources have been optimised and, together with the utilitarian *weltanschaung,* have become the preferred ambition and the ultimate goal [Lefebvre, 1968]. The specific capitalist features of the industrial society in the early 90s, which were mainly interpreted by weighing the available means against the desired goals, have gradually evolved into universal "laws" applied everywhere and at any time [Martinelli, 1999].

In this context, we ought to initiate a process capable of *denaturalizing* the traditional economic model, by highlighting the existence of a relationship based on the mutual influence exerted by economic actions and "community" models. As a matter of fact, both economic (individual) and social (collective) factors are becoming increasingly incapable of finding self-explanatory models, and even more incapable of providing single-cause interpreting solutions [Starobinski, 2001]. Similarly, the connections between public institutions and markets are increasingly presenting themselves as complementary and mutually indispensable aspects of the processes regulating recent transformations at city and territorial level.

A considerable part of social relationships, including the physical processes of territorial and urban transformation, can no longer be solely regulated by simply controlling a model consisting in "an exchange between stakeholders who use allocated resources for process optimisation", i.e. through *the market*. Indeed, the market has proved to be unable to completely assimilate all the aspects of a city, to turn it into space for endless movement, and to endow places and products with the abstract qualities of seamless fungibility, fluidity and transparency, which are typical of *goods*. Nevertheless, it is a unique tool for quantifying the commercial exchange value and defining price-based mechanisms which regulate productive processes and resource allocation. In a short-term perspective, the market is capable of identifying the optimal process and resource configuration. But on its own, the market is not capable of assessing, recognising and measuring long-term values, i.e. when *irreversibility* conditions emerge within non-ergodic dynamic processes, highlighting the potential for process accumulation and the high modification costs. This definition perfectly corresponds to the typical features of economic actions in the context of territorial and urban transformation processes, where these aspects are particularly visible.

In addition to that, such dynamics should be seen in relation to the different stakeholders who, unlike in economism-inspired models, are capable of inducing endogenous changes in preferences and production functions and of adopting decisions bearing irreversible effects. In so doing, they participate in transformations and highlight their influence on the physical dimension of processes and outcomes. Under these circumstances, rationalising and maximising the usefulness of players does not necessarily coincide with the community interest. In this respect, what Benevolo wrote at the beginning of the 80s, on the use of territories as the result of overlapping individual calculations combined with the absolute centrality of the public, is still very topical nowadays: "Public control must respect, at the same time, users' needs and owners' entrepreneurial profits, within the limits that each party is ready to accord" [Benevolo, 1978]. Consequently, the following questions are essential: What is the definition of *public* today? What are the *limits* an individual is willing to accept in order to create a common value? It is clear that the community must play a key role in determining the structural conditions, but it is also clear that the conditions - and perhaps even the places and the instruments - are not available today to create a truly innovative and competitive process between political and technical stakeholders on the one hand, and economic operators on the other. This is shown by the fact that the latter have a tendency to act according to visions and rationales of profit maximisation, which are often very trivial and based on short-sighted perspectives. After all, it is known that long-term perspectives, especially if coupled with irreversibility and innovation phenomena, typically fall within the field of interests of the *homo oeconomicus*, but cannot be properly explored using categories from the neoclassical economic analysis.

I. Urban models

Space *is* organised and *becomes* organised according to the needs of economic processes. The shape of cities and territories - since they are not "alien" to economic and social processes - is also a visible expression of predominating interests and powers. The destiny of cities has always been doubly linked to that of the economic system. In order to interpret the city and its problems, with a view to solving them, contamination is required between architectural disciplines and the principles of economic reasoning. A critical aspect, however, emerges from observing these phenomena: within the transformation of territories and cities, the economic process does not follow a morphological *excursus*, where the "form of the city" is discussed and shared, but it is reduced to a sheer morphological *outcome*. The physical *facies* of the city is the final result - almost the residue, the material deposit - of a very complex economic process following long-term interactions, negotiations and exchanges between stakeholders who often do not think in physical terms. What is left is the series of limits and constraints, often strictly physical, which remain hidden during the process and are almost never expressed through the specific project instruments, especially the design. Such dynamics seem to stem today from a weary and unaware attempt to re-propose Taylorist procedures based on utilitarian models that are more suited to periods of quantitative rather than qualitative growth.

One of the key elements in the shift from a *quantitative* to a *qualitative* urban model is the move away from interpretative models based on *economies of scale* - which are typical of industrial cities focused on accumulating and agglomerating productive factors - towards a model based on *economies of externalities*. A vast economic literature underlines the great potential stemming from an economy based on *interactions*, where the benefits for a player in taking a specific "action" increase proportionally to the number of other players doing the same.

Additionally, we should consider the idea elaborated over the past few decades by Anglo-Saxon thinkers [Arthur, Durlauf, Lane, 1997] challenging a static and exogenous vision of externalities with respect to the system they operate within, and highlighting instead their endogenous and dynamic nature, which is perishable but also operable and nourishable. This aspect is particularly relevant for the physical spin-offs that this never-before-seen model has on the urban form, as well as for the relationships they establish with each other. The industrial city, for instance, can be seen as the cradle of technical externalities [Marshall, 1890], fuelled by the aggregation, in the same city, of many enterprises operating in a specific sector and undergoing a process of spontaneous, mutual "pollination". Similarly, the technology park - a typical instrument of industrial policies in the 80s - is an example of money-based externalities, since it was specifically created to reduce the cost of absorbing certain inputs. The spatial spin-offs deriving from the social interaction model are visible in the evolution of the technology park. Physical contiguity is no longer achieved by agglomerating various interventions on the same "site", but it is the result of connections, nets and fabrics. In other words, isolated episodes are interconnected in a web-based dimension which could be described as that of a *knowledge-based economy* [ref]. The spin-offs and the material deposit of a knowledge-based economy can be seen from multiple perspectives. Gone is the linearity and rationality stemming from the mechanical juxtaposition that used to characterise production processes. Instead, the opportunities of territorial transformation appear in a more fragmented and discontinuous manner, as individual events which are capable of generating great potential and are unevenly distributed in space and time. This potential, quantifiable by weighing the achieved objectives against the quantity of used resources, is certainly higher than in the past, where an intensive use of resources often coincided with the activation of poor territorial potential. The coherent and planned addition of isolated interventions allows for greater results and benefits than what could be achieved if resources and potential were to be concentrated in a single direction. The great undertaking or the great organic transformation, i.e. the "ideology" capable of elaborating an *a priori* order of reality, disappears and is replaced by a plurality of opportunities and interests emerging in isolated situations. In this context, the true resource and mission of a governmental *élite* is the ability to put pressure, to build networks capable of interconnecting different opportunities.

On the one hand, greater organizational capabilities are required, since fragmented processes become more complex. On the other hand, the morphological impact on cities, occasioned by multiple opportunities, is one of the main factors and driving forces to measure the ability to attract capital, particularly "human capital" [Lee, Florida, 2004]. This *dynamic* and *endogenous* dimension of externalities underlines a specific and growing *governance* responsibility on the part of the local society, which becomes increasingly crucial to boost the setting of appropriate conditions capable of transforming the city into the main *interface* between the various "innovative players" [Camagni, 1993]. However, with respect to this new responsibility, the random accumulation and juxtaposition of many different urban projects still seems to be the legacy of processes inspired by Taylorist models: a series of decisions and events raining down without even attempting - and therefore without finding - a true moment of synthesis. The effects of an industry-oriented rationale still reverberate through this model, which is still partially guiding the *GrandeScala* project and continues to be "a trivial machine" [Secchi, 1988] generating progressive phases of rigidity that stiffen until they petrify and ultimately block, before having found consistency among all their parts. These stiff fragments of quantitative town planning and of urban and territorial set-up, where progress and growth continue to be the ultimate and absolute goal, no longer seem to be a sustainable horizon today.

II. Economic processes and morphological dimension of the city
The interpreting model which saw the city as a *production factor* has been abandoned in favour of an interpretation that considers the physical urban and territorial dimension as a fundamental *interface* with economic processes, among other things.
For a long time, the distinction, within the city, between the functions oriented towards external demands and those which, on the contrary, aim at satisfying the needs of resident people has been reductive and simplistic. During the twenties and thirties, in the United States, a conceptual distinction was made between fundamental (*city-funding*) and filling activities (*city-filling*), the former being generally associated with industrial activities and the latter with the service sector. The tendency to focus on basic activities, directed towards foreign markets, has generated interpretation models which are essentially based on the measurement of production capacity as an answer to foreign demand. This approach, which is based on the *demand,* has been progressively replaced by one that is based on the *offer.* As a consequence, the quality of productive

factors, cross-sectoral synergies, economies of agglomeration, technical progress and innovative skills have begun to be viewed as driving forces for greater competitiveness in an enlarged urban system and as the foundations for long-term development capacities in a given territory. Under this new perspective, the residential and the service sectors cease to have a passive function and start to play an active role instead, which has even become a pre-condition for development. The quality of services provided to people and enterprises and, by extension, the living and *urban quality* standards have thus become fundamental elements. This picture clearly shows that there is a need to seize the potential and the implications of urban and territorial transformations on the role and on the future of cities, since optimising the "great production machine" will no longer suffice. Instead, it is necessary to seize the opportunities that are intrinsically associated with every urban transformation, by combining complex processes involving different stakeholders and different timelines, and by designing a system capable of increasing the potential of local economies. This new interpretation model is fundamental to understand what Roberto Camagni defines as "city demands", whereby the principles orienting localisation choices are no longer based on *agricultural* profitability, but rather on the *urban* one. Thus, in order to be able to profit from a true *urban atmosphere,* to be able to "stay in the city" and have access to the synergies it offers, individuals, families and enterprises are willing to recognise a greater value. But to this end, it is fundamental to develop the role of the city as an *interface*.

In this context, the *GrandeScala* architectural project, by shaping and building possible future scenarios, can become today an instrument capable of defining a morphological dimension that can be useful to direct political and economic choices, as well as strictly urban ones. Working opportunities derive from the still notable and critical gap between the dimension and the scale of economic processes on the one hand, and the actual political and administrative capacity to govern these transformations on the other, in terms of urban and living standards. This gap highlights the possibility to use the architectural project in its enlarged urban dimension as a *mediation instrument*, as an imaginary place where different stakeholders and individuals come together to build consensus and agreement, but also dissent and opposition around future city and territorial assets. Of course, to be effective, this approach has to make every critical effort to avoid becoming overpowering in its turn, thus steering clear of the path already traced by the idea of a "total project" [Eco, 2008]. The *GrandeScala* project can instead become a useful tool to orient the economy associated with urban and territorial transformations, by seeking an aggregated and shared answer capable of avoiding the random accumulation of diverse projects, and by exploiting the potential deriving from a more general combination of the multiple interests acting upon the city. Clearly, the objective is not the supremacy and autonomy of the form. Rather, it is to pursue greater integration and interaction between the *economy* and the *form*, where the economic input is acknowledged or denied by the physical image of transformation, in a continuous process of short-circuiting. The objective is a physical and material impact on cities and territories which is not just the sheer residue of reductive and shapeless economic processes, but rather something capable of seizing the potential offered by better living standards, even in economic terms. The recognition of the limits of economic processes, outside the neoclassical model, provides precisely the opportunity for a morphological research that does not withdraw itself behind an autonomous and self-regarding dimension - like in a battle fought exclusively by architects and urban planners alone - but is capable instead of elaborating images that can be presented where decisions are taken, and where the *GrandeScala* project participates as a "guest", rather than as a simple "observer". The morphology or the *morphological prefiguration*, to be more precise, is the field where stakeholders can come together to represent different interests and rights, and which detects and *translates* the different dynamics unfolding on the field according to their disciplinary result: the design of conflict and confrontation.

Bibliography

Marshall, A., 1890, *Principles of economics*, London, Macmillan

Lefebvre H., 1970, *Il diritto alla città*, Padova, Marsilio (1968)

Benevolo L., 1978, *Urbanistica e crisi economica*, Bari, Laterza

Indovina F., 1980, *Base materiale e schema interpretativo per la modificazione dell'organizzazione del territorio*, in Ceccarelli P. (edited by), *Potere e piani urbanistici. Ideologia e tecnica dell'organizzazione razionale del territorio*, Milano, Franco Angeli

Secchi B., 1988, *La macchina non banale*, Urbanistica n.92

Camagni R., 1993, *Principi di economia urbana e territoriale*, Roma, La nuova scientifica Italia

Arthur, W. B., Durlauf, S. N., Lane, D., 1997, *The economy as an evolving complex system II*, Addison-Wesley, Redwood City, CA (eds.)

Martinelli, A., 1999, *Economia e società. Marx, Weber, Schumpeter, Polanyi, Parsons e Smelser*, Torino, Edizioni di Comunità

Starobinski J., 2001, *Azione e reazione*, Torino, Einaudi

Lee S.Y., Florida R., 2004, *Creativity and Entrepreneurship: A Regional Analysis of New Firm Formation*, Regional Studies, Vol. 38.8

Eco U., 2008, *Prefazione a Gregotti, V., Il territorio dell'architettura*, Milano, Feltrinelli (1982)

Bianchetti C., 2008, *Urbanistica e sfera pubblica*, Roma, Donzelli Editore

Part II Devices

Edited by Alessandro Armando and Francesca Camorali

OPERATIONAL STRATEGIES OF THE GRANDESCALA

Paolo Antonelli, Alessandro Armando, Francesca Camorali,
Andrea Delpiano e Roberto Dini

Recapitulation
We tried until now to clarify some issues around the definition of the *GrandeScala*
architecture – while the following appear partial and not necessarily aligned.
The first fundamental aspect is founded on and apparently linked to the
identification of a consistency of territorial form and its transformability through a
project that begins morphologically [De Rossi]; hence it was proposed to discuss
the political importance of this project as a medium and translation of the decisions
and complex chains that lead from political acts – without linearity – that is, all
actions which affect the ground [Armando and Durbiano]. Among the operational
goals of the *GrandeScala* project there is certainly a need to change the scalar
references of urban design, looking at the conditions of living in rapid change which
are increasingly characterized by global processes of building production – with the
consequent disconnection between the project of building components and the
project of manufacture – towards a variable geography of settlement phenomena
in terms of location and size [Bazzanella and Giammarco]. Of course the need to
ask broad questions also stems from the dynamics of construction of dwelling
places, in regards to the close relationship between the atomizing privatization of
space and the crisis of representation of macro-organizations (parties, trade unions,
industries, associations) – with consequences for the construction of forms arising
from delegation policies and collective decisions [Rolfo]. But if on the one hand the
individualization of the forms of employment of places we live in corresponds with
a profound transformation of the geographies of administrative power, on the other
it could be argued that this correspondence also concerns economic dynamics in
relation to the construction of physical space, almost as if the physical appearance
of the city was the result (or the residue) of an autonomous dynamic that is economic
and financial (as well as political) [Antonelli].

It is critical to draw our attention to the close connections between capital, power and physical form in order to consider *GrandeScala* as an attempt to define the social role of an architecture project, without the the pretence of playing the role of teacher, or alternatively to falling dangerously toward the "aesthetic of general observation" [Gregotti 2008]. The need to stress the core of the project as a means of knowledge that has a social function is tied to the limited rationality of decision making and the instability of economic imperatives: in the contexts within which we are concerned probably there are not stakeholders able to exert unilateral power or monopolise transformative events in the territory. Moreover it is unlikely that actions of physical transformation in the area are the direct and linear result of visions and priorities dictated by the actors, not only because of the fragmentation of authority. There is probably an inevitable lag between ordinary politics of arguments, decisions and regulations, and the ordinary material products that constitute the land. The *GrandeScala* project affects the points of equilibrium and convergence between these two levels – and therefore the decisions that occur on the first level. This occurs on the first level through the figures that provide consistency, and on the second level through the figures that give a possible (but open) consistency.

So if this decline to the level of economic imperatives and land administration bureaucracy is transformed into actions, they could be used imprecisely as "figure-metaphors" [Ambrosini and Berta] that the *GrandeScala* project puts at its disposal to construct operating margins between which the "necessity of architecture" (Isola 1999) defines its legitimate place.

Instruments of mediation

The project of the *GrandeScala* constitutes therefore activity primarily aimed at building scenarios – and even possible geographies – through designing a physical form. It should have among its objectives the production of operating conditions for ordering the priorities of decision makers. Indeed, one could say that the *GrandeScala* project begins when determining the themes and issues that pertain to particular processes of space transformation which have not yet already crystallized. It becomes the means through which you construct physical scenarios useful to construct the reality of who, in various ways, performs the construction and modification of territory.

In this sense, it finds its legitimacy – and disciplinary policy – in the specific possibility to establish a conventional plan through the design of a hybrid figure. A figure that is at the same time shaping conflicts and defining the horizons and scenarios for change. The idea of a strategy for a project convention is certainly problematic. Gregotti, for example, maintains that "designers [should] have a conviction as definite as their final proposal, to be considered without alternative" [Gregotti 2008]; and not without reason, since the conviction and responsibility of the designer, traditionally, guarantees the work to be carried out. But who is it that really guarantees a transformation at the local level? Whom, and under what disciplinary legitimacy, can be considered within a context muliplied by mediation and separation (political decision-making, economic, technical production) to establish the conviction that will assure the future of the *GrandeScala* project? This does not mean to delegitimize the consistency of frameworks and knowledge of architecture, which attempt, at least hypothetically, to bend the instrumental aims toward an increased capacity to produce knowledge through design, understood as as a space and place articulated between politics and *physical forms*.

It is not the act of "division" that constitutes the planning process [Mazza 2008], but rather "tidying up" decisions and "putting together" the conflicts through the project. The *GrandeScala* project becomes a conventional instrument of mediation, in procedural conditions with measurable effects in paradigms at odds with the logic of conformity – rules and constraints of the plan, strict regulations – to arrive at forms of negotiation (with all the risks involved) and forms of argument which, in turn, are able to transform specific rules, and make them shared.

This change in the structure of decision-making is linked to two fundamental aspects that concern the government of the territories under our care. First, the progressive enlargement of the public sphere of urban and territorial transformations, which expand the social basis to legitimise a process / project [Bianchetti 2007, cf. also chap. 4 Bagnasco]. Secondly, the metropolisation of the territory that opens and initiates project applications which are often not effective responses to the instruments and dimensions of the current local government. Given these conditions, the action that takes place through the *GrandeScala* project is itself a work of continuous hybridization between technical action and political action, including morphological preconditions – the settlements and landscapes – and processing operations, including design of "places" and the footprints on the ground of power – the administrative boundaries of those owners or uses.

Recognition, recomposition, representation
In an attempt to define the specific requirements of the *GrandeScala* project it seemed useful to examine some research and projects that constitute a shared reference and that better identify the strategies for working together: both methodologically and in terms of outcomes. This is not the place to address the problem of what is the distinction between a compulsion to repeat figural repertories that have marked common experiences and the need for "science" to propose operational categories within which to carry out project actions: inevitably every proposed taxonomy will produce its own autobiography. It is therefore valuable at least to state – and thus distinguish – the horizons of action of the project, with the intent to make the arguments that are in use visible – that is, as conventional instruments for decision making processes.
In considering some of the practices whose implementation recurred intermittently and is always implied, it was decided to establish a pattern that highlights the differences between modes and designs of the project using three main categories: strategies for recognition, reconstruction and representation. Recognition strategies are primarily aimed at defining the terms of reference between the design and physical reality, they determine what is "relevant" (and therefore representative) stating that the extension (geometric dimensions as the variety of processes related to ground) relative to a problem of transformation. Assuming the difficulty of managing the sovereignty of a quadrant of space in a project it is necessary to determine the extention and approximation. So the design of infrastructure and activation of new building areas does not affect established perimeters *a priori,* but it leads itself to project boundaries and perimeters. Very often the recognition of extensive conditions of relationship between neighbouring territories, or the enunciation of a latent forms – which we consider here as an interpretation and revelation of a physical structure, though supported by sedimentation or long-term strategies, in terms of traces recorded over time and in space – might justify a change oriented physically within the sign or, conversely, to produce constraints and resistance in view of its denial or cancellation. The measures of recognition are therefore dealing

with the same collection of maps that are considered relevant to represent the territory in question, but also with the tracking boundaries inevitably interfering with the separation of ownership, sovereignty and also the administrative jurisdiction of other technical tools that always overlap each other (recognition as a classification). Finally, recognition is the possibility of giving meaning and weight to things through design: the work of reference submitted by the project, through the establishment of similar categories of items, but also by establishing what is meaningful or relevant (and thus designed) in view of the changes that you are considering, which is a very powerful active faculty of the same project, often given as implicit and naturalized (recognition as a choice).

The restoration strategies are common to those facing the production of relations (causal links, similarities and differences, contradictions and intersections – and therefore perimeters) between parts or elements that represent of the territory. Reconstruction operations may act horizontally, or by placing side by side, according to paratactic procedures, different representations of the area that have already been produced for various purposes (shifts of construction projects or infrastructure and landscape plans) or by separate administrative bodies (the mosaic of zoning): in any case it is mounted, and can assemble or temporally differentiate sectoral projections (for duration or timing) of parts of land which, in the processing, will be considered in terms of continuity, separations and limits that are not yet established. Likewise, recomposition strategies act vertically, or overlap, through interference and intersection between representations of the structures on the same ground. The very definition of "land as palimpsest" [Corboz 1985] requires first and foremost the concept of superposition and rewriting – something too often forgotten – scraping off the tracks on the ground with a happy ambiguity, put simply: between parchment – *palimpsestos* meaning "scraped away (to write over)" [Deli Etymology Dictionary 2004] – and territory. In our case, the categories refer only to the design, to the "parchment", including its inevitable separation from the physical actions of the transformation. In this sense, the cognitive value bought into force must regard the convention and dimension of the argument, before we can determine the size of executive changes.

This limitation also applies to the operations of representation, that while implicitly proposing visions and projections of future states of affairs, almost never reflect the sum outcome of decisions already made, technical and economic audits already overcome, and processes already undertaken and approved. Almost always – and increasingly, given the exponential increase in power production and reproduction of virtual representations – these figures anticipate complex structures in the form of scenarios which are open, if not arbitrary. Even the great works of urban marketing with systematically extensive and detailed images, discounting future possibilities according to a logic of "putting in a state of becoming" [Cacciari 1982] require less to be verified in terms of their feasibility, while media coverage makes into an instrument of real debate (if not persuasion) figures that are very far from utopian modernist or radical neo avant-garde.

We already mentioned [cf. ch. 1, Armando and Durbiano] and will say again the case of the Corso Marche in Turin and the objectives that the project seeks: a great auction infrastructure that becomes the carrier of a vision of transformation involving the entire western quadrant of the Subway, identifying areas and concentrations for property development, without local governments bound to their implementation, and yet with the ability to synthesize a *GrandeScala* hypothesis, which is intended to influence (but not prescribe) the future.

Certainly, this portrayal not only concerns a provision of synchronous elements in space, to account for proximity, separation, distance and continuity, through strategies of measurement of dwelling places. The strategies of representation refer to the possibility that the project of narrating, showing diachronically the persistence of conditions that produce and identify the places, representing the collective identity and thus taking over symbols to represent the horizon, through what is inscribed in the substrate material, and in the "thick ground" [De Cesaris 2002].

Bibliography

BIANCHETTI, C., 2007, *Giochi seduttivi e politiche urbane*, in LANZANI, A., Moroni, S., *Città e azione pubblica*, Roma, Carocci

CACCIARI, M., 1982, *Nihilismo e progetto*, "Casabella", n. 483

CORBOZ, A., 1985, *Il territorio come palinsesto*, "Casabella", n. 516 (1983)

DE CESARIS, A., 2002, *Lo spessore del suolo parte di città*, Roma, Palombi & Partner

DURBIANO, G., 2009, *Prefazione. Vent'anni dopo*, in ARMANDO, A., *La soglia dell'arte*, Torino, SEB 27 Edizioni

GABETTI, R., 1984, *Il progetto come ricerca scientifica*, in BAZZANELLA, L., *Progetto. Storie e teorie*, Torino, Celid

GREGOTTI, V., 2008, *Contro la fine dell'architettura*, Torino, Einaudi

ISOLA, A., 1999, *Necessità di architettura*, in DE ROSSI, A. et al., (edited by), *Linee nel paesaggio. Esplorazioni nei territori della trasformazione*, Torino, Utet

LANZANI, A., 2007, *Introduzione. Riformismo al plurale*, in LANZANI, A., MORONI, S., *Città e azione pubblica*, Roma, Carocci

MAZZA, L., 2008, *Ippodamo e il piano*, "Territorio", n. 47

RECOGNITION AS CHOICE

1234567

The decision to order these "Keyword" strategies around the *GrandeScala* project is not accidental. We would like to tell thedesigned objects from the built ones with the intention of exploring the relationship between them, which is always uncertain and variable between these two levels. It is a difficult task and somewhat limited: first to say what scenarios and strategies should be preferred we make "limits" to determine which signs are needed to make speakable our projects. We are not speaking of a retreat towards autonomy, indeed: only by dissolving the ambiguity between design and building construction, and showing the limit of one in respect to the other, it seems that the *GrandeScala* project could take accountability and legitimacy within the cognitive conditions of the present.

For these reasons, the issue of choice of what is meant to represent the project design should be relocated within the more general problem and the complex semiotics of architectural design. At least what you mean by "choice" may establish a relationship between a sign and the presence (past, present or future) of an "element" in the physical reality of a place. We might define this relationship as a reference, where the signs (symbols) are repeated in the presence of objects belonging to the same "class" or meaning where each sign (icon) to identify individually the presence of that object [Ogden and Richards 1966, Peirce 1936, cit. either in Eco 1968]. The discipline of architectural design is hybrid, from this point of view, in that it establishes the conditions of reference (the conventions of symbolic drawings, tables and plants, urban and topography, etc...) articulated iconographically (through the laws of descriptive geometry and surveying techniques). These two phases of design always involve a form of "choice", understood in its dual sense of distinction and selection: from one side the drawing distinguished symbolically similar categories of items, on the other it selects what is to be found, compared, evaluated, and represented.

The theme of the centrality of choice through the drawing as "reduction of the phenomena" has been addressed by Gabetti in the course of his reflections on the "clinical method" [cf. ch. 1, Armando and Durbiano]. Indeed, it is consistency from the operations of the technical drawing as a "concatenation of symbols" which introduces the concept of method: "The first step of the method is resigned to not describe all [...] to select aspects sufficiently clear and separate to disassociate without equivocation and transmit the content through language or symbolism created "*ad hoc*" [Granger, cited. in Gabetti 1983]. Gabetti describes the operations of choice that define disciplinary technical drawing as an essential instrument of transfer "without ambiguity" of information for the organization of production. Here, otherwise, you would like to highlight the degree of ambiguity of the choices made by the codes of the project as they become available to the productive game of the argument: it is a complementary and not opposing operation, which involves assuming the same problem.

The tentative attempts – which usually failed – at the turn of the sixties and seventies to encode a semiotics of architecture have always concentrated on the relationship between sign and architectural significance (functional, political, symbolic), always leaving a little aside the subject of semiotics of architectural drawings. Umberto Eco admits his lack of interest in the problem of "how to read a project" declaring what "posed the rules of interpretation of the object, posed the rules for endorsement of the resulting project" [Eco 1968]. Of course this implies a continuity that is necessary and biunique between design and *res aedificata:* that is one of the great issues before us. If the architectural design (and design in general) is not considered to be "closed source" [ibid], where each variation specifies a unique syntax (one code for road engineers, one for planners, one for landscape), then the question arises of what strategies are available in a argumentative context, not independently prepared by the designer as technical data. Unlike the production of the project, which remains the preserve of scientific disciplines and technical codification, the receipt and reading of drawings – and thus their instrumental dimension – also concerns a non-specialist audience with decision-making powers (of various types and grades); From this point of view the project recognises the elements designating a presence that is in fact essential to the argument. In their treatment of the argument (1958) Chaïm Perelman and Lucie Olbrechts-Tyteca cite, regarding the rhetorical power of choice, a Chinese tale "A king sees an ox to be sacrificed. He takes pity and orders it is replaced by a ram. He confesses that this was because he saw the ox, while he did not see the ram". In fact, the *GrandeScala* project poses systematically the problem of what must be seen and what, in the complexity and "disorder", can be concealed.

The definitions of "sprawl" and "spread city" used in different ways, describe strategies related to the representation of territory in discrete parts, almost always in homogenous classes of items (warehouses, houses, fences, junctions...). In this indifferent and dusty homogeneity, the issue of recognition as a choice poses many implementation problems, as often for each identified "class", there was no clear hierarchy between the elements. This was answered in different ways: on one hand trying to leverage the conditions, even in a minor way, the regional planning that guides morphological transformation, and by prevailing strategies of latent pattern recognition (here is the palimpsest, with the plots of channels, the rows, the parcels etc.); the other taking measure of fragmentation and using choice as a criterion of design, but as the election of the key items (or systems) to bring "order" to the landscape, without dwelling too much on the distinction between design and practice, between "words and things."

Arturo Lanzani summarised these interpretations in terms of a "network landscape that warps into a structurally fragmented territory," where "disorder becomes a structural given of the contemporary landscape' and the city appears as "a dust of lonely buildings" or "fragmentation in collision" [Lanzani 2003]. For this class of problems he wishes to "define formally some milestones and jointly, with greater difficulty, build partial relationships between certain spaces...' without distinguishing between the effects of a design which make it, through the decision, a conditional instrument for the practice of politics, and the effects of the actions of a "building site" in response to a decision.

Indeed, assuming that there is no longer a public dimension to the project capable of establishing agreements, everything (almost) seems to be descended from an insightful analysis of individual practices, the "minimal rationalities" that actually make up the framework of physical transformation. Examining the "elementaristic tradition", Cristina Bianchetti has read a kind of critical acceptance of reality: "We do not have a general plan that provides reasons, values for actions which counter the spread. This opens to the difficulty of the project: there is no public contact as in the past...that can guide the project" [Bianchetti 2004]. On the other hand it seems that the public partner is still strong, though perhaps no longer carries the "guide" in unilateral prescriptive and bureaucratic terms, rather, increased availability of local decision making is often not matched by political will already structured, the design decision is thus one of the objectives of the project, which shifts (at least partially) its role from being a binding instrument to become a medium of understanding to provide scenarios, depict structures and balances or explain differences and conflicts in the design of places. In this second sense, the project makes available all the various possible scenarios, which are preferably not the prerogative of the designer as an expert, but the actors as decision makers and stakeholders and values. The responsibility of the designer moves from the floor of the definition of "best of all possible worlds" that of falsifiability (argumentative) and feasibility (technical) of preferred worlds that he anticipates.

If you separate conceptually the phenomena of reading and drawing from models describing the practices, or if you split the time of construction of the decision by the conventional design by the construction of the territory through the working drawing (all scales), the problem of the functionality of the design changes. The reflection should be given the status that is attributed to the "elements", trying to clarify to all users of the design which are the rules that guide the syntax of the hybrid project, which choices of reference and meaning manifest and order the design. From the perspective of the strategies we are trying to define, it is not short to understand directly (or naturalise codes) what is best territories to implement, but rather to include actors in the choice of what is important, design.

Take the case of the design of a constructed fabric: in local projects it is common in a performance of individual buildings to report the dusty quality of the settlement at the same time, however, it is a choice that does not see the degree of soil sealing and texture plates [cf. ch. 3, De Rossi] that make up an urban fabric, leading to confuse volumetric density and surface density (i.e. the occupation of land). Similarly, the the highlighting of green areas may provide false continuity between permeable and impermeable soils, including slabs and green landfill, etc... As in the case of infrastructure, the choice to combine landlocked areas – often treated with a mantle of vegetation – in the class of agricultural or "green" areas – may radically change the representation of continuity and penetration. More generally, the results of selection are reflected in figures of continuity and order of classes of elements (layers), whose consistency is the grammar of design strategies of *GrandeScala*.

The operational theme of the framework taken as an action within a frame that gives limits to the project design, suggests a few orders of implication, related as much to disciplinary reflections as to larger conceptual horizons.

Bibliography
BIANCHETTI, C., 2004, *Abitare la città contemporanea,* Milano, Skira
ECO, U., 1968, *La struttura assente,* Milano, Bompiani
GABETTI, R., 1983, *Progettazione architettonica e ricerca tecnico-scientifica nella costruzione della città,* in GABETTI, R., MUSSO, E., OLMO, C., ROGGERO, M. F., *Storia e progetto,* vol. 6, Milano, FRANCO ANGELI, ora in GABETTI, R., *Imparare l'architettura,* 1997, Torino, Allemandi
LANZANI, A., 2003, *I paesaggi italiani,* Roma, Meltemi
PERELMAN, C., OLBRECHTS-TYTECA, L., 1966, *Trattato dell'argomentazione,* Torino, Einaudi (1958)

Giulio Paolini, *The Simple Truth*, 1994
collage on paper, 4 elements, 15 3/4 x 15 3/4 in. each
Castello di Rivoli Museum of Contemporary Art
Gift of the artist, 1994
Photo Paolo Pellion, Turin

Alighiero Boetti, *Everything*, 1987-1988
canvas, embroidery in colored cottons, 83 5/16 x 76 1/2 in.
Castello di Rivoli Museum of Contemporary Art
Permanent loan
Fondazione CRT Project for Modern and Contemporary Art, 2003
Photo Paolo Pellion, Turin

RECOGNITION AS A FRAMEWORK

2 1 2 3 4 5 6 7

Perhaps a closer disciplinary reference is in the reflection of Gabetti, regarding the possibility of a new design for the city and territory, neither starting from a single public or private set, nor from the big infrastructures, but by direct recognition that all reality, everywhere present, is experienced directly, succinctly by users, beyond the limits of the fences, and the curbs of the road" [Gabetti 1983]. This is an interpretation which highlights the conditions necessary for the continuity of territory, seen as an object of transformation - and then as material relevant to the project on an area of ground, valuing everything, so that "to take a quarter of the city or country and redesign it in a direct or mediated reference to users, can give significant results" [Gabetti 1983, emphasis added]. Given this premise, the theme of the area of land is no longer relevant, at least, as an operation that defines and includes, or "tables" substantial elements (plots, emergencies, critical points...) but becomes a representation that is consistent: a "table" that coincides with potential projects. From this perspective, the framework assumes the continuity of the soil before any hierarchy among the elements is selected and distinguished.

The framework should precede, in logical terms, making it possible to choose many combinations of signs from a significant territorial situation. Conversely, if let's say, an urban edge is taken as a basis for the framework of a project, leaving it excludes other options. That's what happens almost always, to the boundaries between municipalities, where each considers the extent of the problem from a fact of construction (degradation, completion, etc..), or administration (municipal boundaries) which are already selected regardless of the classification of other assets (environmental frameworks, proprietary boundaries, geographies of power and conflict).In this way even local policies identified as positive, especially if they involve borders with other sovereignties, can produce tensions and undermine processing operations which are also interesting (as is the case in recent years, tensions between the towns of Turin and Venaria all around the area of the Stadium of the Alps). It is also possible that these types of contradictions are constituted, in the long run, as a problem for the effectiveness of conceptualizations and of the projects on the outskirts, developed during the eighties.

In some ways it would be useful to compare the problem relative to the perspectives on the issues which have characterized urban planning at both national and European levels over the past two decades: this is only a brief and approximate account. The two-way link between downtown and the suburbs has gone through research and policy in the eighties and nineties – from the studies on "urban regeneration" as Eupolis (1990) to test operations in France as Banlieu 1989 –contributing crucially to broaden our vision of the settlement of the post-Fordist city, to the enunciation of the landscapes of dispersion, without "mass" borders or related smaller lattices – and, some say, "territories without qualities" [Bianchetti 2003]. But whether or not the current sold out investigations into dispersion, the operating horizon of a *GrandeScala* project in any event moves from the edge to the border. The issues are no longer declined in terms of "edge" and "margins" [Giammarco, *Isola* 1993] but within a metropolitan territory, becoming points of contact and sometimes confrontation between different structures – administrative, owners, land users. It is boundaries precisely. So if the borders are multiplying and behind, opening up unexpected but always in binding chains through the framework that you can include all causes and all possible effects, half of which will be articulated for the values and interests that insist on the transformation of that area. More generally, the principle of formal setting leads to issues of art theory and aesthetics: the problem has a long history that is relevant to the extent that was included in discussions of landscape and territory. The commissioning framework is not only verticalised framing, of the implicit recruitment from above of the modern gaze, by aerial reconnaissance of Our World from the air [Gutkind 1952] to the global overview of Google Earth. It is before "symbolic form" as a framing point of view [Panofsky 1961] and therefore horizontal gaze: as Alain Roger poses the "invention" of the window in the fifteenth century depicted the first symptom of the idea of autonomy of the landscape, precisely by means of a principle of framing [Roger 1994 and 2002]. And it is always through an – almost cinematic – sequence of shots which make the designs of Gordon Cullen, in other respects, the analytical framework of the view from the road [Lynch Appelyard and Meyer 1964]. Practices in dealing with the concept of territory within the landscape seem to imply a double meaning: on the one hand becoming the working range of new technical knowledge and specialized ecologies from environmental engineering, and secondly the background, the place of most ancient memory and, as such, a place to store. The output from this dichotomy has attempted to define the landscape as a cogent idea, as a place that is made of things and meanings [Gabetti *Isola,* 1988], requiring a constantly shifting position of eyes – the view from above, flying bird, from the bottom - to guide the action on it. A change of perspective that moves from critical reflection also emerged from studies on urban sprawl: through fragment dispersion, discontinuities become reference figures and types useful to interpret and guide simultaneously thinking forms and physical forms [Secchi 2000].

It is within these conditions that the *GrandeScala* project acquires its scope. The physical boundaries – rivers, mountains, hills – become more legal and disciplinary: the conventional boundaries, those related to land ownership, planning tools, risk constraints, but also the other boundaries, derived from specific knowledge and technical expertise. Boundaries that produce a critical difference between the recognition of a place, a landscape, and the institutional level to which they belong, and which direct and define changing rules. The city and the territory are not monolithic units, but clusters of local situations in themselves more or less homogeneous, "with stability and recognition, both in terms of physical form, and in terms of processes (ecological, social cultural, institutional) from which and by which they change" [Dematteis 1989]. What follows is the need for the project to recognize these situations, which are always of variable geometry, in time and space, producing waste in motion with the conventional boundaries, being smaller or larger scale.

For these reasons the capacity to frame is necessary for activity that is meaningful, and therefore, defensible and falsifiable: a question that is not strictly technical, but rather political in nature and design. The *GrandeScala* project requires a fundamental operation, – the suspension (and continual rewording) of the frame of the problem – and its legal and disciplinary boundaries, to be able to recognize, interpret and design by establishing new borders. The operation of recognition of a framework, away from the myth of a "total project", running always along double tracks, looking on one side to the *physical* data – the photograph of the forms of the territory, their morphology as they have taken shape over time – but keeping in sight of the political – the X-ray of power to the ground, the conventions. In this sense, *recognition* becomes a *framework* for complex representations, but also a starting point from which to reconstruct and reinterpret a design problem.

Bibliography
BERQUE, A., CONAN, M., DONADIEU, P., ROGER, A., 2002, *Mouvance: un lessico per il paesaggio. Il contributo francese*, "Lotus Navigator", n. 5
BIANCHETTI, C., 2004, *Abitare la città contemporanea*, cit.
D'ANGELO, P., 2001, *Estetica della natura*, Bari, Laterza
DEMATTEIS, G., 1989, *Contesti e situazioni territoriali in Piemonte. Abbozzo di una geografia regionale dei possibili*, "Urbanistica", n. 96
GABETTI, R., 1983, *La progettazione architettonica*, in CIUCCI, G., Guida alle facoltà di architettura, Bologna, Il Mulino, ora in GABETTI, R., 1997, *Imparare l'architettura*, cit.
GABETTI, R., ISOLA, A., 1988, *Nuovi valore per l'ambiente*, "Domus", n. 700
GIAMMARCO, C., ISOLA, A., 1993, *Disegnare le periferie*, Roma, NIS
GUTKIND, E. A., 1952, *Our world from the air. An international survey of man and his environment*, Garden City NY, Doubleday
PANOFSKY, E., 1961, *La prospettiva come forma simbolica E altri scritti*, Milano, Feltrinelli (1999)
ROGER, A., 1994, in BERQUE, A., *Cinq propositions pour une théorie du paysage*, SOS Free Stock
SECCHI, B., 2000, *Prima lezione di urbanistica*, Bari, Laterza

Giulio Paolini, *Study for "As Far as the Eye Can See"*, 2007
mixed media on paper
27 9/16 x 39 3/8 in.
Castello di Rivoli Museum of Contemporary Art
Gift of the artist, 2007
Photo Paolo Pellion, Turin

RECOGNITION AS A LATENT FORM

3 1 2 3 4 5 6 7

The possibility of recognizing, by drawing, coherency and causal connections in the traces of the territory was effectively described by Corboz, that "The territory has a shape. Indeed, [...] is a form". It is a condition of textual form, a result of concatenations, necessity, correspondences: precisely the"palimpsest". The textuality of the ground is at the same time reading and writing, project and transformation, that forces you to "scrape one more time the older texts upon which people have inscribed material, over the irreplaceable ground" [Corboz 1985].

It has already been said about this ambivalence of the text as sign and as ground that defines the issue of choice; also the theme of latent form should not be mistaken for an attempt to reveal something objective or essential.

To some extent the possibility of recognizing a shape inscribed in the traces of a territory requires the separation and selection of these tracks: each figure means, first, that the order of immanence of the signs on the ground has been represented then chosen within desired codes and references. This makes each result an arbitrary figure, whose consistency must be argued and repeated for historiographical, geomorphological, economic and political reasons: hence the conventionality of the latent form.

The recognition of a form is a strategy in many ways complementary to the operations of classification: what is limited and clipped within the frame is available as a fragment, and has significant potential as a whole, what is recognized as a form instead of establishing relations and hierarchy of priorities that are not extensive but intensive (edges, nodes, plates, continuity, roofs). The first case defines the scope of the potential action and its orders of reference, the second states of different locations and places in relation to continuity and consistency. For this reason the definition of a latent form can forge a strategic framework, when, for example, the continuous reasons of a given area end up exceeding the "frame" of the project.

It does not appear necessary to establish consecutiveness between two strategies, suggesting a principle detection of the latent form that transcends conventional arguments (including those often established frameworks), the recognition of a form is an open strategy, which may be more or less effective and acceptable. Even the "voluntary geography" - described in 1966 by Gregotti as a specific architectural possibility, a "total figural invention" for the area – evaded the responsibility of arbitrary, although "authentic", intention [Gregotti 1966]. However, the problem of a territorial form of visual gestalt occurs every time you appeal, more or less deliberately, to the alleged evidence of the signs, according to an idea of the "vision" that goes back at least to Arnheim: "To see, is to grasp some compelling features of an object [...] A few simple lines and some dots are readily accepted as "a face", not only by "civilized" individuals in the West [...] but even by children, wild animals".

Cristina Bianchetti has highlighted the inherent risks of a territorial project from a morphological point of view - as is being proposed here - hypostatized and independent of the problems of physical form: "The readings are not always morphological but make explicit economic, social and institutional meanings, the permanences may have different reasons, which may make different imprints [Bianchetti 2004]. Precisely for this reason, the readings of a territorial form, rather than aspire to reveal them, are traced back to their conventional codes and declare their partiality, seen as a declining possibility of transformation of physical scenarios: not in terms of a realization of the design, but of its use as an instrument of articulation of these "economic, social, institutional meanings", which are mandatory carriers for upgrading and transformation of the ground.

To some extent, the aggregated Roman references of the Gabetti and Isola project for the area Bicocca in Milan [cf. ch. 1, Ambrosini and Berta] is a strategy of recognition as a latent form: as in other projects by the same authors, reading a sign becomes "weak"; accepting the changes and contingencies (what is and what will be) is a transformation into a "strong" project [Giammarco 1984].

Latent forms and shapes of transformation are intertwined and therefore interfering: the weight given to the discovery of a text is already inevitably an act of "writing" a project, therefore no deduction or determinism of the palimpsest, both in terms of its objective consistency – as result of the decision of design, as of its importance – as unfit to produce orders and priorities for transformation.

Bibliography
ARNHEIM, R., 1962, *Arte e percezione visiva*, Milano, Feltrinelli (1994)
BIANCHETTI, C., 2004, *Abitare la città contemporanea*, cit.
CORBOZ, A., 1985, *Il territorio come palinsesto*, cit.
GIAMMARCO, C., 1984, *Pensiero debole e immagini forti*, in BAZZANELLA, L. et al.,
Periferia torinese. Progetti per la modificazione, Torino, Celid
GREGOTTI, V., 1966, *Il territorio dell'architettura*, Milano, Feltrinelli (2008)

Luciano Fabro, *Cross*, 1965–86
aluminum, iron, 393 11/16 x 393 11/16 in.
Castello di Rivoli Museum of Contemporary Art, 2001
Photo Paolo Pellion, Turin

Giuseppe Penone, *11-meter Tree*, 1969–89
spruce wood, 2 elements, 203 1/8 x 17 11/16 x 17 11/16 in. each
Castello di Rivoli Museum of Contemporary Art, 1996
Photo Paolo Pellion, Turin

RECOMPOSITION AS MONTAGE

4 1 2 3 4 5 6 7

The conceptual implications of the category of montage are probably related to the debates of historical avant-garde, in particular the definition given by Adorno and the problem posed by Benjamin in his essay, "The Work Art in the Age of Mechanical Reproduction'. But the practice of montage has a much longer history - think of the *Ichnographia Campi Martii Antiquae Urbis* in 1757 [Rossi 1966] - perhaps the first of the iconological studies which tried to evoke this complexity through the definition of the recursive use of the accumulation of the fragment and its ruin over the centuries [Klibansky, Panofsky, Saxl 1983, Benjamin 1971]. These two horizons are also the basis for a definition of the strategy of montage in relation to this project.

According to Adorno, what characterizes the work of non-organic art using the principle of the montage, is the renunciation of the production of the "appearance of reconciliation 'between man and nature', this is a procedure that involves the fragmentation of reality and illustrates the construction phase of the work" [Adorno 1970, cit. Bürger in 1974]. Thus, for Benjamin, the Dadaists obtained the "merciless destruction of the aura" in their paintings, "which montaged buttons or train tickets" [Benjamin, 1955]. The work of assembly of inconsistent pieces expresses its materiality, since the parts do not make a whole, the fragments – newspaper, buttons, but also "word salads" [ibid] – belong to orders irreversibly lost, to the ruins, in the form of hybrid or accumulations.

In some ways, the description of a strategy for the GrandeScala project related to montage implies this condition of the sign without referent, of inevitable hybridization, adopting it as a fruitful principle. Before we deal with the territory in its concreteness as an accumulation of "ruins", we should consider the logic of production of drawings that represent it: where the purpose is to relate the morphological dimension, these drawings hybridize and break all other representations, built on unique disciplinary codes (maps, soil, infrastructure, geopolitical, economic...). Here the principle of representation is georeferential, it is not renegotiating the code place by place or framework by framework. Instead, the *GrandeScala* project is related to the contingency of that place and that frame, and uses this geographical circumstance and the particular established choices, for a convention regarding the real syntax of signs. The montage and duplication, which will be discussed later, are the principles of construction of this syntax.

Naturally, the montage is not only the hybridization of patterns "organic" to their code, but also the consolidation of other hybrid projects, which are in turn assemblies of different codes (eg, the mosaicing of plans to transform an extended area, whose implementation may have degrees of advancement and different textures). Reassembling by montage the issues that pertain to the territorial project requires also a work around constraints and images – and therefore the imaginary – of the transformations that have already "established" in a technical and political sense. local administrative forms of the communal extensions and of the of sovereignty related to parts of land separated by "intangible"borders, based on land ownership, planning tools, but also on the maps of environmental and hydrogeological risks and constraints. The montage strategies of the GrandeScala project differ from other ways of using the "fragment", which featured some great proposals in contemporary architecture: in GrandeScala project there is not autonomy of the code by which the montage takes place. This is not to reproduce the aesthetic principles of montage, with which the theories and manifestos of urban design – Plug-in by-City [Cook 1964] to Delirious New York [Koolhas 1978] to Collage City [Rowe 1984] and beyond – have sought to break the canons (not codes) of languages, editing them for fragments within the linguistic dimension (the autonomous code here) of architecture. What you want is account consolidation and not "settlement" through the montage.

A "non-organic" and "hybrid" assembly therefore does not join different parts in a predetermined order, or unite all the forms and objects of interior architecture [Purini 2006], since this would require an autonomous form of the *GrandeScala*, which is expressed primarily in the ability to determine its own absolute code. Rather, it is a way of working with pre-existing materials, in their morphological and technical-political dual nature, and that's why it does not necessarily belong to the specific disciplinary knowledge. It's that idea of "disassembly, list and reassembly" that Roberto Gabetti [1968] recalled about the eclecticism of the early twentieth century and that can define an action that is both cognitive / analytical and operational / planning, provided that it does not play in the separate sphere of architectural composition, but also it is capable of recomposing orders of meaning and different signs, without reconciliation in an autonomous and definitive order.

In contrast to the idea of the fragment, the juxtaposition of the patchwork [Viganò 1999] – key figures and categories for the description of ordinary practices of transformationthe recomposition strategy as "montage" requires a clear distinction between the cartographic fragment and the physical fragment: each these two dimensions establish references and meanings within themselves, so it could be argued that the "meaning" of a sign of the project is still in the drawing. Similarly, the "fragment" of a hybrid code of the project of *GrandeScala* is distinct from the fragment of an ordinary incision in the ground. The references between foliage and ground will inevitably contract orders and limits of power that govern the transformation.

The mosaic of different planning regulations that guide the transformation of administrative contexts becomes, within the metropolisation territories, a fundamental operation that allows you to recompose and re-read this logic within an otherwise partial framework. As if the synchronic representation of diverse projects – potential or current – affects a given landscape as a central instrument of explication of synergies and critical nodes that produce such planning. And yet, the design of the many technical and political imaginaries guiding the change of a territory is a prerequisite to shared democratic change. This common goal in front of the fragmentary nature of ordinary practices is therefore not simply to impose a new form on the ground – that is self-legitimizing as "architecture" – but rather to reconcile in the design the diverse rationalities that, acting separately, condition physical transformation of territory.

Bibliography

ADORNO, T. W., 1970, *Aesthetic Theory*, Torino, Einaudi

BENJAMIN, W., 1971, *the German Baroque drama*, Torino, Einaudi (1999)

BURGER, P., 1974, *Theory garde*, Torino, Bollati University Press, (1990)

COOK, P., WEBB, M., 1972, *Archigram*, New York, Princeton Architectural Press (1999)

DEMATTEIS, G., 1995, *The geography of urban places* in CAGNARDI, A., *A new sense of the plan. Zoning Gregotti Associati*, Milan, Etas books

GABETTI, R., 1968, *Eclecticism*, in PORTUGUESE, P., *Encyclopedic Dictionary of Architecture and Urbanism*, Rome, IER

KLIBANSKY, R., PANOFSKY, E., SAXL, F., 1983, *Saturn and melancholy*, Torino, Einaudi (2002)

KOETTER, F., ROWE, C., 1978, *Collage City*, NY Cambridge, MIT Press

KOOLHAS, R., 1978, *Delirious New York*, Milan, Electa (2001)

PURINA, F., 2006, *Dial architecture*, Bari, Laterza

ROSSI, A., 1966, *The architecture of the city*, Torino, Città Studi Edizioni, (1995)

VIGANO, P., 1999, *The City Elementary*, Milan, Skira

Giuseppe Penone, *House of Lucretius*, 1981
plaster casts, plaster fragments, fabric, wood, 2 plaster casts, 18 1/2 x 11 x 11 13/16 in. each
4 wood bases, 47 1/4 x 11 13/16 x 11 13/16 in. each
Castello di Rivoli Museum of Contemporary Art, 1986
Photo Paolo Pellion, Turin

RECOMPOSITION AS OVERLAPPING

5 1 2 3 4 5 6 7

The principle of overlapping, like a montage, can define a possible category of the constructive operations regarding the project. By contrast with the montage, however, the acts associated with the heterogeneous fragments, the overlapping presupposes the existence of categories of homogeneous elements that form parallel systems, and that insist on the same site. This means that the overlapping always involves a decision, a selection of what is relevant to the representation and distinct sets of factors associated into sets.

From this point of view overlapping proceeds analytically, the montage synthetically. Unlike montage, overlapping can reconstitute an organic and coherent unity, and indeed the taxonomies of modern science produce sets of "independent *variables* under a "necessary reason" which is the function of variables" [Deleuze and Guattari 1991]: these sets, called layers, would be extracted by choice from the whole territory and organized, according to a criteria – the "function" that unites them. We will then have what represents the cartographic layers of "roads", "green systems", "landlocked spaces", "buildings" etc, according to acts of uniformity imposed in the form of variables, objects and states of things that identify the physical reality of the place. So far, however, the production of layer and the syntax of overlap which describe a resulting logic that could be extended to the anatomy or, better still, the earth sciences - that taking care of "spheres (geosphere, biosphere, atmosphere...) – reason systematically in layers. Yet those sciences that make use of layers are entirely descriptive and analytical, you might say, extreme, in that the natural sciences use vertical layers (cross sections), while only layers in maps really act by overlapping, throught the horizontal plan view (in plan). This is because science investigates the layer (or layers) to create orders of coherence or"tasks", and the project builds layers using conventional functions to create different orders of processing. In other words, the use of overlap to represent the territory defines the interference between the levels set and modifies them. For example, to compare a latent form with a framework by renegotiating its extensions, is an overlapping operation.

Every organic overlapping of layers can be a coherent and stable syntax: topography, agronomy, engineering and road proceed to overlap, with a taxonomy that is stratified in mostly invariant legends. In the case of the *GrandeScala* project however it is really the open construction legends that render it unstable, and from time to time, as a taxonomy of design, they are composed of non organic orders (because diachronically separated, or because the products themselves of mutually untranslatable readings of the territory) which, interfering with each other, produce trimmings, tensions and further orders of differences. So often that the interference between two layers is taken in turn as another layer: it is the case with "settlement matrixes", where the overlap between the built fabric and farmland produces a design, which is the form and the consistency of the thresholds of the settlements.

The paradigm of the overlap is the underlying operational concept Corboz called "palimpsest", with a specificity that he refers to the simultaneous act of rewriting metaphor and scraping. The assumption is the irreproducibility of soil, defined as locus, which persists and is continuously processed (or consumed). This makes the use of stacked layers in the design of territory an ambiguous tool, since on the one hand it separates and distinguishes, and on the other always refers to the same thing.

The overlap may therefore be a strategy of the *GrandeScala* project that is intended as a falsifiable statement of latent interdependencies, such as non-neutral representation of novel hierarchies, chosen from among the infinite possibilities. It should also be considered a poetic description of nature [Dematteis 1986] as it invents new vistas of unexpected aspects, suggests alternative scenarios and "reveals" possible new geographies. Under these conditions, the territory may be regarded as an "object" [Corboz 1985] modified according to a long process of cumulative selection, as a huge database of signs, resulting in concrete projects, intentions, actions by individuals, even whole societies [Secchi 2001].

The construction of overlapping systems is composed of layers of signs, hybrids consisting of physical objects (geomorphological structures, objects, buildings and infrastructure, etc..), signs that abstract in nature (administrative boundaries, areas of influence of various nature themes, etc..) and diachronic stratification of signs.

The overlap of hybrid signs allows a hierarchy of spatial objects, creates new orders of things and sets new priorities, leaving some signs in the background and bringing to the fore others, working also resignification, giving new meaning to things, highlighting the latent values or creating a new dimension.

The overlap between abstract signs (administrative boundaries, constraints and other themes) and physical signs can determine the components of a causal link between political and administrative systems that within a territory, and the morphological configurations of this, reveal "morphogenetic" rules and explicit ways in which policies interact with physical space, in the shaping of different morphologies of settlement (eg the zoning of land use plans) and the formation of negative space (eg areas subject to restrictions of any unbuilt structure, landscape, geological, seismic, etc.). The overlap of boundaries and political, administrative and economic areas of influence made in the form of conflict, gives new meaning to the boundaries that enable territorial objects involved in a tension that transforms and assigns them new roles, becoming the morphologies of settlement, the meeting place between different stakeholders and the physical space, materials for the mediation process [Olmo, 2009].

Finally, the overlap of diachronic signs recounts the evolution of palimpsest through the use of comparative mapping techniques relating to different periods, staging a state of becoming, which processes for differences and interdependencies and constitutes a possible description of the mode of settlement underlying the construction of the territory.

In the diachronic overlapping they will relate, in an archeological sense, the traces deposited over a territory with the movement that produced them. Deciphering the oscillations that touch the past and present of a place you can project the course of some future trends to use as scenarios of transformation, continuously falsifiable through the implementation of the data.

Bibliography

BERTA M., DE ROSSI A., 2004, *It 's possible to design "architecturally" the landscape,* "Controspazio, n.104

CORBOZ, A., 1985: *The territory as a palimpsest,* cited.

DELEUZE G., GUATTARI, F., 1991, *What is Philosophy,* Torino, Einaudi (1996)

DEMATTEIS G., 1985, *the head of Janus,* "Urbanism," No 82

FOUCAULT M., 1967, *The Order of Things,* Milan, Rizzoli

MUNARINI S., TOSI MC, 2001, *Traces of the city: explorations of an area inhabited: the Veneto area,* Milan, Franco Angeli

SECCHI, B., 1989, *A project for the urban,* Torino, Einaudi

SECCHI, B., 2000, *First lesson planning,* cit.

Alighiero Boetti, *Pile,* 1966
34 Eternit bars, 75 9/16 x 39 3/8 x 39 3/8 in.
Collection Margherita Stein
Property Fondazione CRT Project for Modern and Contemporary Art, 2001
Permanent loan
Castello di Rivoli Museum of Contemporary Art, Rivoli-Turin
GAM – Municipal Gallery of Modern and Contemporary Art, Turin
Photo Paolo Pellion, Turin

REPRESENTATION AS NARRATIVE

6 1 2 3 4 5 6 7

Wanting to enunciate a strategy of representation using "Keywords" in terms of narrative/narration may seem ambiguous, if not naive. Philosophical questions and the "narratives" – in relation to the hermeneutical problem of the "temporalization of being", from Gadamer to Ricoeur, to "postmodern" themes of Lyotard and Vattimo, and beyond – are set beyond our control and our intent. On the other hand just a definition of Aimaro Island regarding the "silence, experience and narrative " [Isola 1993] leads us to bring with caution the concept of narrative to the horizon of the *GrandeScala* project: "The project idea alludes to the construction of the plot of a story, but a story that implies the involvement of the novel-reader in the action plan"; and, citing in a footnote Evelina Calvi: "To build a plot, in fact, the architectural design is powered by memory, interpretation of events and traditions, deconstructing them, reworking them, giving them new congruences [...]" [Calvi 1991, cited above. Isola in 1993]. The possibility and necessity of the project to make a consistent story would be in its capacity to weave plots, to become "plot, intrigue leading to language [...]."

Thus understood, the narrative exceeds the total rank of a simple mode of representation, rather it represents the general attitude of the designer and is almost untranslatable, though abdicating the "[...] rank of director, which is often repressive compared to the contribution of individual, cast and crew [...]" [Gabetti 1983] did not waive the "plot" to identify or put links to images. In this sense the narrative stands as recognition, reconstruction and representation, and becomes subject to the overall project.

The degree to which you would like to elaborate the theme is here far more limited than the conditions of the use of narrative strategies through the design. Assuming the overall *mise en intrigue*, with the idea of inalienable *jeu d'Echelles*, you would first make assumptions about the size of the sequential mode of representation within the *GrandeScala* project, then provide some less reductionist clarifications.

In general, the structure of the project has always as a plot of sequences (tables, advancement, approvals, inspections...) while the content in the sense of "projection" of a transformation of physical space is often placed as a state, a point of arrival [Cacciari 1982], but can also be a draft about the becoming conditions of a place in time. The narrative sequence of the project can therefore be spatial or temporal. Schematically, one could speak of synchronic narrative and diachronic narrative.

In the first case are depictions of prevailing "subjective" movements through the extension of the project and the land. Here time (of places) is still "put in the state," only by a spatial sequence from the eye of the observer – through the sequence of representation. The synchronic narrative thus requires an individual point of view amending its terms of framework and framing to articulate the story of a project caught in a "realised instant": as in a cinema "blocked", through control of the framework sequences of magnification are produced, through the framing one obtains sequences of plans and story paths. It is a sequence of the eye.

In the second case it is an objective movement rather than a look outside, it reads the differences in time from a fixed perspective. Here the time of the land is in flux, but is observed and so represented, "in progress" and has been observed - and therefore represented - according to stable spatial coordinates, that make the diachronic narrative lack a true subject who looks at an indefinite place or one in polar aspect to it. The movement therefore no longer affects classification and framing, but changes the states of things in them. The diachronies may include reconstructions of the past – through the consolidation of overlapping different chronological stages – or projections into the future – simulating scenarios linked to the implementation of a project, even the division into "functional lots" of executive plans could be considered a narrative diachronic to "the future". It is a sequence of the place.

From the conceptual point of view the synchronic and diachronic narratives of hybridization are as insignificant as they are feasible: the observation in motion of a phenomenon in flux produces cross-interference in terms of understanding the development of temporal phenomena. The current possibilities of virtual representation allow us to produce these multiple conditions uncritically through animation. But the navigation tools in interactive three-dimensional space – the zoom and pan – reflect a synchronic conception of that space, so in the case of virtual movies, the "becoming" is relegated to the background elements (people, vehicles, location of light and sunlight), while the "setting-in-state" of territory paradoxically becomes the main figure (as an object of description) and background (as motionless). The diachronic narrative is most often used in hybrid form, to represent deterministic scenarios, which represent quantitative data in relation to geographies (urban growth phenomena [Guerra 2009] and animated diagrams of the use of space [Hillier, 1996], etc.); also the diachronies of the *GrandeScala* aggregate data are nearly always around the shape of physical space, but not directly related to the metamorphosis of the soil. The diachronies are used in these cases as "modern geography", where "a fixed point of view is adopted, a global-outside as if the only possible union" [Dematteis 1993], increases the risks derived from the narration.

Very well-known examples are the synchronous narration sequences of Gordon Cullen (in fact already mentioned regarding the frame) which also shifts the framework replicated among other projects at different scales [*Isola,* Giammarco 1993] – acceleration to the top, which creates a "universal narrative" through the pervasive use of maps via Web, like Google Earth.

Some examples are the diachronic narrative, the stratigraphy and the "biographies of places" – like those collected in the book "Linee nel paesaggio" [Lines in the Landscape] [De Rossi et al. 1999], but also the wealth of geo-referenced historical maps available on the web www.davidrumsey.com/view/google-maps, or the digital panopticon made by countless eyes – the camera – through which to view streets, highways, coasts, ski slopes, etc...

So far, the categories presented define patterns affecting the properties of sequential narrative. However, it is clear that for narrative representations, we must also understand the strategies arising from the joint images of the territory taken in their morphological and geographical significance, which are able to derive from the latent forms a narrative, within fragmented and chaotic conditions. It is the idea of a project as a canvas [Giammarco, Isola 1993] that suggests possible stories – interpretations – of cities and territories which seem ever more difficult to be read and designed. A project that attempts to portray an area's topography made up of frames and textures, using pre-existing materials, does not necessarily act by imposing further – perhaps "larger" – forms over the space: through the narrative it is possible to stage the transition from a latent form to a figure of transformation by placing links between temporally different soil structures, framing perspective, axes and points to significant topography of the area. The narration plays through the figures also ambiguities inscribed in plots of ground and plots of narrative: the representation of empty negative spaces and the resignification of related elements present on the ground can construct the warp within which to imagine very different walks of life and liberties of building [Lanzani 2003], laying the foundation for transformative projects focused on sensitive elements (walls, banks, rows of trees, arrays...) in a "morphological infrastructuration" of the territory. The drawing of borders and limits of the built environment, thresholds and the gaps between built landscape and open space contribute to the creation of large-scale spatial stories, where the soil does not simply support the changes but becomes a potential element of plot.

The representation as narrative is then rhetorical and physical at once. It is an interpretive strategy as well as functional, in the "tidying up" of the space, building new landscapes which suggest possible readings and profiles (Lanzani 2007).

But the narration in a dimension attentive to the social practices of transformation of the built environment also creates meaningful places form the point of view of identity, capable of restoring external reality as a dimension of human experience (Sennett 1994), as well as creating recognition and sharing. The ordinary settling "comportments" often imply the assignment of material and symbolic values to places by their inhabitants. The project then explores, through putting them in shape, always new forms of correspondence between population and territory which from time to time are necessary to rethink, reinvent and rebuild. The gaze becomes in effect a project action through the sequencing of signs and spaces, creating landscapes, mediating and converging policies, imaginary identities for shared quality objectives.

Bibliography

CACCIARI, M., 1982, *Nihilismo e progetto*, cit.

CALVI, E., 1991, *Tempo e progetto*, Milano, Guerini

DE ROSSI, A. et al., (edited by), *Linee nel paesaggio. Esplorazioni nei territori della trasformazione*, cit.

DEMATTEIS, G., 1993, *Geo-grafie*, in GIAMMARCO, C., ISOLA, A., *Disegnare le periferie*, cit.

GABETTI, R., 1983, *Progettazione architettonica e ricerca tecnico-scientifica nella costruzione della città*, cit.

GABETTI, R., ISOLA, A., 1988, *Nuovi valori per l'ambiente*, cit.

Guerra-Laq

HILLIER, B., 1996, *Space is the machine – a configurational theory of architecture*, Cambridge, Cambridge University Press

ISOLA, A., 1993, *Pensare il limite, abitare il limite*, in GIAMMARCO, C., ISOLA, A., *Disegnare le periferie*, cit.

LANZANI, A., 2003, *I paesaggi italiani*, cit.

LANZANI, A., 2007, *Introduzione. Riformismo al plurale*, in LANZANI, A., MORONI, S., *Città e azione pubblica*, Roma, Carocci

RICOEUR, P., 1986, *Tempo e racconto*, Milano, Jaca Book

SENNETT, R., 1994, *La coscienza dell'occhio*, Milano, Feltrinelli

http://earth.google.com/

www.davidrumsey.com

Mario Merz, *Time-Based Architecture – Time-Debased Architecture*, 1981
iron tubes, painted glass, clamps, stones, acrylic on canvas, neon, twigs
118 1/8 x 551 3/16 x 157 1/2 in.
Castello di Rivoli Museum of Contemporary Art
Long-term loan – Fondazione Marco Rivetti, 1996
Photo Paolo Pellion, Turin

REPRESENTATION AS A MEASURE OF LIVING

7 1 2 3 4 5 6 7

The definition of GrandeScala put out the problem, among many others, of size and scale, because the "large scale" does not imply, as mentioned above [cf. De Rossi, chapter 1], an immediate geometric data, but rather the size and number of intermediaries making and implementing a project that separates the project of a territory from its physical construction. In this sense the *GrandeScala* project is also always a measure of the relationship between subjects and places they inhabit.

The theme of the measure has to do primarily with the possibility of representing the proportion between man and the built environment: the "human scale" of places. The modern movement has literally interpreted this relationship in quantitative terms (standards), specifications (ergonomics), but also poetics. Consider the proportional Modulor system of Le Corbusier, where the golden section produces a series of measures that give life to the size of the Unités d'Habitation [Le Corbusier 1973]. Here too is the bottom of a picture, but where is the theme of the measure as a condition of development of a system of linear spaces, "from man to city". Not only: determinations governing relations are not built according to an individualized look, but take the value of objective rules: in some way as "modern geography" [Dematteis 1993] that sets the terms of proportion to man (not the subject) and the city.

Here arises also a problem of narrative that pertains to the eye. The representation as a mesure projects the eyes of many subjects into the design to enunciate shared ideas about the place: only this way is it possible bring back the signs of maps with their references of residential place. As recalled by Corboz, citing Raymond Bloch, "the landscape as a whole, exists only in my consciousness" [Corboz 1985], because without individualized looks it is not given the condition of living. The *GrandeScala* project must continually refer to the size of the subject. It is not just to narrate, to sequence and intrigue these spaces and times: it is necessary also to conceive of a strategy portrayed as an instrument for determining the physical relationship between subjects and places.

But here is the second set of problems: the attempt to give a real measure of the places through a figure is basically impossible. Gregotti, for example, considers the realization (line) of the project as the only "substance specification" of architecture. In his view "the delivery of a new thing in the world" [Gregotti 2008] is intended as a physical presence of the res aedificata, which exceeds every performance as a concrete measure of the relationship between person and place. Just because no one can really make this project at the size of its practical implementation, the measure cannot be represented, but only built. For the *GrandeScala* project the problem is indeterminate, because the terms of the measurement of the design may never be falsified (as opposed to a construction project).

However it is within this relationship between place and subject that the representation as a measure of living acts, in rhetorical terms, through the project, and evokes, inside the design, a condition of attendance at places of the subject: so that the controversies that enliven public debates on urban transformations are often conveyed by this type of representation - think of the recent discussions about the impact of new towers in the skyline of Turin, conducted at posed photographic shots of the urban landscape "seen" from the hill [La Stampa 2007].

Within this framework, what is fundamental becomes the experience of architecture through the scales, measuring spaces, objects and distances, observing sights and points of view, interpreting places and uses, in a continuous circuit between residency and shape of the city and territory. The result is dialogue that circulation through figures should make substantial a possible "formal resonance" between the materials chosen in the "palimpsest" [Corboz 1985], identifying those particular measures of space which alternate to bring in various scales that shape the character of the place. These measures of the landscape, and especially the spatial arrangements that regulate the different "grain of texture", are a key input to define the fundamental theme of the "quality" of individual sites and to determine the real scope of the project operability. Which takes as its primary value "respect" the rules of operation of these devices, and their constitution [Mamino 1994], as a field of action and bargaining choices and decisions. Thus the representation as a measure of living renders available the stocks and the orders of the presence of places, through the research of a synthetic look in a way that combines the observations of geographic character of the signs of the palimpsest to a an immersive investigation, based on the reconstruction of a possible application of formal quality.

The process of representation can proceed in many ways: *through the recognition of latent forms,* namely identifying elements "attractors" that allow a regrouping of fragmentary episodes, through the enunciation of particular and recurring scalar sequences of solids and voids, using a choice between deposits of ordinary materials that are sequences of an ordinary landscapes.

The so-called "large regional architectures" are identified by the definition of some sets of evidence to sort the processes of densification and transformation, putting into the background the language of individual objects, with respect to their relationship to the particular character of the structure that holds them. Such a pattern of support has the ability to attract the other elements of the palimpsest, and manages to keep open the possibility of a general reconfiguration, with the objective of creating shared formal organization, which involves the construction of place scales in all their dimensions. Therefore the measure of living is also an immaterial connective tissue, that "holds together" things and acts as Transcal device, finalised in turn to reconstruct potential narrative units.

Large roles in the definition of a "general grammar" of the measure of living have reinterpretated a figurative and technical heritage, "a tradition", which arises from the observation of intermediate places, the transition from a reinterpretation of certain elements or structures as simple as spaces or covered porches, the rows of trees, irrigation paths, the steep walls and containment against the ground. These phenomenological explorations of "weak" signs become a necessary foundation for the establishment of vocabularies of image guidance strongly dependent on attention to the morphology and topology in different places, but attentive to possible "gaps" and fusions that can produce significant innovations in the perception of urban space even with regard to the material nature and three-dimensionality of the various environments.

Bibliography

CORBOZ A., 1983, *Il territorio come palinsesto*, cit.

DEMATTEIS, G., 1993, *Geo-grafie*, cit.

GREGOTTI, V., 2008, *Contro la fine dell'architettura*, cit.

LE CORBUSIER, 1973, *Modulor 1-Modulor 2*, Mazzotta, Milano (1948 e 1950)

MAMINO, L., 1994, *Progetti per una Piccola Città*, in FELISIO, P., edited by, *Il Progetto nelle Tesi di Laurea della Facoltà di Architettura di Torino 2- La Piccola Città*, Torino, Celid

VATTIMO, G., 1991, edited by, *Filosofia 90*, Roma, Laterza

VOLLI, U., 1991, *Apologia del Silenzio Imperfetto*, Milano, Feltrinelli

La sfida dei grattacieli, in "La Stampa", 8 luglio 2007

Sempre più in alto, in "La Stampa", 30 ottobre 2007

Michelangelo Pistoletto, *Architecture of the Mirror*, 1990
gilded wood, mirrors
4 elements, 149 5/8 x 78 3/4 in. each
Castello di Rivoli Museum of Contemporary Art
Gift Gruppo Dalle Carbonare, 1991
Photo Paolo Pellion, Turin

Part III Geographies

Edited by Andrea Delpiano, Roberto Dini and Mattia Giusiano

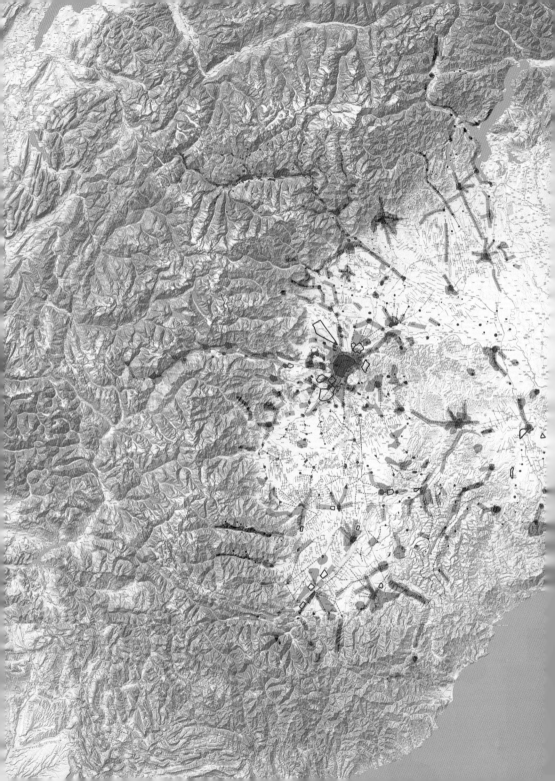

3.1 LANDSCAPE NW

Antonio De Rossi

September 2nd, 1706. The duke Vittorio Amedco II and his cousin Prinz Eugen are ascending the hill of Superga, dominating Turin, in order to study the topography of the plain and the deployment of the French-Spanish troops, which have been besieging the capital of the dukedom since the 14th of May. From the hill they are able to detect the weak point in the enemy lines, between the rivers of Dora Riparia and Stura di Lanzo. On September 7th, the battle of Turin takes place: the Austro-Piedmontese army overwhelms the French-Spanish forces, putting an end to the siege and marking a turning point in the first phase of the Spanish Succession War. To celebrate the victory, Vittorio Amedeo II will contract Juvarra to build the Basilica of Superga which, together with the Castle of Rivoli and the road that visually connects them, frames "the wide area between the buttresses of the Alps and the Apennines". In the words of Leonardo Benevolo, it creates "an extraordinary perspective of 19,5 km, descending from 354 to 248 meters above the sea level, and then ascending to the dome of the church that dominates the wooded hill, at 675 mt". He describes it as "the world's biggest architectonic work ever created through the means of perspective". Several years later, the battle will be immortalized by an extraordinary watercolor painting by Giuseppe Pietro Bagetti, in which a precise view of the landscape is framed by the physical marks of a baroque territorial structure. The four rivers crossing the plain and the agricultural layout on the one hand, the armies and the geological architecture of the Alps on the other: the culture of the Enlightenment is intertwined with a blooming romantic sensibility.

The military tone of the *incipit* should not come as a surprise. The parallelism between topography and military history –that is, between morphology of the land, size and location of the troops, moves and strategies– appears to be a milestone in the history of space, as indicated by works such as *Les Vallées Vaudoises: étude de topographie et d'histoire militaries,* written by Albert De Rochas d'Aiglun in 1880.

We should go back to the hill of Superga, by omnibus if possible, in the company of mayors, technicians, and economic operators. From that point, in between a zenithal and a perspective view, we should make a fresh start and analyze the constructed landscape once again, trying to define strategies and scenarios. We ought to start from the *physical evidence* –which today is often underestimated, or reduced to a pretended objectivity and neutrality of *amorphous* field analysis– of the constitutive elements of the territory: architectural, topographic, geomorphologic, geographical, and tectonic. We especially ought to reinterpret in analytical and planning terms the *stratifications* that have naively been suppressed by the architecture scene of the last years, to try to respond to the anxieties generated by the accelerating transformations. We might not forget the many things we have learned in the last few years through the ambitious analysis of the transformation processes of different places, and through the reconstruction of their territorial biographies: the awareness of a transformation of the space based on the conflict between individual rationalities and immutable self-referential strategies; the importance of precise and minimal tactics and practices aimed at resisting and controlling the space; in spite of the growing rhetoric on places and differences, the prevalence of "reductionist", "by catalog" logics of transformation and predetermination of project topics; the changes in the traditional relationship and dialectic between local and national political powers with respect to project ideas on a large scale –especially in Piedmont, where there are 1206 municipalities in a country where there are about 8000; the prominence –often underestimated– of the collective imaginaries in the process of defining the "fields" of reference for the transformation of the territory; finally, the future of a political and architectural approach based on incrementalism.

I. Tectonics of the territory and polycentric structure
Looking from Superga, you could describe the land of Piedmont as the final part of the long inclined plan that emerges from the Adriatic Sea, stretching across the Po Valley to end abruptly –almost like a *finis terrae*– at the bottom of the massive buttress of the Western Alps.
This geometric plain is framed by the 400 km long line of the amphitheater of the Maritime, Cottian, Graian, Pennine, and Leopontine Alps, and by the streams flowing downhill to merge into the Po and Tanaro rivers, the biggest of Piedmont plain. This connection between constructed border and contained space, *vertical*

margins and *horizontal* interiors, is peculiar to the region of Piedmont, which might be seen as a type of large *room*, or a *mountain theater.*

This dialectic has been wittingly detected by Jean-Jacques Rousseau, who in the *Émile* creates –at the same time immortalizing– the modern image of the landscape of Piedmont:

"Il me mena hors de la ville, sur une haute colline, au dessous de laquelle passoit le Pô, dont on voyoit le cours à travers les fertiles rives qu'il baigne; dans l'éloignement, l'immense chaîne des Alpes couronnoit le paysage; les rayons du soleil levant rasoient déjà les plaines, et, projetant sur les champs par longues ombres les arbres, les coteaux, les maisons, enrichissoient de mille accidents de lumière le plus beau tableau dont l'œil humain puisse être frappé. On eût dit que la nature étaloit à nos yeux toute sa magnificence…".

An instantaneous of the landscape that was revisited and extended in the second half of 18th century by Horace Bénédict de Saussure, in his extraordinary *Voyages dans les Alpes:* "La vu que l'on a du haut de Superga, surtout de la galerie qui est au-dessus de la coupole, est une des plus belles que je connaisse. Les Alpes présentent de là l'aspect le plus magnifique…". Themes that appeared once again in *Alle Porte d'Italia,* by Edmondo De Amicis, indelibly depicting the North-West like "a large bay" surrounded by the "circle of the Alps, from Monte Viso to Monte Rosa".

The importance of geomorphology should not be considered a mere pictorial data, only relevant to the landscape as a background. A background that is marked by the *sublime* of the Alps –the line of the peaks, the sparkle of the snow and the ice– and complementary contrasted, according to the lines of the aesthetic debate of the 18th and 19th centuries, by the *grace* and the *picturesque* quality of the details characterizing the internal plain –crops, rivers, hills and settlements. In this region the decisive factors to guide the transformative and settlement process are tectonics, geomorphology and topography. Furthermore, it is the close interaction between the lines of the large and narrow valley rifts, the terraced sides of the foothills, the plain and the fluvial terraces, the hill crests and the alluvial cones stretching down to reach the internal plain. Here, during the XII and XIII century, a *polycentric* settlement pattern of small and medium centers began to take shape, gradually forming the extensive urban grid –traditionally feudal in the North and communal in the South– of the Piedmont and Valle D'Aosta regions [Dematteis 1989]. The interaction between the geomorphologic substratum and the pattern of the superimposed urban and territorial structure of these settlements is rooted

The polycentric structure of historic Piedmont region in relation to the geomorphologic substrate in the representation of the fresco in the Gallery of Maps in the Vatican Museums in Rome (1580-83)

in the Middle Age [Griseri 1974]. This is evident in cities like Cuneo, Fossano and Cherasco, where the terraces have created orthogonal geometrical patterns. This polycentric system has been designed by the flourishing of settlement patterns of large or medium-sized towns in the western part of the region –Mondovì, Cuneo, Saluzzo, Pinerolo, Ivrea, Biella, and ultimately Torino–, in close relationship with the landscape and the corridors of the valleys behind. This pattern was preserved both during the restructuring phase and the baroque territorial development of the XVIII Century, and during the proto-industrialization of the XIX Century, when the rapidly expanding local railway and the search for water energy sources emphasized the role of the area at the foot of the mountains, consolidating the relationship between the geomorphologic substrate and the settlement patterns. When it became the capital of the Savoia reign, Turin's dominance on the other north-western cities did not imply an actual transformation of the long-term territorial architecture: the infrastructural and territorial hierarchy determined by the *routes royales,* and the rewriting of the plain of Turin operated by the absolutist power were coexisting with the development and consolidation of the polycentric pattern. We could maintain that the great Sabaudian engineers and architects –Ascanio Vitozzi and Ercole Negro di Sanfront, Filippo Juvarra and Antonio Bertola– were first of all the *soil designers,* attentive to the lines of the watercourses, the altimetry profile of the area, and the geologic and pedologic nature of the land.

It was during the XIX Century that this interconnection came to an end. Turin became la *ville industrielle* and the quintessential factory-city, absorbing the populations and the resources from the surrounding regional area and the rest of Italy, like a massive black hole. A type of "gigantic infrastructure at the service of production", to quote an evocative image of the time, that brought to life, in morphological terms, a "spatial form typical of a Fordist local society" [Lanzani 1996]: it combined productive areas and factory-work barriers, infrastructural systems and social housing areas. The polarization process around the company town caused the exodus from the mountains and the countryside, which for tens of years remained white, almost invisible spaces. On the other hand, the road network, the penstocks, the power lines began to adventure far from the city, delineating a new geography. The factory of the Fiat Lingotto with its race track celebrated by Le Corbusier, the huge plate of 3 square kilometers of the Fiat Mirafiori became the physical symbols of Turin in the XIX Century. But the deepest change was in the way of interpreting the geomorphologic substratum and the pattern of the soil, brought

The central component of the geomorphological structure of settlements in the north west in scientific studies of the nineteenth century. Panorama views of the Alps. Viewed from the astronomical observatory in the Alps in Turin, the Italian Alpine Club Publication, 1874 (detail)

about by the Fordist organizational cultures [Gabetti, Avigdor 1977]. The rapidly expanding Turin metropolitan area generally interpreted the physical elements of the territory like a mere *tabula rasa,* or like obstacles to be crossed or removed. The rivers of the city were reconverted into backyards for the factories, and on occasions they were covered with plates of reinforced concrete to create space for the needs of the industry.

This extraordinary mechanism started to jam up in the second half of the Seventies. Therefore, while Turin was reflecting on the crisis of the big industry and the need to radically rethink itself [Bagnasco 1986], only few were aware of the deep transformation of the settlements in the North-West of Italy.

II. Interpretations of the transformation
Contrary to what was going on in the North-East and in the so-called "Third Italies", the processes which were taking place outside the well-known and quite reassuring scenario of the polarization on Turin were not being analyzed in the light of the spreading of settlements and the extended city. For a long time a strongly *Turincentric* perspective prevailed, and the new settlement geographies, rather than being regarded as a phenomenon that might not be really new and alternative but it is surely complex and multifaceted, were seen as the result of the deindustrialization and the decline of the city (its population, from a record figure of over 1.200.000 people in 1974, constantly kept decreasing for about 25 years, until the recent increase to more than 900.000). From this point of view, a reconstruction and periodization of the modalities of the expansive and spreading processes in the North-West still has to come [Olmo 2009]. The decentralization and rebalancing, the changing collective imaginary regarding the environment and the real estate of the Seventies were all important actors on the stage. Nonetheless, the key was understanding the geographical and organizational changes of the industrial production (peculiar elements of the north-western space) that, before the *Just-in-Time* Revolution and the productive disarticulation of the Eighties, experienced radical modifications which deeply affected the settlement structures.

In addition to this, we must not forget the consequences of the spreading process caused by the *take off* of the small and medium family enterprises in the Sixties and the Seventies in essentially rural areas, such as the province of Cuneo [De Rossi, Durbiano, Governa, Reinerio, Robiglio 1999]. All these processes, based on the movement of the individuals rather than on politics of mobility, not only take the reuse of the territorial capital assets as a crucial and generative factor, but in a paradoxical way –on the encounter between the spreading of the settled areas and the morphology of the space– they give back to the land "the consistency of a physical fact, the evidence of a *constructed form* that had been kept in the shadow by a perspective dominated by the socio-economic disciplines". Their main focus is on the structure of the substratum –the lines of the valley sole, the fringes at the foot of the mountains etc. A further peculiarity is the extraordinary "passive" capacity of the geomorphologic frame to guide the geography of the transformations. The foothill area is thus reconfirmed as a place to live in the long term because of the traditional drive to settle down of the XVIII and the beginning of the XIX Century –the promise of a productive structure related to the presence of water, a prosperous fruit growing activity etc. To this we should add some new elements: the location of the land, between the Alpine system and the plain, the improved quality of the environment, the landscape and, most of all, the microclimate. Living in the foothills means to stay at a slightly higher altitude than the internal plain. Only a few meters, which are nonetheless sufficient to emerge from the autumn and winter fogs. A small geomorphologic and climate difference thus becomes a decisive factor of settlement, which is often underestimated by the ordinary planning practices. As it has been said, this ongoing transformation is better interpreted through the lens of the environmental consequences than through an in-depth analysis of the changing settlement structures.

This metamorphosis was first indirectly unveiled by the effects that the *architectural exploitation* of the soil had on the agricultural land and its hydro-geological structure [Ipla 1982]. This particular point of view is peculiar to Piedmont –especially to the Regional Technical Board, deeply influenced by the crusades for urban parks and against pollution –, and has been forged by specific lenses through which to observe the phenomena of the territory. In this context, the spreading of settlements was seen as an issue essentially concerning urban expansion and housing speculation, and the rarefied –yet structured– nature of the phenomenon kept being ignored.

A first shift in the interpretation, though limited to the academic world, took place between the Eighties and the Nineties. The study *It.Urb. 80,* part of a *case study* regarding Piedmont, describes the expansion of the urban area which, from the western side of Turin, spreads out across the low Susa Valley to create original settlement structures; these in turn are deeply affected by mobility and accessibility, but also by the forms of territorial substrate. At this point thinking in terms of a mere expansion of the metropolitan area becomes impossible [Astengo, Nucci 1990]. An important project on this respect is the collective research *Progetto Torino* [Città di Torino, 1982-85]. Moreover, the works of Giuseppe Dematteis [1998] show an original settlement pattern of the north-western spaces, based on the encounter between the foothill area and the big transalpine corridor valleys. Turin metropolitan area is in a very strategic and sensitive position within this territorial re-conceptualization, as it lies in the crossroad between the East-West axis of the Susa Valley and the urban foothill area, from North to South. The same issue is dealt with in *Itaten*, a monographic work dedicated to Piedmont, which nonetheless lacks the elaboration of an overall figurative conceptualization, able to identify and define the transformation [Diter 1995; Spaziante 1996]. The appearance of a new generation of technical maps and satellite images will in the following years confirm the results of these studies, finally conferring visibility and scientific dignity to phenomena which – here more than elsewhere– were kept in the shadows by the rise of the *company town*. The new settlement architecture that has been adapting to the territorial scale does not come in contact with the projecting of new communication infrastructures [Ires 1989; Ires 1995]. Now like before the prevailing idea of infrastructure –such as the Susa Valley's highway, the enlargement of Caselle airport, the high-speed railway Lyon-Turin-Milan etc– is essentially that of a strategic tool aimed at connecting Turin to other European regions and cities. In a time where it is crucial to promote the Italian North-West after the long economic and productive restructuring phase of the Eighties and early Nineties, the goal for Turin and Piedmont is essentially to regain its position in the international rankings and in the European map, emerging from marginalization. The infrastructure, apart from being a service for the productive structure, is thus mostly seen from a supra-local perspective, as it is the notion of an Alpine macro-region with Turin and Lyon as the points of reference. The interconnection between the infrastructural projects and the redefinition of the settlement practices remains unexplored, also because of the lack of a clear framework –a planning framework and at the same time a political one, to deal with the vertical and horizontal fragmentation and competition between the different levels of local governance. A base upon which to start a comprehensive debate on the peculiarities of the constructed territory of the North-West.

The first instruments of regional and provincial planning came to light in the second half of the Nineties. They are interesting to analyze rightly because of the territorial

A typical case of contemporary transformation of the Northwest Territories: the foothills Pinerolo. In dark purple - built before 1945; in dark pink – the changes until the late eighties, in light pink - contemporary changes (graphics processing Annalisa Dry, 2008)

images they suggest. The Piano Regionale Territoriale approved in 1997 provides for some "compensation ridges" –which usually coincide with the foothills area– and for "systems of urban expansion" around the regional poles. The Piano Territoriale di Coordinamento adopted by the Province of Turin in 1999 follows the same line, and articulates the idea of systems of urban expansion relying on the creation of a "foothills ridge", an element of reorganization of the new settlement environments. The image of Turin metropolitan area described by the PTC is that of an essentially compact conurbation, rather different than the north-eastern and Adriatic settlements upon which the icon of the extended city was built. Among the most problematic issues lies the crossing of radials and rings in the areas where Turin settlement system meets the foothills. As it is highlighted by the Plan, "the especially critical points" are "where the valleys turn into flatland, where the conurbations of the valley sole clambers up the foots of the mountains and the hills, interrupting the continuity between the mountain and woodland areas and the river bands".

The possibility of an intersection between the environmental frameworks and the morphological aspects of the settlement system is still more a suggestion than a reality. The rationale behind the urban expansion systems is still the *macro-zone:* the identification of rebalancing areas, inside which to implement rearrangement and consolidation measures. The identification of the punctual problems and the strategic topics, upon which to build an overview of a redevelopment and reconfiguration at a territorial scale is far from being a reality: the potentially positive consequences of the new territorial relationship between infrastructural lines, settlement practices, and territorial substratum are still deeply underestimated. The *solid* of the constructed land and of the settlement is essentially seen as related to its effects on the environment, and not as a value in terms of territorial and landscape architecture. At the same time the infrastructures keeps having a strictly functional connotation, and the strategic nature of the open environmental spaces is kept in the background.

Yet this situation is an effect, not a cause. We could say that the political and technical worlds ignore "a priori" –that is, in the initial phase of visualization and setting of the problems– the problem of morphology and settlement architecture of the territory, because the conceptual and interpretative parameters that allow to understand the urgency of the issue still do not exist. What is missing is essentially a geographic comprehensive vision that allows for a better understanding and critical interpretation of the consequences of the territorial transformative processes. The critique to the negative transformations of the landscape is therefore a generic and sterile one, deprived of a technical insight. The responses to the modification of the structural elements of a landscape are the *best practices* for the recovery of the architectural heritage. The building processes are observed in a punctiform manner, i.e. starting from a center outward, or related to the impact on "nature" and the environment, but they are rarely analyzed in terms of a comprehensive evaluation of a constructed landscape.

What seems to be lacking is essentially a conceptual place, a panoramic point from which to have an overall view of what is usually seen as fragmented, reductive and incomplete. But there is also a strong need for a *political place* able to restore a comprehensive vision of mutual glances and shared intentions, in a context that, as soon as you leave Turin metropolitan area, is clearly dominated by a myriad of tiny local realities which measure the world exclusively from their own perspectives.

III. Recent trends

This way of looking at the territory and its transformation reflects itself on the many political initiatives of territorial governance that have been implemented in the last decade, almost a vice of origin. The north-western space for instance has been widely promoting the liaison between the territory and its history, culture, the parks and the environment, the wine and food traditions. The hilly area of the Langhe and the *Corona di delitie* –constituted by the Sabaudian residences which are now a Unesco world heritage site– have finally acquired a status of "excellence", able to promote the territory as a whole. Despite all this, these projects rarely accomplished to affect the usual, specific modalities of transformation –maybe with the exception of the food and wine routes on the hills and of Slow Food, aimed at reinventing a traditional rural scenario. This constitutes a limitation for a territory that, lacking the great historical and artistic milestones of the rest of Italy, has based its peculiarity on the *average quality* of the overall geomorphologic landscape and its consequent interpretation.

This average quality of the historical panorama was thrown into a crisis by the new wave of transformation of the last decade, whose momentum was in 2000, and whose full dimensional and quantitative extent has only recently begun to be appreciated. To give a few examples, in the Turin province the percentage of utilized land between 1990 and 2000 was 5.4%, which corresponds to 2.656 hectares, whereas in the shorter period between 2000 and 2006 it increased of

9.3%, 4.822 hectares [Provincia di Torino 2009]. These data do not concern only the metropolitan area, they take into consideration the areas at the foot of the mountains and the hills, showing once again how the presence of sophisticated planning tools leads nonetheless to mere assessments of procedural compliance. The causes of this important territorial transformation –comparable in magnitude to those of the Sixties and Seventies– are not univocal: the low cost of money and the "real estate bubble", attracting new population groups towards the single family property house; the wide offer of building land, sold by local authorities to increase incomes related to the municipal real estate tax (Ici); finally, the presence of rationalizing tendencies such as the creation of new production areas in order to increase external economies, and contain the *sprawl*.

The percentage and absolute increase, if analyzed out of context, can only deal with part of the problem. What have not been evaluated yet are the results of this transformation, in terms of organization of the space and settlement architecture. Previously, the exploitation of the fixed territorial assets, the incremental approach, and the transformations adapting to the territorial substratum and to the infrastructural pattern used to create a dialogue –although at times ambiguous and twisted– between the programs and the transformations; on the contrary, the present transformative trend seems to be more self-sufficient. The trend is towards introflexion, towards the construction of "other" entities, isolated from their environment: residential *enclaves*, huge enclosed spaces for trade and production, theme parks. This indifference to the physical data is deepened by the "processing of space" which is present in every intervention: the imposition of boundaries and of separating elements, the destruction of pedologic factors and of altimetric and topographic diversity. Once the relationship with the territorial patterns and background has been eliminated, the only geometrical and relational connections left are the changes of the last decades.

In this scenario the infrastructural projects can play an extremely positive part, both in terms of a functional reorganization, and of a potential modeling of the transformations. Nonetheless, the difficulty of building positive interaction between great public works and ordinary extensive works is evident. The case if the Susa Valley is paradigmatic in this respect: the extensive practices and the incrementalism on the valley sole of the Sixties and Seventies were followed by a project for a highway crossing the valley in the early Nineties. Instead of trying to adapt to the settlement structures which were already there, the highway defined its relationship with the territory in terms of an obstacle to be overcome, pursuing the image –a physical one as well– of a self-sufficient and self-referential corridor. This very same vision was represented to the nth degree on the occasion of the project for the Turin-Lyon high speed line: the results were the uprising of the valley's residents and the clashes with the police which took place in December 2005 in Venaus. In the words of Luigi Bobbio e Egidio Dansero [2008], the contrasting reactions to that project, before being a matter of track lines or environmental sustainability, have been revolving around two ideas of the territory that are irreducible and irreconcilable: instead of considering the topic of the crossing as a chance to reflect on a project for the territory, the focus has entirely been on the *ad libitum* building of the great tunnel, regardless of the context. Therefore the issue has become "a solution seeking a problem". Such a deficit of perspective characterizes the local communities as well. While negotiating, the municipalities of the Susa Valley have been incapable of looking beyond the request for facilities, services, reductions of impact, thus recreating the same refund logic of the Nineties, when the highway was built. This opens a door for architecture and the other disciplines dealing with the connection between politics and the physical transformation of the space, since the quality of the landscape goes hand in hand with economic competitiveness and the preservation of the *well-being.*

The same problems keep reappearing in all the great projects, be they infrastructural or not: for example the "retroporto", a logistic platform connecting Alessandria to Genoa harbor, or questionable initiatives such as "Mediapolis", the projected theme park in the Eporediese area. Nevertheless, some of the typical features of the north-western constructed space, which radically differentiate these places from the central-eastern Po Valley, could become the testing ground for an effective experimentation, able to combine the transformation processes with the geographical scale of the territory. The point of departure is the dialogue –a conflictive but also necessarily complementary debate, started in the second half of XVI Century– between the regional pole and the polycentric and extensive settlement pattern that marks the national territory.

The redevelopment of Turin, started in the mid-Nineties, whose main *atout* is the reintroduction of a continuous and compact urban fabric, may constitute a good start to rethink the structural geographic features of the plain of Turin, at a point where the metropolis has spread so much that the environmental and geomorphologic substratum must be regarded as projecting material. On the other

Icons set	Integrated Territorial Program (PTI) networks 2001	Urban Regeneration Scheme and Sustainable Development Planning	Borgaro-Settimo-Turin (Bor. Set. to.) in-between area	"Green Lagoon" project	Botticelli street	Stura downfields	Metro 2 underground line
Built areas inside open spaces							
Built areas on the edge of open spaces							
Open spaces as a connection							
Repetition scheme of the concept							

The relationship between the design of buildings and open spaces in recent transformation patterns in the zone north of Turin metropolitan area (graphics processing Susanna Tubiana, 2008)

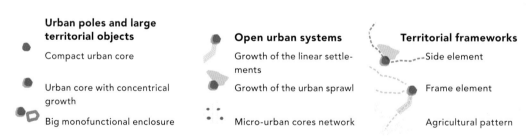

Urban poles and large territorial objects

Compact urban core

Urban core with concentrical growth

Big monofunctional enclosure

Open urban systems

Growth of the linear settlements

Growth of the urban sprawl

Micro-urban cores network

Territorial frameworks

Side element

Frame element

Agricultural pattern

On the right: map of the settlement structure of the north-west region, designed by Dipradi-Polytechnic of Turin for the Landscape Plan of the Piedmont Region (graphic processing Andrea Delpiano, 2009)

hand, we can consider this polycentric and extensive trend not as the deterministic realization of the extended city, but as a complex and well structured configuration which has been frequently taken as a model throughout the North-West [Dematteis 1989]. If we do so, the expanding interconnection of the low density urban fabric with the historical projects can turn into a positive chance for the territory and its inhabitants. This idea of space and local society is seen as conservative and distant –both in political and "figurative" terms– by the inhabitants of Milan urban fringe, as recently narrated in *L'ubicazione del bene,* a book by Giorgio Falco. Despite the limits and the ambiguities, this local horizon has been seeking its own model of development and organization of the space in a spontaneous manner, resisting to any planning framework. The main features of this spatial organization are: the horizontal interpenetration of the constructed and natural structures, the vertical reconnection of the working and living places, the creative coexistence of different spaces, times and cultures, and finally the possibility of experiencing different activities and lifestyles. Yet the fortunes of this model could take a turn for the worse.

IV. The design of the territory as an act of construction and substruction
In order to overcome this mechanicistic and deterministic scaling process which has generated the current crisis of transformative intentions, and to bridge the immeasurable gap between the individual transformations and the overall result on the landscape, it is crucial to develop a vision that highlights the problematic relationship between the settlement patterns and the geographical and geomorphologic structures. Despite the lack of a tradition of local studies in the fields of city-planning dealing with these issues, the north-western space can constitute a very fruitful laboratory. On the other hand there is a *fil rouge* that historically connects the different studies on the territory, from the Sabaudian architects and engineers to the studies of Mario Passanti e Augusto Cavallari Murat and the *analogical landscapes* of Roberto Gabetti e Aimaro Isola. In addition to this, Turin has a polytechnic tradition which has been building its field of action and theoretical speculation on the very relationship between the project and the transformation of the physical environment.
But there are several more threads to follow and interweave, using as a loom the same north-western territory, on which so many glances and interpretations have been cast. For instance a well-known cartographic and knowledge practice was able to conjugate the "topographic mastery" with "the brilliance of the landscape architect" to build the

very idea of landscape [Romano 1978]. And a few geographical and geological studies deepened the readings and interpretations of the territorial substratum, unveiling new meanings and paving the way for its transformation. If the North West does not have a masterpiece such as *Notizie naturali e civili su la Lombardia* by Carlo Cattaneo, it can boast works such as *Geologia della provincia di Torino* [1893] by Martino Baretti, *Les Alpes occidentales* [1913] by Federico Sacco, *Il Piemonte e i suoi paesaggi* [1935] by Carlo Fabrizio Parona, but also Le massif du Mont Blanc [1876] by Viollet-Le-Duc.

The interconnection between architecture, settlement patterns, geographical and geomorphologic structures is of a *metaphorical*, yet at the same time concretely *operational* nature. It is metaphorical because the eye of geomorphology and geography leads the language of architecture to the dimension of the territory, at the same time modifying its rationale and vision. A shift that is not only of a linguistic and metaphorical nature: it transforms the very rationale and visions of architecture. In this scenario the interpreting and projecting activity are not confined to the mere delineation of an object and the consequent risk of self-sufficiency and metaphysical absolutism; they open up to a vision of transformation of the physical space that affects, and indissolubly binds, the notions of construction and substruction. This last term denotes the capacity of the substratum to be not only a territorial feature affecting the construction activity on the territory, but a *construction activity in itself,* a pre-existing structure that must be regarded as *active material* internal to the building processes on the territory. Seen together with the substratum, the very statute and meaning of *construction* undergo a radical change. The interaction between construction and substruction brings about a new, extended vision of the principle of settlement, which through a radicalization of the elementarist mode [Viganò 1999] presents the territory and the landscape as a composed structure of *plates*. Plates and scales that are deeply affected by the *continuity of the soil,* and not only of the surface. They are denoted by the tectonic and topographic patterns, the pedologic profile, the microclimate and cycle of the waters, and by their constructive human interpretations in terms of deposits, intervals, grain, and distribution pattern. A very evocative image can be found in Hegel's *Aesthetics*, when the author describes the "architectural cultivation" of the space.

It is concrete because to think of the substratum as a *building material* analogous to architecture extends Bernardo Secchi's reflections on the urban environment, dealing with the "architecture of the surfaces" and the "architecture of the spaces of mediation" [2001], to the territory and the landscape. It is the architecture of the territorial *surfaces*: it deals with levels and plans, differences in height, ground elevation contours and open spaces, and at the same time it is a type of soil predisposition –through a project of *morphological infrastructuring*– aimed at receiving the objects. It is the architecture of the *relational* spaces, a borderline project in between the settlement and the territorial plates: interweaving routes and crossings, spaces *in between* the sequences and the narrations.

To consider the territorial substratum as building material does not necessarily mean paving the way to the inevitability of its relentless transformation. On the contrary. Against the background of the contemporary modes of transformation that are pursuing the conceptual and physical removal of the soil, the inclusion of the substratum –and its diversity– in the project can contribute to expanding the field and deepening the analysis. The aim is a project that prefers the interpretative data to the transformative ones, the signification process to the modification one, and finally the choice of the point of view and the position of the frame to the manipulation of the materials contained in it [Dematteis 1986; Olmo 1991]. It is an active interpretation of the dialogue between construction and substruction, which refrains from both a mimetic and merely conservative attitude and from the recent "creative destruction" trends. This analysis "by settlement plates" is also far from a vision of the territory based on the definition of landscape units. If the analysis is focused on the elements of internal homogeneity and continuity –since the landscape units are conceptually rooted in the zoning approach, based on the imposition of limits–, then the eye is caught by the fault lines, the overlaying of the plates, the points of discontinuity and rupture, and, especially, the *metamorphic* processes. This necessarily entails a strong project-related attention also to the long-term, durable elements, contrasting a vision that only highlights the novelties and the recent transformations; it also implies a deep attention to dynamic states, seen as strategic factors, as opposed to a vision that regards the improvement of pre-existing elements as a preservation of the fetishistic simulacrum of the external quality of things.

Finally, it underlines the notion of *limit,* to the detriment of the uniformity and homogeneity.

Not because these are not important features themselves. The reason is that one of the problems of the contemporary approach lies in its incapacity to conceptualize the topic of the limit, be it of a morphologic, legal or normative nature –as clearly shown by the studies on the scattered settlements.

V. For a reconceptualization of the geographies of settlement in the North-West
To go back observing the space of the North-West from Superga, using as a lens the crossing between construction and substruction, means to radically modify the conceptual and interpretative categories for the territory. The settlement landscape looses that heterogeneity and fragmentation that crosses most of the contemporary descriptions, and revolves around some essential topics and questions, which in turn acquire a superior strategic value. As for the case of the 1706 battle of the plain of Turin, when Vittorio Amedeo II and Prinz Eugen identified a definite spatial interval between the Dora and Stura rivers to launch the decisive attack, here too it is a matter of carefully defining the limits of the field on which to play the match of the territory and the settlement landscape of the North-West. To describe the emergent problems and the possible territorial planning strategies some documents have been prepared, on the basis of the preliminary studies for the Piano Territoriale Regionale of the Region Piedmont and for the Approfondimento del Piano Territoriale Regionale, regarding the Susa Valley. The following description is not meant to be a typological taxonomy, but rather a representation of the fundamental project themes. Within the game of the transcalar perspectives, it is blatant how a place can be interested by more than one topic, though preserving the material quality of the physical phenomenon.

1. The encounter between the foothill area and the valley systems. We have seen that one of the decisive data is the encounter-clash between the urban area at the foot of the hill and the mountain and, orthogonally, the settlement systems on the valley floor. The settlement as a crossroad, determining the definition of the north-western space, assumes distinct shapes and salient features according to the different contexts.

1.a. The most frequent case is the mix between an essentially linear foothill settlement and the development of the settlements along an alluvial cone, which tends to stretch from the foothill to the entire valley floor. A similar situation can be found in the Varaita and Po valleys.

1.b. A variance of the previous case is when the settlement system of the valley keeps stretching down after the foothill settlement throughout the valley floor, for instance following a river corridor. This is the case of the Sesia Valley debouching into the Plain of Vercelli.

1.c. Another situation is that of a medium-sized urban center that is part of an inhabited foothill strip, at the junction between a few valley settlements; usually

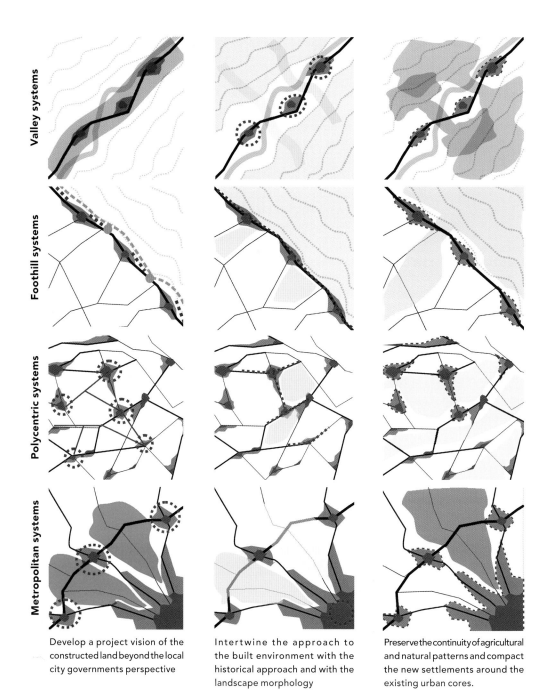

Valley systems

Foothill systems

Polycentric systems

Metropolitan systems

Develop a project vision of the constructed land beyond the local city governments perspective

Intertwine the approach to the built environment with the historical approach and with the landscape morphology

Preserve the continuity of agricultural and natural patterns and compact the new settlements around the existing urban cores.

The settlement environments (horizontally) and the strategic actions planned for each environment (vertically)

Valley systems

Foothill systems

Polycentric systems

Metropolitan systems

Exploit the new built interventions in order to recover the critical settling situations

Avoid the new cases of urban sprawl along the infrastructural axis and in the countryside.

Hierarchize and reorganize as a grid the recent built fabric creating public spaces and environmental connection elements

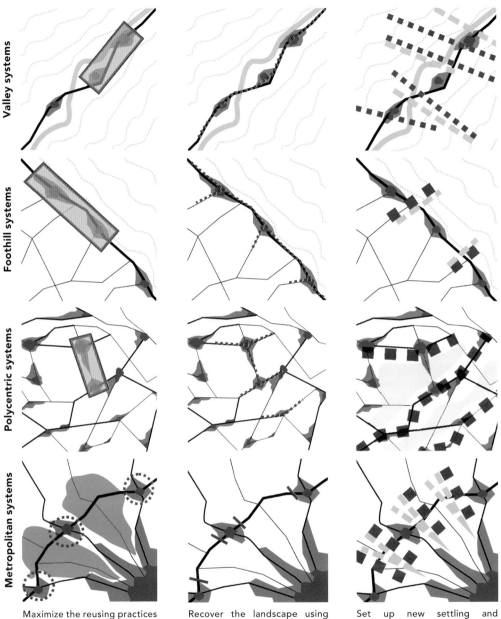

Valley systems			
Foothill systems			
Polycentric systems			
Metropolitan systems			

Maximize the reusing practices of the built heritage and of the urban areas

Recover the landscape using the existing infrastructural plot

Set up new settling and typological models and work on density it tends to assume a radial-centric pattern towards the valley floor. This is the case of the complex systems of settlements of Biella and Cuneo.

1.d. An even more complex situation is when the valley system stretching along the valley floor and the foothill strip coincides not only with a urban center, but also with a great valley corridor, a transalpine crossing. The system created by Turin metropolitan area and the Susa Valley is, despite its peculiarity, paradigmatic in this respect.

2. The linear foothill city. Another essential, though underestimated, issue regards the settlement patterns of the urban area at the foot of the hills and mountains, which faces the plain: a real linear city, spreading out for most of the north-western territory. The points of connection between the hills and the internal plain are generally constituted by ancient terraces, carved by the main river lines and the minor valleys. They are sloping geometric plains of ecological and environmental importance, where multiple uses and functions are condensed along transversal sections of a few hundred meters.

2.a. A representative case is the uninterrupted urban/foothill belt connecting Piossasco-Pinerolo-Barge, Saluzzo-Busca-Cuneo-Mondovì, and Santena-Moncalieri-Turin-Chivasso. An alpine example is the Biella-Romagnano Sesia strip –and the specific environmental topic of the crossing of the Baraggia–, stretching out to reach the of the Maggiore Lake. In this case the physical and environmental specificity is magnified by the fragmentation of the local political visions, which prevents the creation of an overall planning and strategic framework.

2.b. More complex examples are the foothill areas that tend to assume branched configurations, spreading downhill towards the plain below, as for the case of the Cuneese and Biellese.

2.c. A particular case of foothill linear settlement is constituted by the inhabited areas surrounding the lake, such as the south-western side of the Maggiore Lake.

3. Urbanized valley corridors. The third, essential topic is the structure of the settlements along the great valley corridors, be they alpine or hill routes. The key element here is the progressive occupation of the land, from the foot of the valley and the lateral cones to the *thalweg* –that is the line crossing the lowest level of the valley– and the base of the mountainsides. Another essential aspect is the transversal and longitudinal territorial fragmentation, caused by the changing infrastructures. These physical features are magnified by a peculiar conflictive approach between the local urbanization and the supra-local transport infrastructures, regarding the use of the land, the territorial patterns and the systems of ideas. The risk is that the valley floors are progressively transformed into "mid-lands", spaces in between the metropolitan areas and the Alpine tourist destinations.

3.a. From this point of view the most significant cases are the Susa Valley and the Valle d'Aosta, respectively the Rivoli-Avigliana-Susa and Saint-Vincent-Aosta-Sarre strips, even if in both cases the relationship between construction and substruction originates radically different forms of settlement. Analogous topics, although in a lower key, can be observed in the Ossola Valley, spreading almost uninterrupted along the western side of the Maggiore Lake.

3.b. The hill-valley system Bra-Alba-Asti represents a unique case in terms of settlement and geomorphologic characteristics, since it has been modified by the infrastructural and settlement changes –as showed by the tragic flooding of 1994. The same problems affect minor hill-valley systems, such as the Scrivia and the Belbo valleys.

4. *Turin metropolitan system*. Turin metropolitan area is equally affected by the abovementioned issues; nonetheless, it also presents a few specific problems, determined by the progressive "metropolization" of Turin among other factors. These are mainly problems of a political nature –the organization of a metropolitan area lacking a reference framework– and of a physical one –the need to rethink *tout court* the geographical structure, in the light of the balance between construction and substruction. They are determined by the scale of the future infrastructural and settlement changes, which can no longer be referred to Turin alone. 4.a. A metropolitan topic is the structuring of the constructed land in relation to the geomorphologic substratum –the alluvial cone of the Dora River that contains the whole metropolitan area, the interaction with the foothills and the Alps–, and to the line of the four rivers crossing the city. This could bring about a new relationship between the constructed land and the environmental spaces, and therefore a new metropolitan "nature", also with respect to the parks of the Sabaudian palaces –the so-called Corona Verde 4.b. Another issue is the clash between the westward expansion of the metropolitan area, the flowing of the Dora River, the spreading of the East-West settlement system of the Susa Valley into the plain, and the urban foothill belt stretching from North to South. A quite similar issue is the encounter between the linear settlement system at the foot of the hills and the city, which is the alluvial gutter of the cone of the Po River –the actual *thalweg* of the Turin area. 4.c. The last issue regards the

northern and south-western areas of the densest metropolitan area, which despite undergoing different processes of substruction and construction share the same problem: the junction of radial roads leaving the city and intersecting urban strips, and of agricultural and natural remnants that are now part of the constructed area. To these four topics, which define the fate of the planning of the north-western territory and landscape, we must add other issues, more circumscribed and specific.

5. *Distribution of the low density rural settlement.* These areas, that can be assimilated to large, fairly homogeneous plates, are defined by high-quality agricultural practices and relatively moderate dynamics of settlement. The problematic spots are the borderline areas –for example the urbanized foothills– and the internal infrastructural crossings, which tend to condensate the main changes.

5.1. A typical case, which can be found in other areas of the region, is the agricultural plain stretching from the southern metropolitan area of Turin to the northern plateau of Cuneo: based on a polycentric grid, it spreads along the North-South crossing lines of the Po River and the infrastructures.

5.2. A very different case is constituted by the Cuneo plateau, characterized by a specific configuration of the substratum: alternate river lines and southwest-northeast terraced structures, in the area comprised between Cuneo and the interior hilly area of the Langhe. Similar features can be found in the low-middle Canavese, although on a smaller scale.

5.3. A specific typology is that of the rice fields of the Vercelli area, structured on a sophisticated hydraulic mechanism in close relationship with the territorial substruction; this in turn is determined by the strong connection between the shape of the settlement structure and the morphology of the crop arrangement patterns.

6. *Hill settlements.* These large hilly areas, typical of the inner core of the north-western space, are of a particular interest insofar as they are affected by the transformative dynamics. This is the case of the valley systems of the Roero ridges and the Langhe area, interested by the changes in the Bra-Alba-Asti corridor and throughout the provinces of Alessandria, Novara, Asti.

7. *Moraine settlements.* Despite being limited in space, these phenomena have a great environmental value: located at the end of large valley corridors, they present the features of the typical foothill settlements. Due to these reasons, and at the same time to a lack of ad hoc analyses on the specific connection between forms of settlement and territorial substruction, the moraine system of the Serra d'Ivrea – with its gentle, 25 km long slope– and the terminal moraine of the Susa Valley need

specific project-related actions, aimed at preserving the landscape and image unity of the two environments.

VI. Strategic territorial actions
As we said, there are three main linear topics, of which the first is the overlapping and the trans-scale underlying of the second and the third one. They constitute the skeleton of the territorial and settlement system of the North-West, to which we must add two important territorial features (the hill plates and the agricultural plains), the moraine environment, and Turin metropolitan area, which is a junction between the western territories and the Po Valley.

To analyze by lines, strips, and single points means to prepare for a strategic planning vision, more focused on the relational data and the conflictive elements than on the mere identification of the continuity and homogeneity of the landscape. Therefore to work on the territorial scale means in the first place to develop an intense metaphorical-interpretative and denominating activity: this is a rather ambitious task, since it has a direct influence on the –often naturalizing– rhetoric that legitimate the choices of the great territorial and infrastructural projects. It means to overcome the zenithal vision of the institutions and the national and regional technical entities –but also the centripetal vision of local communities– to promote a "flying bird" perspective, structured and not reductionist. It means to use the language of geography and geology to identify the opportunities in terms of an interweaving process between territorial construction and substruction, but also to use the images and the metaphors of the urban project to the *GrandeScala* –the doors, edges and borders, etc.– in order to provide identification clues and physical evidence of the emerging problems of settlement. Most of all, it means to build in political terms a possible alternative to the deadlocked situation of the local territorial governance, which has now turned into a mere clash between the procedural and authoritative stance of the supra-local entities, and the self-referential and circumscribed stance of the local communities. The path to follow is definitely the one of the more articulated programs, that favors the logics of sharing and creation of common, inter-sectoral perspectives.

The different aforementioned topics go hand in hand with a few *strategic territorial actions,* showed by the cartographic representations on these pages. They are considered vital for the future of the physical space of the North-West. The representation, in line with what we have been saying, has a descriptive and planning value, since it describes the great urban polarities, the open (linear, extended, grid) urban plans, the massive instruments and the monofunctional areas. The project-related perspective stresses the importance of the territorial skeleton, which is divided into side elements –geomorphologic or orohydrographic structures functioning as bearing elements for the settlement phenomena– frame elements –infrastructures and not only– and the agricultural patterns. These elements are essential both for interpreting the construction modalities of pre-existing territorial structures, and to guide the contemporary ideas and plans concerning the settlement process.

Then there are the so-called project-related actions: consolidating urban borders; preserving the individuality of urban cores; limiting the spreading of settlements and creating open agricultural spaces, to pursue a continuity in the natural networks; finally, reinterpreting the territorial frame, a major feature in the redevelopment processes.

To these actions we must add the even more specific ones of the urban integration of specialized facilities and big urban enclosures, and also the particular attention to the green corridors and to the areas where the valley corridors meet the plain.

As we have previously underlined, this perspective trying to define the planning actions for the redevelopment and the enhancement of the north-western territory is really different from the approaches revolving around the identification of a landscape and territorial homogeneity, or based on the use of good practices to be uniformly "spread" across the territory. The core is the sequence identification-recomposition-representation, and the subsequent clinical, ad-hoc definition of the individual planning actions to be taken. It is around these actions and topics that today, looking at the settlement landscape of Piedmont and Valle d'Aosta from the Basilica of Superga, we should try to redefine an effective military strategy for the north-western territory.

Urban cores and big territorial objects

Compact urban core

Urban core with concentrical growth

Big enclosure and monofunctional equipment

Open urban systems

Linear urban fabric growth

Urban sprawl growth

Network system of urban cores

Armature territoriali

Elemento sponda

Elemento telaio

Trama agricola

Design actions

Compacting of the urban edges

Preservation of the urban cores separation

Restraint of the sprawl and improvement of the open country spaces

Restraint of the sprawl along the infrastructural axis

Reuse of the territorial framework in the recovering processes

Map of the strategic planning actions of the north-west region, designed by Dipradi-Polytechnic of Turin for the Landscape Plan of the Piedmont Region (graphic processing Andrea Delpiano, 2009)

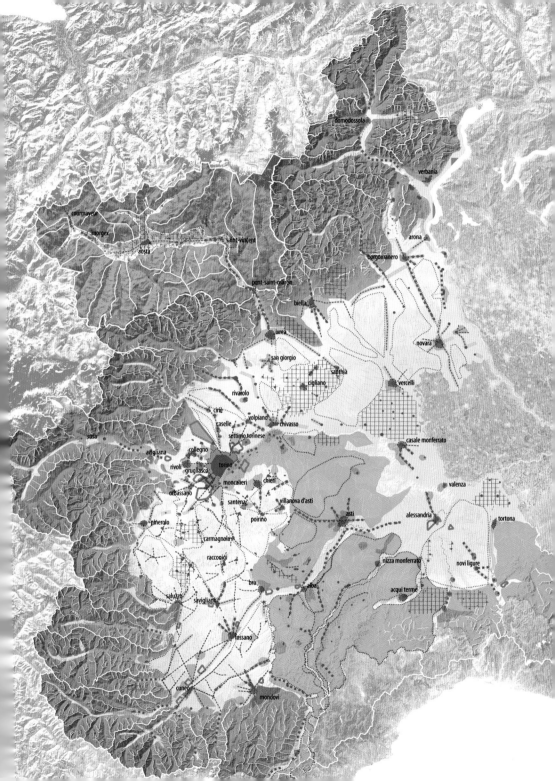

Map of the strategic planning actions of the north-west region, designed by Dipradi-Polytechnic of Turin for the Landscape Plan of the Piedmont Region. Enlargement of the northern sector (graphic processing Andrea Delpiano, 2009)

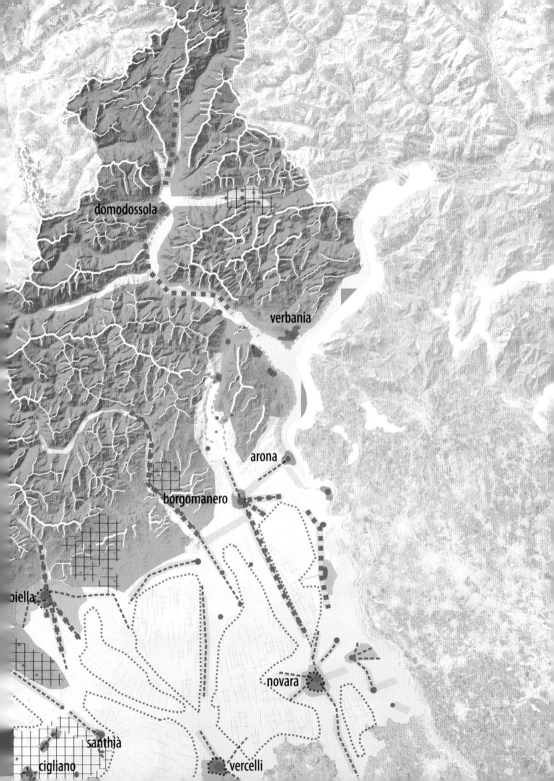

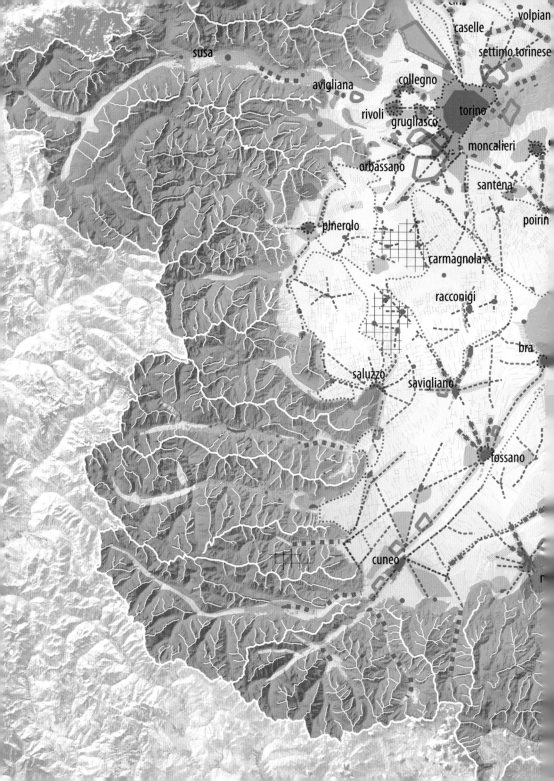

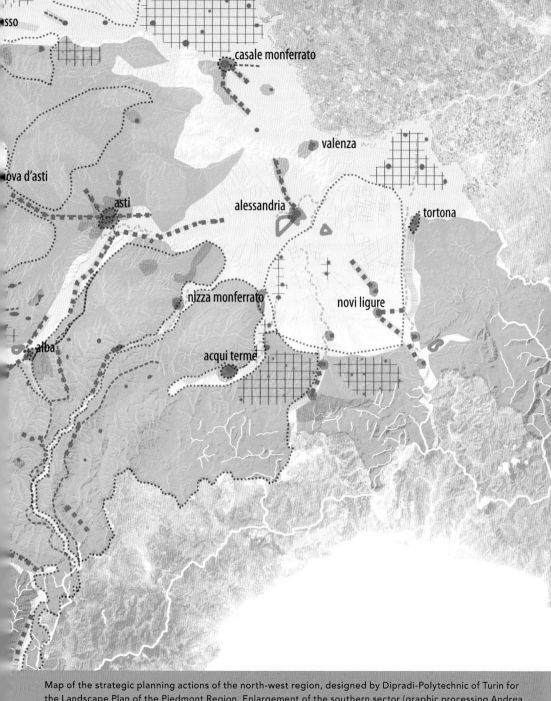

Map of the strategic planning actions of the north-west region, designed by Dipradi-Polytechnic of Turin for the Landscape Plan of the Piedmont Region. Enlargement of the southern sector (graphic processing Andrea Delpiano, 2009)

Bibliography

ASTENGO, G., NUCCI, C., 1990 (edited by), *It. Urb. 80*, in "Quaderni di Urbanistica urban planning Informazioni", 2 voll.

BAGNASCO, A., 1986, *Torino. Un profilo sociologico*, Einaudi, Torino.

BARETTI, M., 1893, *Geologia della provincia di Torino*, Casanova, Torino.

BOBBIO, L., DANSERO, E., *La TAV e la valle di Susa. Geografie in competizione*, Allemandi, Torino.

CITTÀ DI TORINO, CENTRO DI COLLABORAZIONE TRA LE CITTÀ DEL MONDO, 1982-85, *Progetto Torino. Sette ricerche per una città*, 6 voll., Franco Angeli, Milano.

DEMATTEIS, G., 1986, *Nella testa di Giano. Riflessioni sulla geografia poetica*, in "Urbanistica", n. 82.

DEMATTEIS, G., 1988, *Valorizzazione e trasformazioni territoriali. Problemi teorico-metodologici con riferimento all'Italia centro-settentrionale*, in U. Leone U. (edited by), *Valorizzazione e sviluppo territoriale in Italia*, Franco Angeli, Milano.

DEMATTEIS, G., 1989, *Contesti e situazioni territoriali in Piemonte. Abbozzo di una geografia regionale dei possibili*, in "Urbanistica", n. 96.

DE ROSSI, A., DURBIANO, G., GOVERNA, F., REINERIO, L., ROBIGLIO, M. (edited by), 1999, *Linee nel paesaggio. Esplorazioni nei territori della trasformazione*, Utet, Torino.

DITER, 1995, *ITATEN. Indagini sulle trasformazioni degli assetti del territorio italiano. Programma 1994/1995. Rapporto sulla Regione Piemonte*, dattiloscritto.

GABETTI, R., 1977, *Architettura Industria Piemonte negli ultimi cinquant'anni*, Torino, Cassa di Risparmio di Torino

GRISERI, A., 1974, *Itinerario di una provincia*, Cassa di Risparmio di Cuneo, Cuneo.

IPLA, 1982, *La capacità d'uso dei suoli del Piemonte ai fini agricoli e forestali*, Èquipe, Torino.

IRES, 1989, *Progettare la città e il territorio. Una rassegna critica critique di cento progetti per Torino e il Piemonte*, Rosenberg & Sellier, Torino.

IRES, 1995, *Cento progetti cinque anni dopo: l'attuazione dei principali progetti di trasformazione urbana e territoriale in Piemonte*, Rosenberg & Sellier, Torino.

LANZANI, A., 1996, *Tra analisi sociale e indagine morfologica*, in CLEMENTI, A., DEMATTEIS, G., PALERMO, P. C., (edited by), *Le forme del territorio italiano*, Bari, Laterza.

OLMO, C., 1991, *Dalla tassonomia alla traccia*, in "Casabella", n. 575-576.

OLMO, C., 2009, *Architettura e Novecento*, Bollati Boringhieri, Torino.

PARONA, C. F., 1935, *Il Piemonte e i suoi paesaggi: impressioni e riflessioni geologiche*, Paravia, Torino.

PROVINCIA DI TORINO, 2009, *Trasformazioni territoriali della Provincia di Torino*, Quaderni del territorio n. 2, Provincia di Torino, Torino.

ROMANO, G., 1978, *Studi sul paesaggio*, Einaudi, Torino.

SACCO, F., 1913, *Les Alpes occidentales*, Collège des Artigianelli, Turin.

SECCHI, B., 2001, *Nuovi luoghi della sociabilità: il progetto della discontinuità*, in U. Trame, *Città e territori. I nuovi spazi del commercio*, Ed. Compositori, Bologna.

SPAZIANTE, A., 1996, *Piemonte*, in CLEMENTI, A., DEMATTEIS, G., PALERMO, P. C., (edited by), *Le forme del territorio italiano*, Bari, Laterza.

VIGANÒ, P., 1999, *la città elementare*, Milano, Skira

VIOLLET-LE-DUC, E., 1876, *Le massif du Mont Blanc. Étude sur sa constitution géodésique et géologique, sur ses transformations et sur l'état ancien et moderne de ses glaciers*, J. Baudry, Paris.

Ndt: Regional Territorial Plan
Ndt: Coordination Territorial Plan
Ndt: Further studies on the Regional Territorial Plan
Ndt: Green Crown, a green belt surrounding the city.

3.2 TOWARD THE GRAND[A]STAD?

Marco Barbieri, Andrea Delpiano, Mattia Giusiano

Why is it interesting to refer to the *GrandeScala* in order to read and interpret the transformation processes affecting the Cuneo geography? The territorial area that we will be dealing with, which is called "la *Granda*" because of its wide extension, offers a good reason to qualify as a case study. Here again, the presence of settlement phenomena and forms of territorial reorganisation suggests an overcoming of the local dimension towards a new potential metropolitan scale. But in our geography, this new enlarged idea of the city tends to overlap with the boundaries of provincial administration in a rather clear manner. The opportunity offered by the presence of a clear political stakeholder, who could seize this new operational dimension of the territory, is faced with a lack of useful reference imageries that would shape the set-up of this new enlarged city. This is precisely why it is important to observe more closely its constituting materials and express the hidden images capable of describing its profile.

I. Great territorial architectures: the comb shape, the weaving and the arches.
Compared to other geographies, defining a suitable framework to collect the transformation phenomena and the territorial set-ups of the Cuneo area is a rather simple exercise. This simplicity derives both from perceptive conditions related to a strongly characterising orographic structure, and from bedded images related to historical representations. The geography of the *Granda* is clearly and neatly defined by a wide flat surface surrounded by the Alpine region in the west and in the south part (particularly by the Cottian Alps, in the west, and by the Maritime Alps, in the south), which then smoothes down into softer forms towards the east and becomes the hill system of the *Langhe* and the *Roero*.
Our framework is therefore suggested by the layout of the reliefs that border the sub-region under study, defining a "U"-bend that leaves one side open towards the

north, towards the Turin metropolitan system, and keeps a clearer edge towards the west, the south and the east, which is only developed through "filaments" working their way through mountains and hills. The neat southern edge and the more nuanced connection with Turin can also be inferred from the representations concerning the morphological context and land use modalities. Moreover, this set-up is already clearly visible in cartographies and historical views, where the specificity and the separation of the Cuneo "sacca" form the Po valley are synthetically expressed, as it can be clearly observed in the so-called *Carta dei Cappuccini* [1600] and the *Carta Generale de' Stati di Sua Altezza Reale* by Tommaso Borgogno [1680].

From the crown of mountain reliefs, many watercourses flow in a north-easterly direction into the "sacca" and then merge into two main basins: the *Po* and the *Stura-Tanaro* basins. The former runs through the province in the north-west corner and collects the system of watercourses that dig the main valleys of the Cottian Alps in that area, while forming an arch which slowly moves northward, thus defining a wide surface of irrigated flat land.

The *Tanaro* basin, which is called *Stura-Tanaro* in the Cuneo area because of the important role played by the two rivers merging in this portion of flat land, runs through our geographical area in a diagonal way. The powerful eroding action exerted by the watercourses generates a deep incision dividing the "sacca" into two terraces: the former corresponding to the aforementioned irrigated surface, the latter coinciding with a wide triangular surface incident on the hill-foot line, under the strong presence of the western *Langa* slopes. The two basins represent the true support to a fabric endowed with a high natural value, which from the vast alpine ecological surfaces then penetrates into the plain. Moreover, it unveils its great agricultural vocation divided between the intensive cultures in the "humid" flat land (fruit-farming) and the extensive cultures in the southern terrace.

The shape of our framework also affects the functioning of the infrastructural system. A dense web of local road connections, mainly used to organise journeys between urban centres within the sacca, is opposed to long crossings going beyond the borders, in order to ensure communication with the external world.

These are based on a system that develops along two axes criss-crossing the plain: the north-south motorway and railway corridor connecting Turin to Savona by crossing the free-zone enclosed between the borders of some major cities and the course of the *Tanaro* river; the east-west motorway axis, which has been in its completing phase for many years and will have to connect the provincial capital with

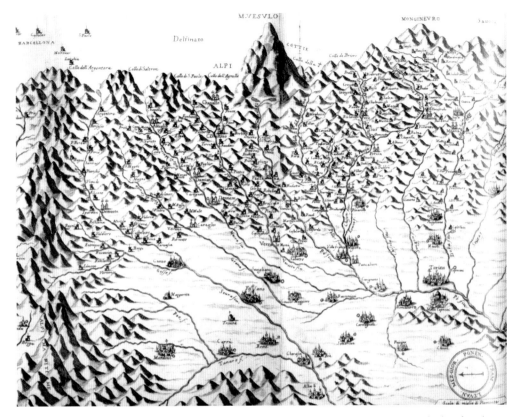

The conceptualisation of the relationship between internal structure and polycentric margin "built" after the major historical representation of the territory. Charter Capuchin F.P. Latha, Turin, Private Collection, 1600

Asti, by approximately following the contours of the river terrace on the *Stura*, but then veering away from it near the entrance to the *val Tanaro* hill stretch.

Viability on a local scale is defined by a dense web that tends to saturate on the central plain by concentrating itself along the foothill line next to the reliefs, thus intercepting the infrastructural corridors of side valleys and adding itself up to a local railway line which is partly disused.

Upon observing the settlement systems, the lack of a main urban hub capable of determining strong attracting hierarchies emerges clearly within the *sacca*. The whole weight of the urbanised area in the *Granda* is sustained by seven main small-medium sized agglomerates (*Alba, Bra, Cuneo, Fossano, Mondovì, Saluzzo* and *Savigliano*) immersed in a constellation of smaller centres. Even in the face of considerable urban growth and urban sprawl phenomena over the past forty years, the foothill border has acted as a catalyst generating some conurbation situations. It is not a coincidence that some of the major centres can be found along that line or have established with it a privileged relationship with regard to growth dynamics. This has determined situations of progressive unity between urban fringes that also involve intermediate minor centres - such as the sections departing from Saluzzo towards Cuneo or from Bra towards Turin or Alba - or has simply been the result of the particular expansion of some major centres - such as in the case of Cuneo and Mondovì. As it can be easily inferred from previous considerations, minor centres - the "constellation" - adopt different behaviours in growth processes according to the attractiveness of the main centres, but tend, however, to reuse long-term territorial structures, such as valley floors, hill ridges, agricultural organisations on the plain. We could therefore conclude that the phenomena of "metropolisation", which are currently under way in the *Granda,* seem to follow a direction that adheres to land conformation and to the routes characterising both the inside of the *sacca* and the surrounding reliefs, thus maintaining settlement development patterns somehow rooted in the great environmental and infrastructural "frames" that we have previously described. This description of land layouts, infrastructures and settlements seems to reveal a

The foothill "combs", arches, plains and the plot of the Cuneese "Beetle"

form of settlement base where everything finds its place. Thus, defining a frame for such a geographical surface would seem not only a simple act, but also an obvious one, given the circular connection between territorial morphology and transformation dynamics. However, it is precisely the elaboration of the settlement situations concurring to the foregoing picture which makes such description interesting. Thus, it ceases to be a sheer geometrical exercise, but becomes the true definition of three major complementary territorial forms or "architectures". The *foothill comb-shaped layout* takes its form from the intersection of the alpine valley floor systems with the interweaving of open spaces, infrastructures and settlements permeating the area where the reliefs merge with the plain. This is the context with the highest density of built surfaces, where most of the production and trading activities are concentrated, in a sequence of *façades* built on the road side, interrupted by small open intervals through which the rear agricultural features of the plain pop out.

The *woven plain* includes the flat land around Mondovì and the settlement which starts from the river terrace on the *Stura di Demonte* and then tends to merge, in the north, with the southern part of the Turin metropolitan area. In this context, the polycentric structure is clearly visible, being made of many centres scattered across the cultivated plain, amongst which Fossano and Savigliano emerge as the main catalysts attracting people and activities.

Finally, the system of *hilly arches* encompasses the valley floor between Bra and Alba, and the settlement systems of *Langhe* and *Roero*, characterised by settlements which are

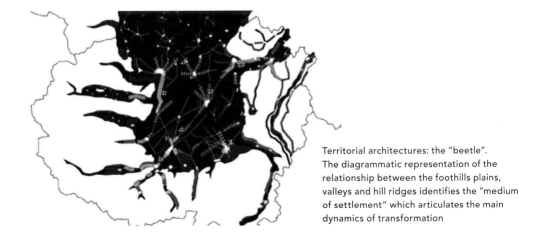

Territorial architectures: the "beetle".
The diagrammatic representation of the relationship between the foothills plains, valleys and hill ridges identifies the "medium of settlement" which articulates the main dynamics of transformation

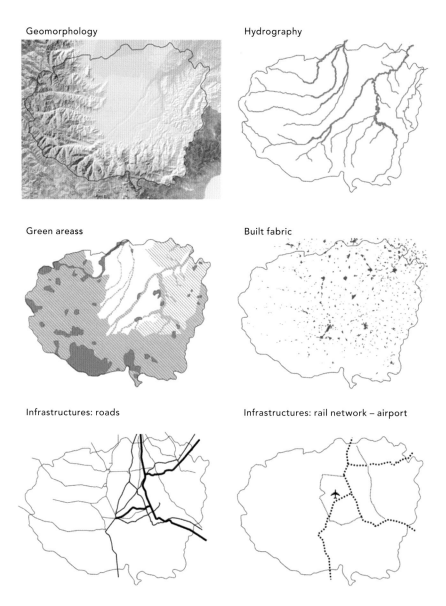

Geomorphology

Hydrography

Green areass

Built fabric

Infrastructures: roads

Infrastructures: rail network – airport

Territorial matrices. A reading schedule shows the characteristic themes of evolution across the main environmental matrices and the lattice structure of the frame that infrastructure tends to arrange, a "comb" at the foothills

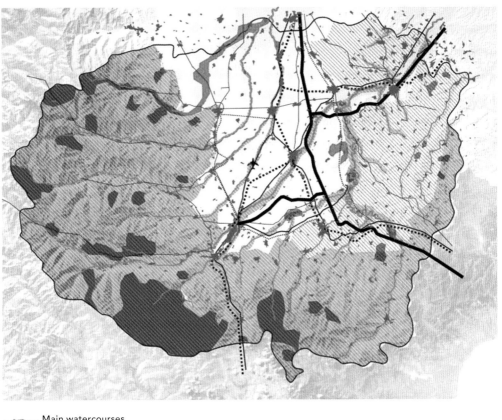

Main watercourses
Urban areas
Motorway lines
Main inner road system
Secondary inner road system
Main railway lines
Secondary or dismissed branches
Provincial airport
Protected areas and wildlife oasis
Mountain and river areas of medium-high wildlife value
Hill areas of medium wildlife value

Physical palimpsest. The recomposition of the different layers renders explicit the different "materials" which are composed of the three main territorial architectures described diffusely scattered or situated along ridges and valley floors, integrated in an excellence landscape associated with the production of renowned wine labels.

II. Hidden images

As previously mentioned, these three great *Grand Scale* architectures seem to be so naturalised that they organise territorial developments and orient their long term future. But is the efficacy of such a short-circuiting process, between territorial form and "identity", a precondition for the definition of a coordinated political project applicable to the whole "geography"? The policies that pre-ordain the Cuneo territorial development provide us with different views on the three identified territorial architectures. These blurred views highlight only some structural elements, while leaving others in the background, or merge everything together except for the borderlines, thus questioning the seemingly closed set-up of these three great complementary forms. Consequently, the ensuing picture does not seem to be capable of combining the intermediate organisational scale, existing among different local entities, and the big large scale infrastructural set-ups. This scenario can be illustrated through three images resulting from a crossed interpretation of the reference political programmes and of the orientations given at different planning levels.

III. Islands and Archipelagos

The first image conveys the local individualism that characterises a polycentric organisation with little hierarchization, such as Cuneo. As a matter of fact, the settlement system revolves around few main centres, mainly the "seven sisters", which often recur in the programming documents for provincial planning and correspond to as many influence areas. The territory is therefore characterised by a series of local "islands" - the "saluzzese", "braidese", "monregalese", etc. - which can be partially aggregated in archipelagos that have variable proportions and are activated by specific sectoral policies.

These mosaic pieces shape their edgings in a quite heterogeneous way with respect to the settlement patters identified above: either by fragmenting them internally, like in the *foothill comb-shaped layout*, where *saluzzese, cuneese* and *monregalese* are side by side; or by connecting them transversally, like with the *saluzzese*, which extends both towards the *foothill comb-shaped layout* in the west, and towards the flat land in the east; or by tracing their borders in a quite effective way, like with the *Fossano-Savigliano* system with respect to the *woven plain*, or the *albese-braidese* with respect to the *hilly arches*.

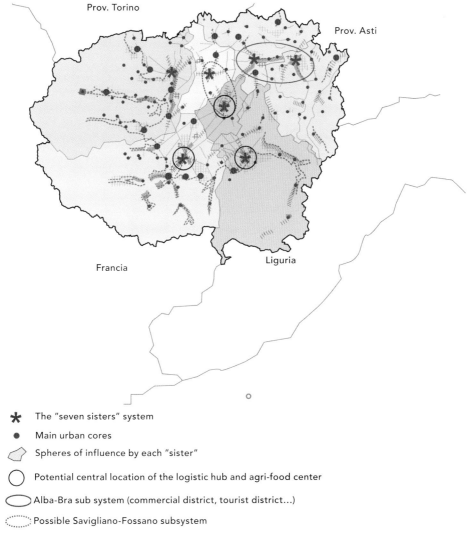

Prov. Torino

Prov. Asti

Francia

Liguria

* The "seven sisters" system
● Main urban cores

Spheres of influence by each "sister"

◯ Potential central location of the logistic hub and agri-food center

⬭ Alba-Bra sub system (commercial district, tourist district...)

⬩⬩⬩ Possible Savigliano-Fossano subsystem

Island and archipelago. A local representation of individualism that returns the low level of the hierarchy of the Cuneese polycentrism

The polycentric nature of this territory is the result of a long structuring process which originated in the medieval feudal organisation and was consolidated by successive local power structures: from the bishop's sees and the Savoy provinces, to the districts of the seventies and the current Territorial Integration Areas proposed by the new Regional Territorial Plan. [Piedmont Region, 2007]
This internal fragmentation is made all the more visible today by the aggregation of municipalities, as a result of their participation to regional and European calls for territorial development. By way of example, we could mention the Integrated Territorial Programmes presented in 2007 [De Paulis, De Paulis, Peyracchia, 2007]: if we observe the contours of the various inter-municipal alliances, we can see that they follow the aforesaid influence areas of the main centres. Only in some cases do we notice processes of aggregation and cooperation between different spheres, particularly with Fossano-Savigliano and Alba-Bra. The latter is perhaps the most consolidated "archipelago" within the Cuneo territory, since the two centres have initiated a shared line of sectoral programming - especially as far as trade, tourism and health are concerned - which has led them to propose the creation of a new province. The programming and planning instruments at higher level, particularly the Territorial Plan for Provincial Coordination (PTCP), basically confirm such a territorial organisation by presenting the "network of cities in the Cuneo area" as a model of inter-institutional cooperation, based on a true leadership exercised by the main centres with respect to the minor centres revolving around them [Piedmont Region, Province of Cuneo, 2004].
All the analysed instruments outline the existence of a polycentric model which is, however, more aimed at legitimising and fostering the role played by the main centres, than at organising the system of mutual relationships between them. It is a polycentric model where competition seems to prevail and finds its breeding ground in a form of local patriotism, rather than in the cooperation and complementarity between centres.
Moreover, the difficulties in adopting a systemic approach within this polycentric structure are also visible if we closely analyse the content of the projects included in their policies.
For instance, within the Integrated Territorial Plans (PTI), every "island" proposes its own intervention lines on recurrent issues - the agri-food sector, tourism, infrastructural developments - in a run-up to widely distributed investments, which culminate when a plurality of suitable candidates emerge for the localisation of large scale services: mainly, the issue of a logistic platform disputed by various centres.

This context reveals an inherent inability to seize dialectic opportunities capable of transversally involving all the systemic hubs, by reflecting upon the potential complementarity of the centres around specific sectors, or by indentifying common issues and projects around which they can confront themselves, and which are sometimes already suggested by recurrent local experiences.

IV. The tube and the cross

The second image encapsulates those policies dealing with the definition of the role played by our geography in wider scale scenarios. This role has been progressively emerging as that of a potential strategic hub between the surrounding "strong territorial systems": the arch of the Ligurian harbours in the south-east; the French coast in the south-west; the Turin metropolitan area in the north; and the Po Valley system in the east. This image is mainly based on large scale viability policies, both on road and rail, and takes the shape of a "cross" generated by the intersection of the two motorway axes.

This image was conceived after the Second World War, when the Italian motorway network was being defined, and develops in two phases coinciding with the construction of the two motorway axes. The first phase coincided with the construction of the Torino-Savona axis, whose main objective was not really to free Cuneo from its infrastructural and economic isolation, but rather to draw the industrial metropolis closer to the Ligurian harbour. At this time, our geography was only viewed as a "crossing area". During the second phase, the idea to connect Cuneo and its Alpine passes to Asti, and thus to Milan and the Po Valley, was symptomatic of the emerging economic development in the Cuneo area and of the need to come out of its historical marginality.

As the "tube" image gradually weakens in favour of the "cross", the Cuneo area becomes a "space to connect" and takes up the role of a "hub" used by current policies and programming experiences. By way of example, we could list: the Programme for Urban Requalification and Territorial Sustainable Development (PRUSST), jointly created by the three southern Piedmont Provinces (Cuneo, Alessandria and Asti); the definition of a pilot project inserted in the S.I.S.T.e.M.A. (Integrated Development for Multi-Action Territorial Systems), created by the Ministry for Transport and Infrastructures; and the proposal to organise the Cuneo territory as a potential inner harbour for Savona. These experiences define the area as a strategic connecting hinge between neighbouring territorial systems. [Ministry for Transport and Infrastructures, 2007a; Ministry for Transport and Infrastructures, 2007b]

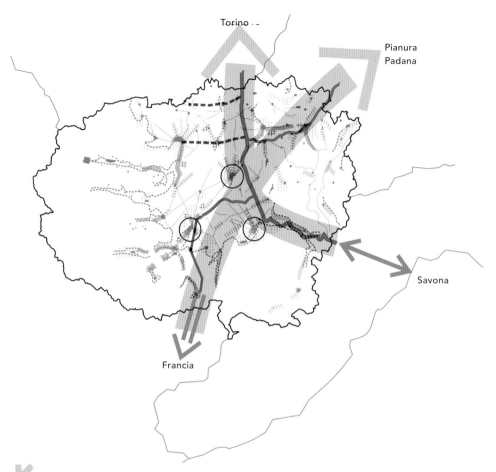

Torino

Pianura
Padana

Savona

Francia

Main setting axis of the motorway system

Designed connections with the motorway system

Potential central location of the logistic hub and agri-food center

Motorway network (Turin-Savona and Cuneo-Asti)

Col de Tende Road Tunnel, lane doubling in the direction of Nizza

The district of Cuneo as a back-harbour of Savona

The tube and the Cross. The separation of major infrastructure in relation to the reticular plotted road and low ranking railway

"A natural door towards Europe, and Cuneo as a cross-border door between the southern Piedmont territorial system, the Nice territory and the Ligurian arch". These are the subheadings of the programmes which concentrate the common macro-objectives in this field, and which recurrently use, in their documents, words such as door, border, hub or hinge, associated with Cuneo even in contemporary experiences of territorial interpretation at regional and provincial scale.

The image of the "hub", as outlined by the different policies, is added up to the three settlement situations and initially runs through them indifferently, before evolving in two different directions. It can either follow a specific path according to the particular configuration of the environmental features - for instance, the woven plain represents, in its least urbanised belt, the ideal setting for the marks of wide viability and acquires a particularly strategic role under this perspective, by encompassing the intersection of the criss-crossing axes. Or instead, it can come close to the relevant urban hubs, thus touching on all the three settlement situations. Particularly, the south-east/north-west connection policy, which is only today near completion, represents one of the most visible issues where the relationship between territorial forms and policies, specifically the infrastructural ones, is at stake. Indeed, this connection cuts transversally across the three territorial architectures: across the foothill comb-shaped layout, from the valley system near France to its convergence on Cuneo; across the woven plain, by touching on Fossano and Savigliano; and across the system of hilly arches, by plunging into the Tanaro Valley narrow passage in order to go through Bra and the Alba area.

Despite being the result of partially outdated sectoral planning methods and referring to territorial organisational models at a higher scale than the sub-regional one, this image continues to be strongly reflected upon the local political choices, where infrastructural aspects continue to be solely perceived as a way to boost connections towards external systems. By way of example, we could mention, in particular, the PTCP infrastructural proposals based on a series of transversal connections between the main centres and the "cross" system, through ex novo building interventions or by reinforcing existing road and rail axes, such as by laying a second track on the Cuneo-Fossano rail line; by widening the Saluzzo-Savigliano road and the Tenda tunnel towards the Ligurian coast and the south-east of France; or by building a new motorway junction near the northern border of the province. Such an influential image ends up overshadowing equally important issues which concern mechanisms for geographical internal organisation. Firstly, there is an issue concerning the local rail network, which could potentially become a frame capable of structuring settlement developments on the *foothill comb-shaped layout*. Moreover, even though it has currently initiated a process of slow dismantling, it could also connect the main centres of the polycentric grid through an independent network of public mobility. Secondly, there is the problematic isolation and the ensuing underutilization of the *Levaldigi* airport terminal, situated at the very centre of six out of "the seven sisters". Finally, we need to reconsider, in logistic terms, the whole territory and its main centres, particularly the Cuneo hub, which is presented in some documents as the very southern door to the polycentric grid, and Fossano, which has come forward several times as the ideal setting for the potential logistic platform for goods exchange.

V. Fences

The third image emerges from an observation of the protection and enhancement policies, which operate according to different rationales and scales, reflecting the dichotomy enshrined in our civil code between these two terms. Every territory delineates "static" fences, in order to preserve certain features, certain environmental frames, and hand them down to future generations. But they also define "dynamic" fences, which are intended to trigger inclusion and cooperation at local level, to focus on the problems of a territory considered approximately "homogeneous" to the appropriate scale, and to support projects that work on quality aspects in order to turn them into points of "excellence". However, the common denominator, shared by both types of fences, is precisely the definition of a limit: defining what lies inside and what remains outside, the selection criteria, the features on which the idea of "homogeneity" has to be based and which should facilitate surveillance and improve governance. Several methods can be used to trace those limits around the Cuneo "geography". Some of them are based on the uniqueness of environmental features, stemming directly from the idea of delimiting a "framework endowed with a high landscape value", which was the basis of the first National Protection Laws in the first half of last century (from the Rosaldi proposal for "landscape protection" in 1915, to the 778/1922 and then the 1497/1939 laws).

We are dealing here with National and Regional Parks, but also with Nature Reserves dotting the province reliefs and the river courses, such as the *Park of Maritime Alps*; the

Natural Park of the Upper Pesio and Tanaro Valley; the *Special Nature Reserve of the Augusta Bagiennorum Area*; the *Special Nature Reserve of the Belbo Sources*; the *Gesso and Stura River Park*; the *Po Park* on the Cuneo side. As we already know, these fences are faced with a historical obstacle concerning their integration in the "contouring" territory: their delimitation is the result of a difficult attempt to superimpose a "nuanced" vision (the landscape framework) onto a technocratic one (the border), which often generates uncertainties related to the discontinuous application of protection rules among strongly interweaved fabrics. In this respect, river courses are a good example where the integration between built surfaces and natural contexts is a delicate and inescapable project theme.

Mountain Communities
Hill Communities
Areas involved in the nomination to the Unesco World Heritage
Parks of National Relevance
Parks of Regional Relevance
New safeguard proposals

Fences. An image of the major policies of protection and enhancement expresses an idea and use of land that puts the focus on their proper excellence and removes the parts apparently "without qualities"

Another criterion used for the definition of limits is based on the way in which event programmes are physically structured, in order to aggregate different stakeholders around strategic objectives for territorial development. The fences that fall within this category are the Mountain and the Hill Communities created in 1971. All these fences obviously describe the relief area, leaving outside the central "sacca" of the plain. In a sense, the strong political component of such inclusion modalities between different municipalities, together with the established Local Action Groups (Gal) as operational centres for the management of European funds, have favoured a continuous redefinition of the borders and of the composition of individual communities. At the same time, the separation between the "high lands" and the plain has also contributed to characterising the mountain and the hills as excellence zones associated with a strong territorial identity, as opposed to the plain which is apparently devoid of specificities capable of aggregating supra-municipal interests. In addition to these two modalities for fence definition, there is a third approach, a more recent one, which tries to combine the previous two. This delimitation technique is based both on the idea of "protection" and of "enhancement". In other words, it tries to combine the "nuanced" vision (but also the technical one) of the landscape framework with a strategic vision converging on common requalification objectives. The nomination of the hilly territories as Unesco World Heritage contains both aspects, because it starts by recognising a strong circularity between, on the one hand, the specificity and the excellence of the landscape forms and, on the other hand, the reasons for agriculture and food production. Although they are not always integrated in current development policies, these aspects are hand in glove with each other, as it is illustrated by the recent success stories of these places in local tourism and in the wine and food sector. Unfortunately, this intention is mostly disregarded in the outcomes of recently published delimitations. Leaving to one side the claims of the excluded, they seem to be the result of excessive technical simplifications on border structuring, and provide an excessively vague definition of the context.

VI. Shaping the gRAND[a]STAD
In the light of the foregoing political images, the Cuneo geography is characterised by a strong fragmentation, due to processes of territorial organisation which are structured, more or less formally, according to very heterogeneous objectives and reference scales. As previously stated, such processes overlap with the support structure provided by the three *forms* - the *foothill comb-shaped layout*, the

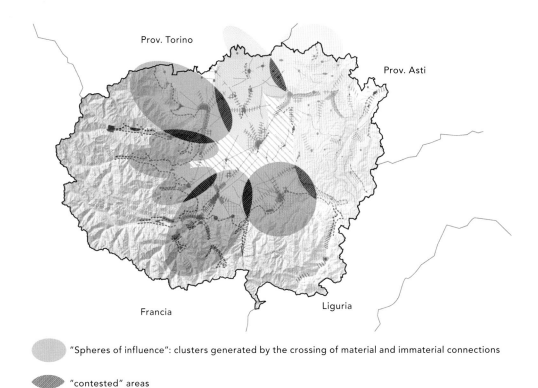

Prov. Torino

Prov. Asti

Francia

Liguria

"Spheres of influence": clusters generated by the crossing of material and immaterial connections

"contested" areas

"forgotten" areas

Actual metropolitan functioning. A superimposition of three different images returns conflicting aspects and dynamics of inclusion in place of the main urban centers and various local situations woven plain and the system of hilly arches - thus defining further internal divisions or cutting them transversally, without highlighting specific correlations.

Therefore, within the political processes of territorial transformation, the three big "architectures" do not seem to express either their pervasiveness with respect to the whole geography, or their complementarity, which is only highlighted at local level.

It is possible to suggest another representation model, by trying to reconstruct the "political palimpsest" in Cuneo. Through the combination of the elements that we have called "islands", "archipelagos", "crossings" and "fences", it could be possible to generate a potential framework for the organisational processes acting on the territory under study.

This perspective is particularly suitable to grasp the Cuneo "metropolitan functioning", which has taken a concrete shape via the cartographic transposition of the "influence areas" acting on the aforesaid processes.

Drawing such a map is an extremely useful operation, because it highlights critical or particularly efficient situations that can be observed at local level.

The physical dimension of these hubs corresponds to distinct spaces, reflecting the degree of proximity or of overlapping between influence areas: shared, disputed or forgotten spaces describing central or peripheral areas in our geography.

Although such a reconstructed "event programme" is still strongly centred on the leadership of the major urban centres, with respect to the surrounding environment, their contours sometimes become blurred and merge with each other. This happens when they identify shared political issues, such as the protection of mountainous environmental quality - a potentially shared issue behind the distributional areas along the foothill axis - or the strategic localisation and the excellence of eastern territories, which could justify the definition of a single sphere encompassing the Alba-Bra system and the hilly areas of Langhe and Roero, essentially corresponding to the hilly arches system. Conversely, in some other cases, the overlapping of different spheres becomes a source of potential tension, where one of the three forms - particularly the foothill comb-shaped layout - is fragmented through different political choices. Examples are the foothill infrastructural hub between Saluzzo and Cuneo, where fragmented settlement choices have engendered an almost continuous dispersion along the supporting structure, which also hinders environmental continuity with regard to the mountain system; or the belt between Mondovì and Cuneo, which shares similar features with the previous case and could also be partially extended to the plain section limited in the north by the Stura.

Finally, the map shows some territories which do not seem to fall under any territorial organisational scheme: areas belonging to "everybody and nobody" which can be especially spotted in the "woven plain" section, surrounded by Savigliano, Fossano, Cuneo and Saluzzo. In a territory which, as previously stated, founds its territorial organisation on a polycentric, non-hierarchical set-up, bearing considerable forms of local individualism, the reconstruction of the more general political programme, and its confrontation with the major territorial architectures, can only increase the general impression of fragmentation.

This highlights the difficulties in balancing out both the perspectives of the seven main urban centres and the more pervading criticalities, so as to find shared issues around which the "polycentric system" can be organised, while adopting a metropolitan perspective to govern the territorial transformations affecting the whole area. Defining a reference territorial image is therefore a fundamental step towards designing a shared outline capable of orienting the different political and sectoral policies. As for Cuneo, this image reflects the shape given to those project issues which are mostly capable of overcoming identified fragmentation aspects, by restoring continuity between the three major territorial architectures. What is then the form of the *Granda* metropolitan area? In the title of this essay, the reference to the *Randstad* model (the "ring city" embodied by Amsterdam, Rotterdam, The Hague and Utrecht) could seem rather strained, certainly not appropriate to the scale. However, leaving aside the differences in the settlement patterns of the Dutch conurbation, which tends to close in a ring shape and projects itself on a large rail network, there are many similarities with this potential hidden city, half-revealed in the set-up of the Cuneo geography. The latter could also be founded on a big ring structure: a hinge connecting the foothill line to the foot of the hilly arches or, even more, a new settlement frame capable of supporting conurbation phenomena along its edges, but also of encompassing the polycentric woven plain together with the large continuous agricultural and natural fabrics running across it.

One first theme capable of moulding this new idea of city could certainly be the restructuring of the internal connecting system. This could serve both to boost the role of large-scale infrastructural "hub", pursued by the area, and, particularly, to create a policy of shared mobility that would allow us to tackle the pressing inadequacy of some sections. To this end, it would be interesting to assess the possibility to create a system of "light underground", particularly by exploiting the network of rail connections which are partly unused or underutilized between

Cuneo, Mondovì, Fossano, Savigliano and Saluzzo, and the possibility to open them towards the east (also by exploiting the old *Bra-Ceva* line).

Another issue concerns the opportunity offered by the environmental continuous areas which transversally cross the whole territory: the river axes. Indeed, they could interestingly inspire future projects both as real physical connections between the major territorial architectures, but also for their power of "shareability", due to the fact that they border on many of the major centres, thus increasing their potential driving role for the creation of wider cooperative processes. The west-east course followed by the *Stura*, and its continuation in the *Tanaro* river, seem to be particularly effective under this perspective, by actually representing the main connecting belt with the mountainous nature reserve and touching upon four of the seven major centres.

The big "central void" between Cuneo, Mondovì, Fossano, Savigliano and Saluzzo, which we have previously described, can also be interpreted as one of the hidden planning elements which are mostly useful for the elaboration of a metropolitan context around Cuneo. The presence of a big rural *enclosure* provides an opportunity to reconsider the plain as the "heart" of the polycentric Cuneo system. This area is capable of collecting the images reflecting the historical vocation of this territory and can therefore become the object of policies that promote its use as an "agricultural park" situated between two other main "parks": the "natural" park of the mountain, and the thematic park of the wine areas. At the same time, the strategic central position of such a "void", with respect to the main urban structures, increases its potential as an ideal location for wide-ranging services, related precisely to the agri-food and logistic sectors. This is particularly important with a view to enhancing the provincial airport terminal, which is situated right in the middle, but also because it identifies this area as a place where new settlement patterns can be experienced, by adjusting the relationship between built areas and open spaces in order to "complement" existing centres.

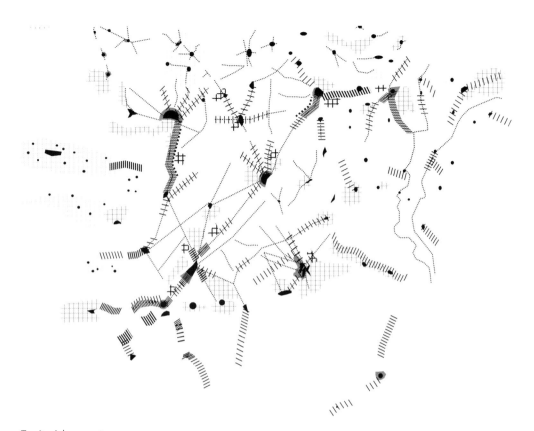

Territorial support

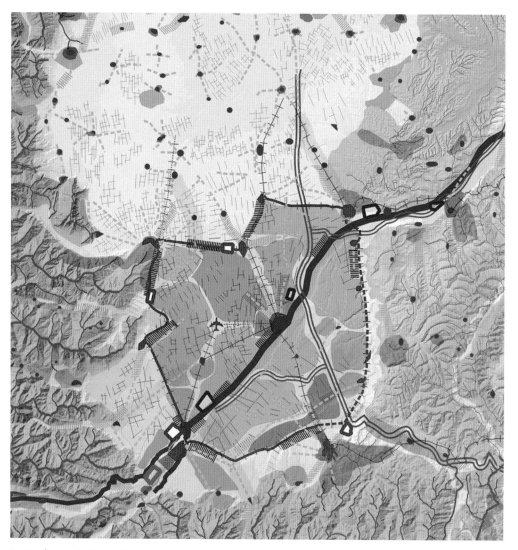

Design figure: the Grand[a]Stad

Existing "metropolitan" micro-systems

"contested" areas

"forgotten" areas

Critical cores/intervention strips

Metropolitan ring

Motorway network

Rail network to be enforced/maintained

Rail network to be built/recovered

Operating rail network

Airport

Compact urban cores involved

Big monofunctional enclosures involved

Urban sprawl growing phenomena involved

Linear urban fabric growing phenomena involved

Green backbone

Green river backbone

Compact urban cores involved

Big monofunctional enclosures involved

Linear urban fabric growing phenomena involved

Cuore Agr **Agricultural core**

Agricultural areas differently valuable

Agricultural plot considerable for the settlement

Bibliography

BORGONIO, T., 1680, *Carta Generale de' Stati di Sua Altezza Reale,* Biblioteca Reale di Torino, Incisioni, III, 311 (1-15), foglio 8

DE PAULIS, E., DE PAULIS, U., PEYRACCHIA, M. (edited by), 2007, *Le stelle dell'orsa. Riflessioni sui Programmi Territoriali Integrati della Provincia di Cuneo,* Quaderno del Territorio n.1/2007, Associazione Culturale E. Bafile, Busca (CN)

DE ROSSI, A. (edited by), 2002, *Atlante dei paesaggi costruiti. Le trasformazioni del territorio operate dall'uomo,* ed. Blu, Peveragno (CN)

MINISTERO DELLE INFRASTRUTTURE E DEI TRASPORTI, 2007a, *2007-2013. Il territorio come infrastruttura di contesto,* ed. Ministero delle Infrastrutture e dei Trasporti, Roma

MINISTERO DELLE INFRASTRUTTURE E DEI TRASPORTI, 2007b, *Reti e territori al futuro,* ed. Ministero delle Infrastrutture e dei Trasporti, Roma

REGIONE PIEMONTE, 2005, *Per un nuovo piano territoriale regionale. Documento programmatico,* Torino

REGIONE PIEMONTE, 2007, *Piano Territoriale Regionale. Quadro di riferimento strutturale,* Torino

REGIONE PIEMONTE, Provincia di Cuneo, 2004, *Piano territoriale provinciale,* Cuneo

3.3 AOSTA VALLEY: BIG VALLEY, LITTLE COUNTRY

Roberto Dini

I. Autonomy as a summation of elements
When dealing with the settlement transformations in the Aosta Valley territory, with a particular reference to the *Grand Scale* topic, one cannot disregard the political and identity issues that have characterised the administrative and cultural specificities of the Region. A specific model of territorial management and transformation has spread in the Aosta Valley. According to this model, which is strongly built around regional autonomy, the fine-tuning of territorial policies is closely related to the landscape vision elaborated by the local society. Understanding the concept of autonomy, as a key to interpret settling transformations, has therefore never been so crucial in order to shed light on their relationship with the institutional and administrative *autonomy* regimes from which the Region benefits. Equally important is the analysis of cultural interaction models through which a specific idea of autonomy has been consolidated over time, translating itself into specific territorial transformation and usage practices, by means of *"unlikely iconographical and cultural syntheses"* [Janin Rivolin, 1995]. First of all, it should be reminded that regional political autonomy has always acted in defence of the right to individual land use. Over the years, the attachment to the land property system has been a fundamental value, strategically guaranteed by the regional authority in order to safeguard autonomy, thus preventing any opportunity to aggregate individual interests for the collective elaboration of development policies. Autonomy is therefore intended as the *summation* of individual interests, rather than as an opportunity to reflect upon a shared territorial project. Settlement expansion was therefore achieved by pasting together pieces of constructed areas and territorial objects. Rather than by following a coherent design, proportionate to

their territorial scale, the new urban fabrics have developed in an incremental way, according to principles of sheer conformity with the *zoning* established by Town Planning Schemes and individual building permits. A low building index – which seemed to be a territorial safeguard in the 70s – applied for more than thirty years without monitoring or questioning its effects, has indeed generated a situation which is the exact opposite of what was initially intended, thus wasting a limited and valuable territory and producing heavy public and social costs.

Secondly, as the Aosta Valley economy becomes increasingly focused on the touristic sector, it is important to understand that territorial enhancement and promotion – as a landscape resource – have of course become an essential and distinctive part of the touristic offer, as well as becoming primarily a key element of the local identity. During the great cultural and social transformations of the last century, the Aosta Valley landscape continued to play mainly a strong identity role for local people, thanks to its real or supposed physical, geographical, cultural and ethnical standard features [Cuaz, 1994]. Epoch-marking changes, such as the transition from an agricultural economy to a tourism-based economy, as well as the major environmental and social transformations, have been cushioned by a widespread feeling of "cultural sustainability", based on continuity with the past. The landscape or, even better, the idea of its conservation has been used to legitimise and make modernisation processes socially acceptable. The transition from a farming economy towards a tourism-based tertiary economy has taken place in the name of a culture which is strongly based on traditions. Since local political life could not directly affect the transformations under way, because they were due to a general trend of market liberalisation and internationalisation that is hardly controllable locally, it acted on their representation by cushioning their effects [Celesia, Dini, Ducly, Fracellio, 2006].

Territorial images, with the complexity of their physical and cultural significance, have therefore played a vital role in creating effective icons for those coming from abroad, and a strong identity for those living within the Valley. Thus, the comforting image of an *international rural* landscape seems to find consensus both among tourists and local people [De Rossi, 1999] by ensuring, on the one hand, considerable autarky in land management practices and, on the other hand, by reasserting the idea of an alleged sustainability in transformation processes. The territory has therefore been constituted through the summation of minimal events,

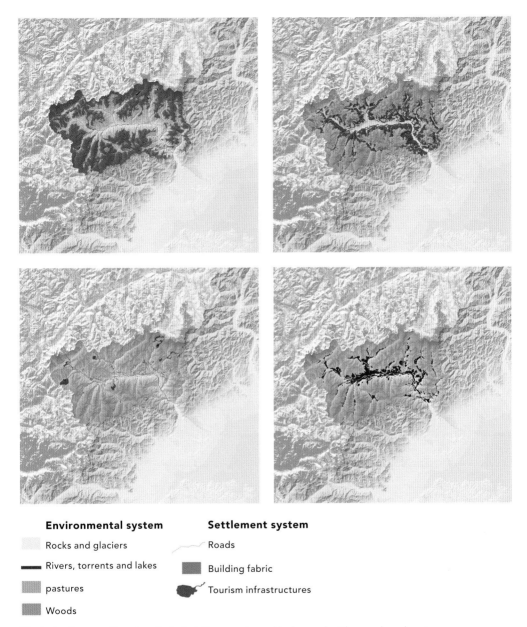

Environmental system

Rocks and glaciers

Rivers, torrents and lakes

pastures

Woods

Settlement system

Roads

Building fabric

Tourism infrastructures

Physical palimpsest (from top clockwise). Topography and hydrography. The woods and pastures. Infrastructure. The built.

Environmental system

Rocks and glaciers

Rivers, torrents and lakes

pastures

Woods

Settlement system

Roads

Building fabric

Tourism infrastructures

Physical palimsest. Recomposition of the settlement

in the belief that a considerable number of small qualitative acts can lead to a *beautiful landscape*. In other words, the small scale is viewed as a remedy to modern "evils".

Nevertheless, if analysed together with the real physical outcomes at a territorial scale, the apparent convergence of policies, images and transformations, with a view to reinventing local traditions and identities, highlights an increasing lack of correspondence between images and concrete transformations. In spite of the image engraved in consolidated representations and in the most traditional iconographies, i.e. the image embedded in *"brochures' stereotypes and rhetorical descriptions of illustrated guidebooks"* [Cuaz, 1994], today's Aosta Valley is a land characterised by considerable changes.

At a closer analysis, current territorial decisions and policies appear to be little sustainable in the long term. Today, building sites within the municipal territories down the valley are being used up. Securing new building sites will require huge costs for the implementation of territorial safety measures, as well as for the exploitation of areas which, for geo-morphological and hydro-geological reasons, are not yet exploitable. As a consequence, all possible real estate operations become extremely inconvenient. Moreover, a fake rural nature would not satisfy tourists either, since they are becoming increasingly attentive to the "authenticity" of places [Montanari, 2007], whilst environmental costs would make the landscape less attractive and, consequently, less useable in tourist advertising.

All this coincides with a particular moment of crisis, where the regional system appears to be extremely vulnerable, since local governments, particularly the welfare system erected around the Aosta Valley autonomy, are being seriously questioned today by global economic and political structures.

Today more than ever, these factors urge the Region to carry out a large scale analysis on its territorial management, in order to be able to adopt a critical position both on the simple transposition of urban models in a mountainous valley, and on the enhancement of a mystified landscape, almost suitable for museum exhibition. The hypothesis of a *third path* [Camanni, 2002] seems to be today, both for the Aosta Valley and for the Alpine valleys in general, one of the few viable routes, since it makes it possible to avoid radical oppositions, such as forced modernisation on the one hand, and the ideological rejection of change on the other hand [Bätzing, 2005]. In the first case scenario, the Aosta Valley territory would indeed be limited to an extremely weak economic, cultural and political role, whilst continuing to be complementary to big metropolitan areas. Conversely, in the second hypothesis, isolating the Valley from the economic hubs of the plain would jeopardise its very existence as an autonomous working and living environment, thus becoming exclusively devoted to tourism and increasing even more the intensive exploitation of its resources. By means of a political and cultural project for the construction of collective visions, it is therefore necessary to focus on transformation models that are capable of keeping images, representations and projects together with the different dynamics and stratifications that characterise and run across the Aosta Valley territory.

In terms of large scale planning, the issue is not just about managing territorial resources in a right and sustainable way, but it is mainly about identifying settlement morphologies that are capable of overcoming the traditional opposition between urban and rural world, between seemingly opposed identities and living habits, by turning the mountain into a *contemporary habitable territory*, in the complexity of its physical and cultural values.

II. New images of the Valley
Because of the deeply rooted political and cultural reasons mentioned above, the *Grand Scale* project seems to encounter some inertia in the Aosta Valley, due to the radical mistrust towards any attempt to build a collective territorial vision. Simply by looking at the developments and outcomes of some recent projects and planning experiences, which have been confronted with the territorial dimension of transformations, one can realise that they have never been strongly rooted in the local contexts: such as the project for the motorway connection between Aosta and the Mont Blanc Tunnel, or the plan for the productive requalification of *Area Cogne* by Luigi Mazza.

Large scale projects have always been treated like purely engineering or sectoral problems, by adopting a passive approach geared towards impact mitigation and technical solutions, but never as an opportunity for wider reconsideration of regional territorial set-ups, nor as a *process* capable of producing shared scenarios and triggering widespread forms of territoriality.

Today, in terms of territorial scale policies, we can observe two seemingly opposite cultural lines developing within regional administration, which are based on two extremely different visions of the Valley future. On the one hand, there is the policy pursued by the *Urban Councillorship Directorate for Territory and Environment*, the Authority dealing directly with regional territorial planning; and on the other hand, there are the strategies pursued by the *Department for Structural Policies and European Affairs of the Presidency of the Region*, which are more concerned with community programming through the *Regional Development Policy 2007/2013*.

The former is oriented towards safeguarding a certain image of culture and landscape - somehow more conservative - and is mainly centred on operations aimed at adjusting local planning instruments to the Territorial Landscape Plan (PTP, 1998) which still remains the main reference for large scale territorial management. The landscape rationale behind the plan seems to have been translated into the local imagination as a collective need to preserve an inevitably idealised landscape, which has to be combined with the typically individual needs for land transformation [Janin Rivolin, 2006]. The conflict that broke out between the regional authority and the municipalities at the time of its approval did not lead to a redefinition of local competences and responsibilities in territorial management; nor did it lead to a general reconsideration of the idea of territorial planning as an implicit representation of property interests. Even the currently difficult process of adjusting local planning schemes to the PTP (ten years after its entry into force, only a few municipalities have changed their urban planning instruments according to the PTP rules) is symptomatic of the extremely difficult dialogue between regional institutions and municipal administrations, which directly represent the interests of local land owners.

The PTP is essentially a wide planning scheme, without a strong project vision, exclusively centred on landscape protection. Since it is precisely an orientation plan devoid of shared transformation images, it was unable to convey the transformation needs of local stakeholders, both public and private, towards overall quality objectives. Even the *Integrated Projects* (the so-called PTIR, PTIL and PMIR) have been mostly disregarded, since they lacked a real structure and were not rooted in the territory. Once again, the image of the Aosta Valley appears to be naturalised, and is essentially that of an "uncontaminated territory", where urban systems are treated like alterations of the physical-formal set-up, rather than as a key element for the strategic reorganisation of territorial structures.

Conversely, the second cultural line develops on a more dynamic idea of territory, which is more geared towards innovation, and aims at promoting regional development by strengthening cooperation opportunities with other European regions, as it emerges from the Single Planning Document (DUP). The objective is to convey the joint contribution of community, state and regional resources (coming from different programmes, such as those for Regional Competitiveness, Employment, Territorial Cooperation, Rural Development and the Fund for Underutilised Areas) to create centres of excellence and the necessary infrastructures for the development of concrete projects. In particular, through the coordination of financial resources, numerous Cornerstone Projects are expected to be launched in the next few years, which will widely trigger new infrastructural interventions, as well as territorial enhancement in some areas, and the recovery and reactivation of brownfields. However, the weaknesses of both strategies are to be found, once again, in the lack of a set of physical transformation images, which would make it possible to asses both their degree of appreciation within local societies and their morphological value with regard to the territorial scope of the project.

It seems then that, in the Aosta Valley, the shared visions capable of orienting the transformation of built areas can mainly be observed in representations that have been settling, layer after layer, in the collective imagination, rather than in large scale projects and programmes. By way of example, we could think of the polarised images associated with the big touristic resorts in the *Piano Olivetti* (1937) – which definitively destined the Region to a touristic monoculture - or the fruitful intuition, by geographer Janin, of the Valley as *a cell and a cross-roads* [Janin, 1968], which is so far the only seemingly possible synthesis between tradition and innovation. What kind of images can today be so strongly rooted in the imagination of the Valley inhabitants and, at the same time, constitute a reference scenario capable of generating territoriality? What kind of images can virtuously interweave the strategies pursued by different cultural lines and different policies coexisting and conflicting within the region?

In order to try to respond to these questions, it should be possible, as an indication, to establish three categories of issues with which the *Grand Scale* must necessarily

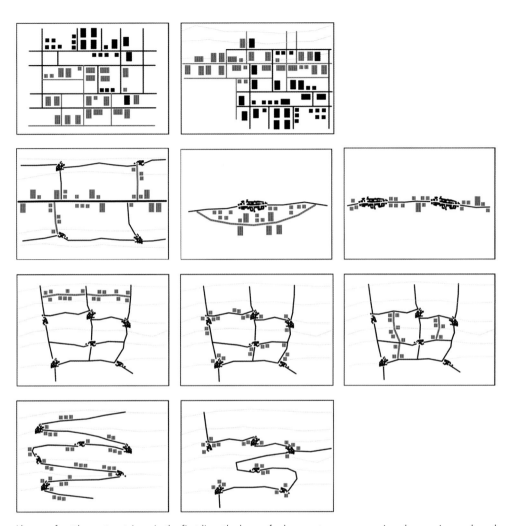

Abacus of settlement matrices. In the first line, the base of urban centers: compression along major roads and modular expansion. In the second line, the urban centers in the valley: linear development along valley roads, new road development along the ring road, development along existing roads. In the third line, the villages on the polycentric fan: new development along main roads from the foot of the fan, density around most villages, development of new road sections along the line of maximum slope. In the fourth row, polycentric settlements on slopes: density around existing villages, development along existing roads.

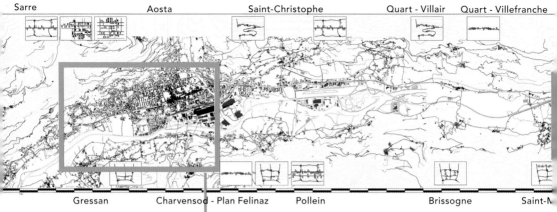

Sarre Aosta Saint-Christophe Quart - Villair Quart - Villefranche

Gressan Charvensod - Plan Felinaz Pollein Brissogne Saint-M

Zoom 1 (Aosta)

Urban growth from 1965 to 2003

■ Buildings and infrastructures until 1965

▨ Building and infrastructures from 1965 to 1975

▨ Buildings and infrastructures from 1975 to 2003

Diachronic map of the urban growth

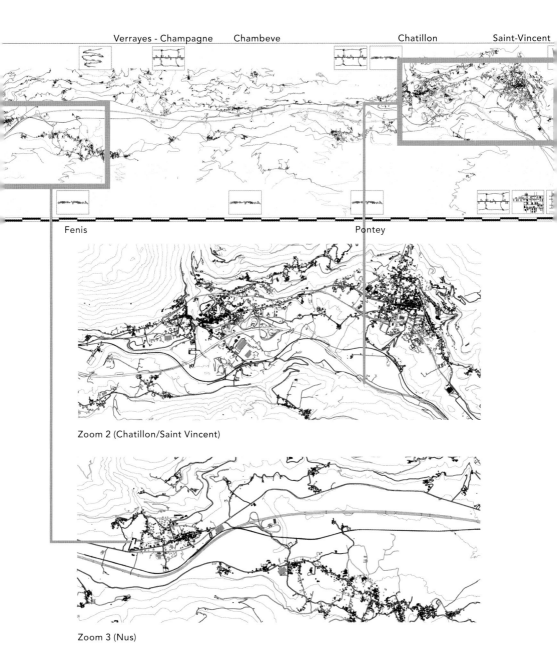

Verrayes - Champagne   Chambeve   Chatillon   Saint-Vincent

Fenis   Pontey

Zoom 2 (Chatillon/Saint Vincent)

Zoom 3 (Nus)

be confronted: *reinventing* and *recognising* the geographical syntheses through which the territory is represented; *representing* wide continuous spaces and physical structures used to organise transformation; *recomposing settings* and *framings* to find a new synthesis between *zenith* territorial visions and *perspective* ones.

III. Geographical territorial reinventing

Besides orienting the outcomes of urban transformations, the geo-morphological structure of the regional territory has also contributed to reinforcing their representations in a univocal way.

The Valley has historically been described by opposing the two major environmental frameworks, the *plaine* and the *montagne* – the former corresponding to the flat territories of the main valley corridor, and the latter embracing approximately the mountainous territory situated at more than 1000 meters above sea level. These settings can be differentiated not only for their landscape and weather features, but mainly for the diversity of their social and economic environment and for the life style they have developed [Cerutti, 1971].

As a consequence, mountainous areas, which are mainly covered by rocks, glaciers and woods, have been viewed as *territorial scenery* [Lanzani, 2003] destined to the touristic monoculture, whereas, on the other hand, the central valley has been deemed to be more suitable for urban development. Even the theory of geographer Janin – which claims that the Aosta Valley harbours a dualism as a result of its own natural conditions, being a *cell* and a *crossroads* at the same time [Janin, 1968] – has strengthened this representation which is now deeply rooted in the local collective imagination. For many years, this seemed to be the only way to combine tradition and renovation, thus legitimising even more the touristic monoculture, as the only synthesis possible between local and supra-local interests.

In particular, the naturalisation of the *corridor* image in the central valley has contributed to an urban expansion model which is flattened on the valley floor - where the various infrastructures and urban settlements concentrate – as well as around the heads of side valleys in the vicinity of big touristic resorts for winter sports.

Therefore, the representations produced by past and current territorial policies have rarely diverged from the image of the *eaves* - representing settlements *streaming down* towards the central valley – and from that of the valley floor as a *back space* serving the excellence landscape, or as a cross-border *connecting hub*.

In a continuous process of short-circuiting between representations and real territorial transformations, territorial images have increasingly stiffened over time, petrified by a sort of inactivity, without ever overcoming the dichotomy between the intensive creation of infrastructures on the valley floor, and the conservation of archaic landscape images, which can only be used for touristic advertising.

The current saturation on the valley floor requires the territory to be *geographically reinvented* so as to question the traditional conceptual separation between, on the one hand, the mountainous area, perceived as being marginal and weak, but with a high landscape value, and on the other hand, the urban areas on the valley floor, which are economically strong but less environmentally representative. In order to do so, we should come up instead with more elaborated set-ups that are capable of taking into account the complexity of the Valley settlement patterns.

The image of a corridor which is hyper-equipped with infrastructures, as opposed to that of an uncontaminated landscape suitable for museum exhibition, seems to be reductive today, since it does not account for other forms of territorial set-up that are emerging in areas so far considered to be marginal. By way of example, we could think of the slope areas, the orographic terraces or the side valley mouths which were intensively provided with infrastructures and densely populated over a long period of time, and were then progressively abandoned during the short-lived Alpine industrial phase. Although, for some decades, these areas were only doomed to abandon, today, thanks to a progressively different approach towards the possibility of living and populating the mountain, this "middle land" is again attracting projects, dynamics and transformations which highlight the emergence of new development forms, of never-before-seen cultural approaches and, therefore, of new settlement opportunities.

In this respect, we could mention the new forms of suburban residential life along the slopes, the achievement of landscape requalification interventions linked to agricultural practices, the appearance of new hybrid forms of agricultural tourism, as well as the increasingly widespread interventions for the recovery of abandoned architectural heritage and for territorial enhancement through extensive projects on trekking paths, eco-museums and thematic areas.

By *reversing the framework,* and therefore also the usual way of interpreting the Aosta Valley territory, it is possible to look at the central valley from a different perspective, which reveals new geographies aspiring to emerge from the closed main valley corridor and open themselves up towards above and towards the slopes. Recognising the existence of some *intersecting routes* in the valley is a way of accounting for some transversal *settlement situations*, which insert themselves into wide linear spaces on the valley floor, thus highlighting elements of current and potential continuity between opposite slopes with regard to the valley floor, between the *adret* and the *envers*.

Even the way in which the borders of some political entities are defined according to territorial divisions, such as the Mountain Communities, seems to underline, also from a technical and administrative point of view, the need to look at the territory in a "transversal" way, thus redistributing local opportunities and resources over the *intersecting routes*, without being exclusively focused on the valley floor.

In so doing, it is possible to identify local specificities which lead up to the recognition of different settlement environments and establish a vertical connection with the settlement systems along the slopes and with the high mountains.

These hubs emerge as being doors to the side valleys, favouring a sort of "slow" infrastructure creation, as opposed to the "fast" connections and development of the *plaine* along the main valley axis.

IV. Representing wide continuous spaces

In a context where the regional authority guarantees a true urban autarky, thus nullifying any attempt to apply top-down planning models, one cannot but accept the "grassroots" territorial building modalities and, in a reformist approach, decide which elements can be considered as negotiable and which ones as nonnegotiable. *Wide continuous spaces* may be built from elements which, for their own nature, can be considered to be "nonnegotiable" to all intents and purposes, since they are supposedly essential for most of the community, such as big natural and environmental frames (woodland belts, pastures, torrents and water systems, rocks, glaciers, etc.), but also areas exposed to hydro-geological risks, protected zones and natural parks. The next step is then trying to develop figurative images (the edge, the head, etc.) capable of giving shape to such material values, in order to provide the territory with a "morphological system of infrastructures".

The technical nature and ecological value of such themes and constraints are shared within local communities and could therefore help hierarchize the territory, if translated in morphological terms.

The physical representation of hidden territorial images - by delimiting areas at hydro-geological risk, river systems, protected areas and parks, as well as borders contouring fast-flowing infrastructures, power transmission lines or ski installations – makes it possible to morphologically define some wide continuous spaces, while defining some specific related figurative images. It is possible to outline a "hard" structure representing the land framework, within which negotiation opportunities

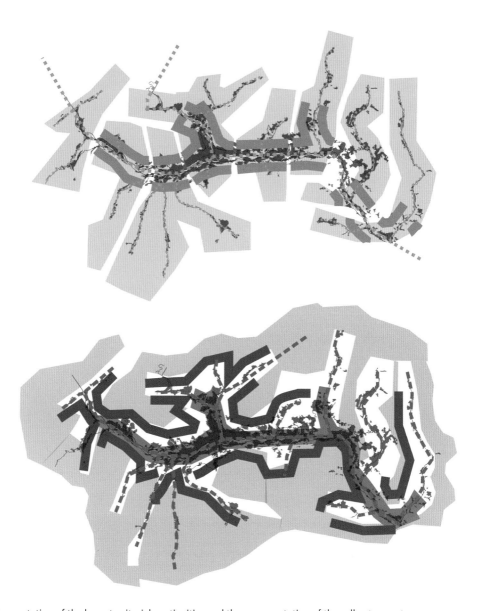

Representation of the large territorial continuities and the representation of the valley transects

Wildlife parks and protected areas

 Wildlife parks of National and Regional relevance

 Protected areas

 Environmental areas

Crossing

 Crossing lines

- - - - - Turin-Aosta-Morgex railway line

Turin-Aosta-Courmayeur turnpike

Mountain Communities

1_Aosta
2_Valdigne
3_Grand-Paradis
4_Grand-Combin
5_Monte Emilius
6_Monte cervino
7_Evancon
8_Mont-Rose-Walser

Settlement systems of the Landscape Territorial Plan

 High mountain wildlife areas

 Traditional settlement: "integrated development" subsystem

 Urban system

 Traditional settlement: "touristic development" subsystem

 Traditional settlement: residential development subsystem

 Pastures

 Woods

Pivotal Projects

 Areas involved in Pivotal Projects

 Spot projects

Political palimpsest (from above, clockwise). Wildlife parks and the protected areas. Crossing. The settlement systems of the Landscape Territorial Plan. The flagship projects for 2007-2013. Mountain communities. Recomposition of the political palimpsest can be created for the "soft" territorial elements which are extremely fragmented, in terms of processes and physical outcomes, but must converge into general patterns. Ordinary processes of infrastructure creation can thus virtuously converge in a *Grand Scale* design, defined by successive phases of implementation, which are concerted every single time, and where *ex novo* interventions simultaneously generate and strengthen the "backbone" image at a larger scale.

In terms of territorial architecture, the issues around the relationship between negotiable elements and *Grand Scale* images open up to numerous morphological themes, thus widening considerably the range of possible settlement configurations starting from the use of ordinary materials, as opposed to an incremental and atomised building production. Representative examples are the construction of *territorial tales,* where the alternation of built zones and natural areas provides the territory with a narrative element; or the construction of mediation systems by working on the borders of wide continuous spaces, in order to experience hybrid settlement patterns that play on the rural-urban mix.

V. Recomposing zenith visions and perspective ones
An elaborated growth, which could be defined as *multi-speed,* is highlighted by recomposing the planning of physical elements (geo-morphology, built areas, infrastructures, etc.), as well as by diachronically recomposing territorial set-up developments expressed through settlement matrixes in the central corridor [Ambrosini Berta, 2004]. Some "rapid" transformations connected to touristic presence and exploitation – including supra-local route connections, production and marketing sectors, big infrastructures such as ski lift facilities and ski resorts – follow a rationale that can be ascribed to an enlarged use of the territory. Others, which could be defined as "slow", are mainly linked to individual initiatives and are characterised by incremental settlement patterns.

For the former type of transformations, the territorial geo-morphological configuration represents an obstacle to overcome and the land is reduced to a *tabula rasa.* Conversely, for the latter, it becomes a supporting element on which new settlement patterns have to be grafted, by creating new meaning and changing the semantic value of the historical traces of land planning and design, with respect to the new spatial needs. The territorial substratum, in its new configuration, becomes a true building material for *Grand Scale* architectures. The different orographic conditions and the traces of previous infrastructures constitute the matrix for a wide range of possible settlement situations, corresponding to as

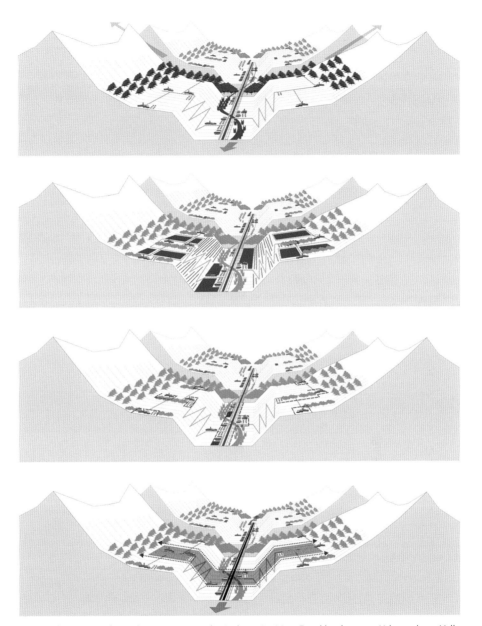

Architecture of transects (from above). Large ecological continuities. Rural landscapes. Urban edges. Valley floor connections and crossways

Territorial architectures

many different ways of treating open space and land. If interpreted in "architectural terms", this variety can lead to never-before-seen settlement patterns capable of combining land morphology, consolidated territorial structures and new developments.

Future project visions should precisely be based on the idea of planning continuity, both physically and in terms of images and identity. As a matter of fact, if we observe the Aosta Valley landscape from different *framings*, we realise how the aforementioned tendencies of territorial transformation produce a strong imbalance between the *zenith vision* - that of real physical transformations – and the *perspective vision*, i.e. the real space as it is perceived by inhabitants and tourists [De Rossi, 2006]. By comparing territorial zenith images, for example aerial photos, with perspective images taken from the ground, we realise that recomposing *zenith* and *perspective* visions represents a key aspect for the *Grand Scale* territorial project.

The tendency to listen to a certain territorial identity - that of the "mountain", which is artificially achieved through *typical* and *folkloric* traits at the level of space characterisation – still awaits to be translated at the intermediate scale, which consists in the organisation of settlement fabrics. If it is true that the process of iconographic production for touristic purposes continues to play a strong identity role for local people, by supporting a stereotyped use of traditions with respect to the nature of architecture and of the single building elements, the same cannot be said for settlement models, which instead continue to be uncritically developed as a sheer application of the limits and rules stipulated in town planning schemes.

By recomposing layers of different nature, the aim is therefore to elaborate rationales that combine territorial objects and *ruralising* objects which are typical of ordinary building practices, in order to create more complex settlement models, where local identities can be achieved through the integration between settlement patterns and living habits, rather than through a-topical growth rationales disguised under pseudo-traditional stylistic elements.

In terms of individual, but also technical and political imagination, a great deal of work is needed in order to fine-tune reference images at intermediate scale (between the territorial dimension and the "*villetta*"). These images should, on the one hand, enrich individual *repertoires* and enable local identities to position themselves also with respect to environmental and sustainable issues, and on the other hand, support the dialogue between local and supra-local planning bodies. In some ways, the Aosta Valley is a unique territorial problem, but, in other ways, it resembles other Alpine valleys. When faced with "high lands", the *Grand Scale* project must necessarily come to grips with some great contradictions, such as the conflict between innovation and conservation, between local habits and global dynamics, between quality of physical projects and robustness of collective identities, which are also common to other contexts, where modernisation processes intertwine with significant bedding of environmental and cultural values.

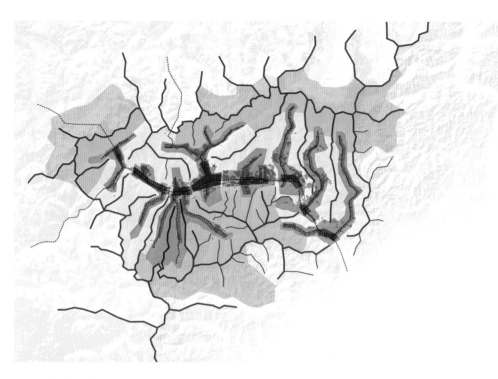

Design Figure

Transects

Large environmental continuity

Pivotal valley floor elements

|||||||| Crossways

---· Main infrastructures

Crests

Design figure: the Transects Valley

Bibliography

Janin, B., 1968, *Le Val d'Aoste. Tradition et renouveau*, Allier, Grenoble

Cerutti, A. V., 1971, *Le Pays de la Doire*, ITLA, Aosta

Cuaz, M., 1994, *Valle d'Aosta. Storia di un'immagine*, Laterza, Bari

Woolf, S. J., (edited by), 1995, *Storia d'Italia. Le regioni dall'unità a oggi. La Valle d'Aosta*, Einaudi, Torino

Janin Rivolin, U., *Valle d'Aosta*, 1996, in Clementi, A., Dematteis, G., Palermo, P. C., (edited by), *Le forme del territorio italiano, II. Ambienti insediativi e contesti locali*, Laterza, Roma-Bari

Gambino, R. (edited by), 1997, *Piano Territoriale Paesistico della Regione Autonoma Valle d'Aosta*, Quaderni dell'INU

Regione autonoma Valle d'Aosta, Assessorato Territorio, Ambiente e Opere Pubbliche, 1998, *Sguardi dal cielo sulla Valle d'Aosta*, Aosta

Diamantini, C., Zanon, B. (edited by),1999, *Le Alpi. Immagini e percorsi di un territorio in trasformazione*, Temi Edizioni, Trento

Camanni, E., 2002, *La nuova vita delle Alpi*, Bollati Boringhieri, Torino

Dini, R., Hugonin, D., 2003, *Paesaggi della dispersione insediativa: il caso della Valle d'Aosta*, Tesi di laurea, relatori: Isola A., De Rossi, A., Politecnico di Torino

Bätzing, W., 2005, *Le Alpi. Una Regione unica al centro dell'Europa*, Bollati Boringhieri, Torino

De Rossi, A., 2005, *Architettura alpina moderna in Piemonte e Valle d'Aosta*, Umberto Allemandi & C., Torino

Celesia, P., Dini, R., Ducly, G., Fracellio, F. (edited by), 2006, *Guardare da terra. Immagini da un territorio in trasformazione. La Valle d'Aosta e le sue rappresentazioni*, Tipografia Valdostana, Aosta

Vallet, M., 2007, *Nuovi paesaggi insediativi della "plaine" di Aosta: analisi e linee guida per il progetto*, Tesi di laurea, relatori: De Rossi, A., Dini, R., Politecnico di Torino

3.4 SUSA VALLEY: PROJECT VS COMPENSATION?

Massimo Crotti

17, 18 and 19 September 1871: Bardonecchia and Modane are celebrating the opening of the Fréjus railway tunnel, at the time still called "Cottian Alps tunnel". As a local reporter wrote, the tunnel meant "the fall of the Alps, that is to say, nature corrected by the human hand". The building site called the attention of journalists and visitors from all over the world; Edward Whymper -who first conquered the top of Mount Cervino in 1865- portrayed in a wonderful drawing the compressed air drill created by Germain Sommeiller, a true technical fetish during the second half of 19th Century. The Fréjus tunnel is one of the important elite projects that left a mark on the positivist season: "It is an achievement of our time to have started and built some of the greatest works that honor the wit of man, such as the connection of two continents through the transatlantic line, the Suez Channel, the Pacific rail line, the Cottian Alps tunnel".

December 8th, 2005: an incensed crowd, composed by thousands of the Susa Valley residents, is picketing the building site of the "basic tunnel", the first work in schedule for the Turin-Lyon high-speed line (TAV). This area had been taken over by the police -in a rather violent action- only a few hours earlier, at night. It is the so-called *battle of Venaus*, from the name of the site. The news spread around the world, and the images of the clashes between the residents and the police were broadcast by the televisions of the entire planet.

In about 130 years the Susa Valley has witnessed the life-cycle of two opposing visions: on the one hand the infrastructures, and on the other the development and transformation of the territory. On the second half of 19th Century, the railway and the tunnel under construction were generally seen -despite some criticism- as an opportunity for growth and emancipation of local society. On the contrary, the project for the TAV -the high speed line moving downstream from the highway that was hardly criticized in the Nineties- is perceived as a simple act of belligerence, with no positive effects on the territory. The inhabitants of the valley know very well that, for all the *non-local* actors, the valley territory is just a *corridor* for the passage of goods, objects and people, with no connection to its own environment.

This is not an overstatement. For those who, in the years preceding the battle of Venaus, stopped by the office of the Lyon-Turin Ferroviaire (LTF) –the designated subject for the realization of the infrastructure- the memory of the *modus operandi* still persists: to define a geometrical axis on which the rolling stock could be moved, through radii of curvature and areas with a steady grade ("the steady gradient"). Around this geometrical axis *the territory does not exist*, if not as a problem of disposal of the excavation material (the "spoils") or as change of position between the parallel infrastructural axes (the so-called "buck jumps"); to its best, the territory -houses, factories, natural features- turns into an obstacle to be overcome. And in case the population -an abstract, at times even bothersome actor, as the LTF has long claimed- poses any problems, there are always the compensating works. The same chord, compensation, was hit several times during the construction of the highway by SITAF: the local communities, instead of asking for a comprehensive *territorial project*, acted on their own to obtain link roads, ring roads, cycle lanes, sports facilities, even vehicles for city services. In this respect, it is illuminating to read the archive files on the negotiations between SITAF and local administrations. Things were not as legal sometimes -these were the years of the Tangentopoli scandal- and one of the mayors even committed suicide.

To understand this *partition* of the valley terrain in two irremediably different perspectives -from the one side the corridor, from the other the living environment-, it is enough to compare the different perceptions of the territorial space, opposing the geography of crossing to the geography of local settlements. On the one hand the glance of the passer-by, above and separated from the ground —from Turin citizens, who on weekends rush to the ski facilities in the high valley, to truck-drivers venturing along the highway stretch. They see the surrounding space as a simple, inconsistent background, a sort of *wings* framing the valley bottom settlements and foothill structures, up to the profile of the peaks. On the other hand the glance of the residents, who from their houses or from the local roads along the foothills stare at the passers-by: they rarely stop and generate lots of noise, traffic congestion and polluting emissions.

The low Susa Valley is a mid-land with a rich historical and settlement tradition, which is getting more and more vulnerable, and is seeing its own identity weakened; an identity that is connected to the physical places of living. It is not a mere juxtaposition between the "authentic" legitimacy of the inhabitants of the place and the aggressive indifference of the supra-local rationale. If we look at it from a wider angle, analyzing the different transformations that have started in the Fifties, the situation is even more complex and articulated, like in the aforementioned case of the highway.

I. Between incrementalism and settlement specialization: half a century of new territories
Until the end of the world war, the area of the low Susa Valley basically remained the one immortalized by the photographer Mario Gabinio in 1925 from the top of Mount Pirchiriano, where lies the Sacra di San Michele: an agricultural valley plain, with few settlements on the valley bottom, crossed by the river and by the infrastructural *bundle of nerves* constituted by the Napoleonic road and the historical railway.

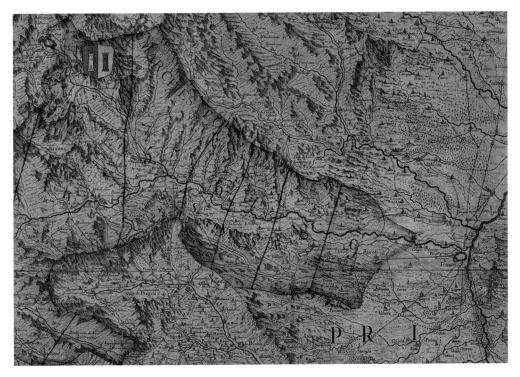

The 'entrance corridor of the Susa Valley in spatial representations of the eighteenth century. Topographic map of the extent of the Susa Valley and those of Cezanne and Bardonecchia divided into nine parts, 1764-1772 (detail)

The attention given to the relationships between human settlement, geomorphological, infrastructure and river basin as a basis for planning actions in spatial representations of the eighteenth century savoy. Topographic map extent of the Susa Valley and those of Cezanne and Bardonecchia divided into nine parts, 1764-1772 (detail)

It is an almost abstract image, which well depicts the co-existence of two different visions of the territory that in just a few decades have been growing and overlapping, without ever confronting themselves. The situation finally culminated in the *territorial antagonism* that burst forth only a few weeks before the Winter Olympics of 2006, to oppose the opening of the exploration works for the TAV tunnel.

In the first decades of the post-war period, the high valley saw the development -due to the massification of winter sports- of a process of invention and construction of the mountain of *loisir*, which had started at the beginning of the century. On the other hand, the low valley witnessed a transformative process that in a few decades eroded most of the fertile soil of the valley bottom, mineralizing almost a 40% of the soil of the aggraded valley plain.

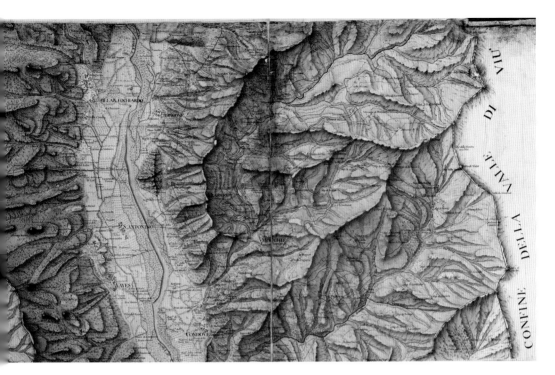

In the context of the radical transformations of the low valley in the post-war period, the decade of the Eighties -which saw the birth of the Turin-Lyon highway- marked a threshold between two different forms of settling dynamics: first the expansion of the settlements on the valley bottom, then their transformation into consolidates *plates*. Nevertheless, the territory is "not a disposable container that can be replaced" [Corboz 1985]. Therefore what we read and live today is a single result, that is the progressive transition of the valley from a landscape of extraordinary environmental, climatic and historical qualities to a *collage* of lost identities. A territory oscillating between a nostalgic, slightly regressive recovery of the values of the past and the incapacity to reinvent, to create new settling patterns as a strategy to react against both the indifference of the external actors and the short sight of the local ones: in other words, the incapacity to *re-territorialize itself* [Bobbio Dansero 2008].

From the post-war to the beginning of the Eighties, during the construction of the highway, a settlement increase took place. It started from the historical villages along the foot of the hill, lapped and framed by the two main roads: the Napoleonic one (renamed S.S[1]. 25 since the creation of A.N.A.S[2]) and the S.S. 24, built in the Thirties for military purposes. It subsequently stretched to the agricultural areas of the valley, longitudinally crossed by the Dora Riparia River. Thanks to a season of indifferent local planning that determined a "strong process of settlement condensation at the bottom of the valley" and "extensive phenomena along the infrastructural lines", that "process of physical evaluation of the fixed capital of the soil through the architectural (or simply building) cultivation of the soil" took place [De Rossi et al 2002 (a)]. A process that generated a radically different territory, modified according to logics of incremental growth -often individual houses- and of exclusive attention to the accessibility of the main roads. The ordinary settlement principles that tried to interweave soil, orography and pedology with the road system were rapidly set aside.

Since the end of the Eighties there has been a growing welding process between the infrastructural pattern and the settlement activity; today it seems to be blatant and, in a way, irreversible. The motorway was built, definitely confirming the ancient function of the Susa Valley: an *infrastructural cable duct*. The layout of the highway first unfolded on the agricultural plain, often over the watercourse, using all the few areas still untouched by the recent constructions and by a landscape rich in marks and heritages. Once in the high valley, the highway needed trestle bridges and important works of engineering in order to overcome the problems posed by the complex orography of the territory, and guarantee total accessibility to the *domaine skiable* branching up towards the slopes and the crests until the French border. At the same time the systematic building activity along the valley continued: more compact in the high valley centers, it occupied new areas surrounding the older centers. On the other hand, the low valley witnessed a season of monofunctional plans and projects that tried to limit soil consumption by creating places; these were often in the form of fences, framed by the new residential, productive and commercial settlements.

The incremental logic of the previous season seemed to have shifted from *micro* to *macro* scale: the interventions, also the public ones, followed "an idea of space construction based on separation and specialization" [Id.]. This in turn highlighted the conceptual independence of the projects for settlement environments from those concerning the infrastructural fabric.

---

[1] Ndt.: Strada Statale: State Road
[2] Ndt.: Associazione Nazionale Autostrade: National Association of Highways

Paradoxically this distance -of territorial vision, of knowledge and technical cultures- did not prevent the chances of capitalizing the territorial substratum; on the contrary, it accelerated and multiplied them. The highway consumed the land, taking over the soil it needed for the building sites, the complementary areas and appurtenances (some of them still in the waiting line), the many interchanges, and the road platform. The result was the proliferation of areas confined within the infrastructures, the reduction of the agricultural land and their decreased accessibility and profitability. At the same time the local administrations were asking and obtaining the construction of linking roads between the highway and the two state roads, and the beltway around the populated centers (following highway-based, oversized models) as compensating works.

This *hyper-infrastructuring* of the territory has enabled to implement new settlement strategies, designing new geographies that transversally invaded the valley, favoring the growth, and in some cases the "welding" of the settlements at the foot of the two sides of the mountain. At the beginning of the new millennium, the Susa Valley appears as a discontinuous, compressed and fragmented territory. A territory completely transformed by half a century of projects, chances provided by internal and self-referential logics, be they isolated structures or important infrastructural works.

What has always been missing is an overall morphological framework and, as a consequence, the (political and cultural) possibility to use the topic of the physical form of the territory to combine the specificity of the places with the many ongoing transformation works. Even big events such as 1997 Alpine Ski World Cup and 2006 Winter Olympics were not enough to bring about a real reflection on the asset of the territory, or on eventual overall planning proposals, able to adjust and orient the territorial patterns of the entire valley. The logic of accumulation of the punctual interventions -especially in the high valley- for sports and tourist accommodation facilities and for the infrastructural works (the Olympics of 2006 meant the conclusion of the works started for the World Cup) has always prevailed. It was seen as the "resolution of a technical problem that basically consists in crossing space and overcoming obstacles through the separation from the context." [Id.].

Even the planning framework implemented in recent years through the preliminary studies for the *Approfondimento Valle di Susa*[3] in the *Piano Territoriale Regionale*

---

[3] Ndt:Discussion Group on the Susa Valley

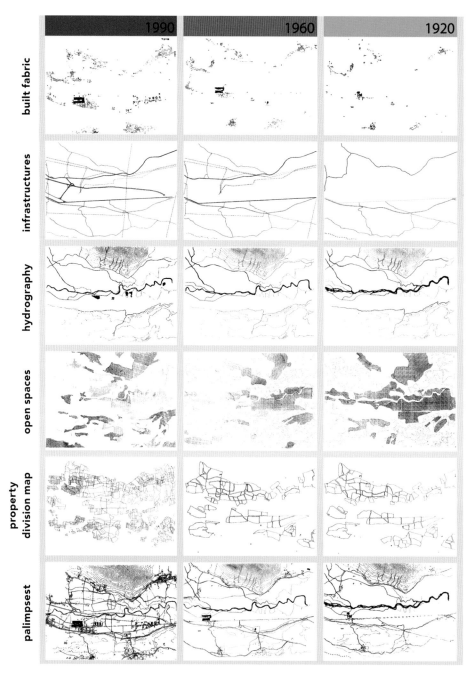

A representation of the study on palimpsest and settlement transformation of the lower valley of Susa, achieved at the end of the nineties

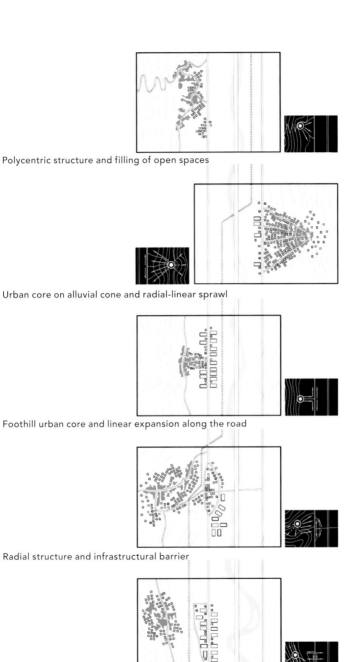

Polycentric structure and filling of open spaces

Urban core on alluvial cone and radial-linear sprawl

Foothill urban core and linear expansion along the road

Radial structure and infrastructural barrier

Hill structure and commercial strip at the valley floor

Abacus of transformation dynamics of the lower valley of Susa in the relationship between infrastructure and housing boards (graphics processing Mauro Berta, 2002)

(PTR)[4] [Regione Piemonte 2005] -based on the general settlement pattern and on the local specificities and aimed at presenting territorial images and planning action on a *GrandeScala* -, could not manage to find a correspondence in the local planning strategy, or in the isolated transformative practices carried out in recent years.

The works for the Olympics, for example, avoided dealing with the project of public space in the locations that were hosting competitions, even when it was tightly related to accessibility and tourist accommodation. It is paradigmatic that the only case reflecting the strategies presented by the *Approfondimento Val di Susa* of the PTR is the planned situation of the "snow front", a urban border in terms of public and functional space: parking lots, accessibility and services at the ski lift facilities and a urban *promenade* combined to the beltway system. It was situated in *Montgenèvre*, the French ski location adjacent to the Olympic sites.

II. TAV / NO TAV: *the revelation of the territory*

The situation described until now should not lead us to think that all is lost, that the territory of the Susa Valley does not have images and resources to compensate the damages and the missed chances of the past, in terms of both opportunities and implemental modes of projects and interventions. The experience of the *Osservatorio per il collegamento ferroviario Torino-Lione*[5], promoted by the national government after the violent opposition to the TAV project of December 2005, shows that "the adequate setting can bring about visions that in a reasonable time can be put in common on a technical level; this would pave the way to common solutions on a political level as well" [Bobbio Dansero 2008].

The work of the *Osservatorio* from 2006 and 2008, despite being still on a technical level, has essentially enabled "the analysis on what the problem, and the possible alternative solutions, might be": on the potentiality entailed by the use of the historical line, on the carriage of goods along the Alpine arch, and on its relationship to Turin metropolitan area and the alternative paths. It has tried to open a technical debate with all the institutional and territorial actors on the high speed line; a topic intentionally avoided by the proponents until that moment. This has enabled to suggest new alternative paths, lengths and localizations of the base tunnel, to the extent that it has turned the very idea of a high *speed* railway line into a high"

[4] Ndt: Regional Territorial Plan
[5] Ndt: Platform for the Turin-Lyon Railway

capacity one (TAC). It has especially underlined the need to overcome radical positions "for or against" the TAV, rooted in divergent territorial and geographical views more than in ideology. Finally, it has highlighted the need to turn the page in favor of a territorial project on the *GrandeScala*; a project combining and interweaving the geographical, social, cultural and economic reasons of both stances, able to read "the potential contribution of a territorial approach in defining the territorial peculiarities operating behind the great project. The goal is to identify a possible common ground on which to build a geography able to deal with both perspectives" [Id.].

Therefore a different glance on the complex and articulated physical reality of the Susa Valley becomes a possibility and a necessity. The implementation of a new railway line -together with the improvement of the historical one- can represent a chance to *re-territorialize* the valley. Mario Virano, coordinator of the *Osservatorio*, claims that we need to accept a shift in our perspective on the project, moving from a mere *infrastructural project* –sectional and specialized- to an inclusive, multifunctional and transcendental *project of territory* [Id.]. This seems to be the underlying rationale of the *Piano Strategico per il territorio della direttrice Torino – Lione*[6], set up by the Province of Turin after the protests of the end of 2005. The initial phase of consideration, analysis and evaluation of the suggestions was concluded in 2008. The many actors involved -from the institutional and administrative levels to the social, economical and cultural forces- have been taken into consideration, which has helped to identify some common guidelines and established some primary objectives. The goal is to develop vocations, overcome difficulties and open the dialog to planning perspectives and strategic measures, by dividing the territory defined by the infrastructural project in three macro-areas: Turin and its metropolitan area; the low Susa Valley, and the Cernischia, Ceronda, Casternone y Sangone valleys; the high Susa Valley.

Among the different guidelines and the primary goals of the *Piano Strategico* for the Susa Valley -especially the low valley- the principle of *territorial quality* seems to be the fittest to meet the demand of compensation for the landscape, urban and environmental damages. In order to explore the guidelines of the *Piano Strategico*, oriented to programming a polycentric, sustainable and highly relational future, and to move on to a planning and implementation phase, it is necessary to define some method and content-related pre-assumptions.

[6] Ndt: Strategic Plan for the territory of the Turin-Lyon line

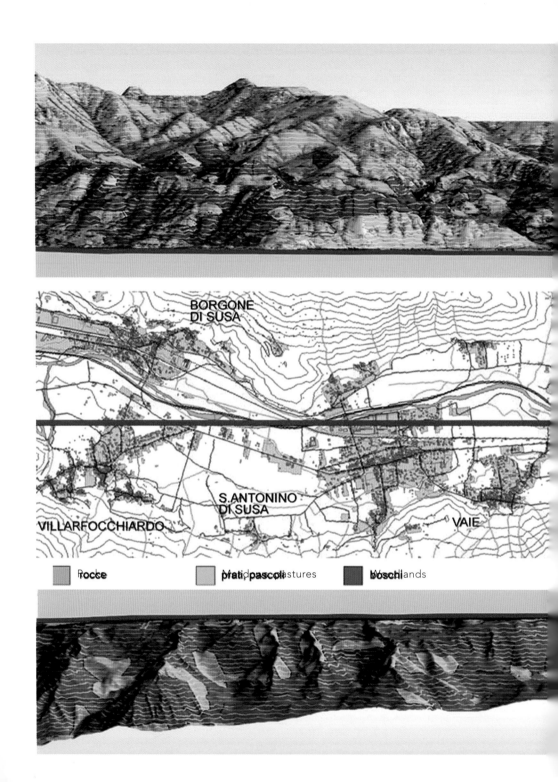

BORGONE
DI SUSA

S. ANTONINO
DI SUSA

VILLARFOCCHIARDO

VAIE

Rocce / rocks   prati pascoli / pastures   boschi / woodlands

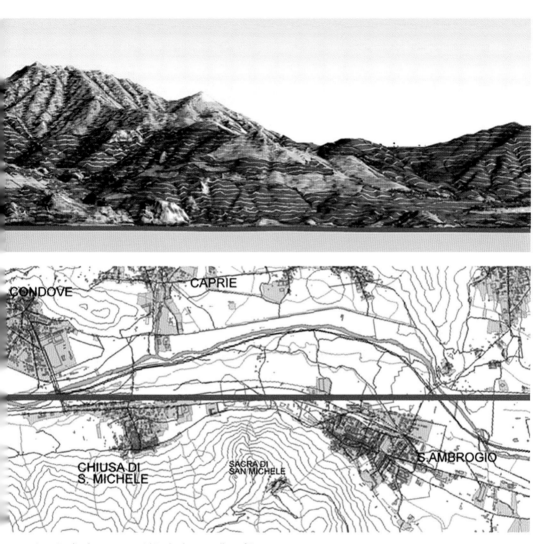

Longitudinal transects within the lower valley of Susa

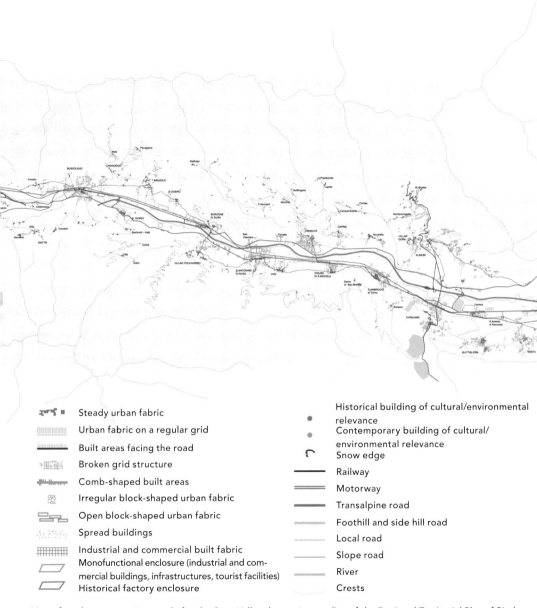

Steady urban fabric	**Historical building of cultural/environmental relevance**
Urban fabric on a regular grid	**Contemporary building of cultural/ environmental relevance**
Built areas facing the road	**Snow edge**
Broken grid structure	**Railway**
Comb-shaped built areas	**Motorway**
Irregular block-shaped urban fabric	**Transalpine road**
Open block-shaped urban fabric	**Foothill and side hill road**
Spread buildings	**Local road**
Industrial and commercial built fabric	**Slope road**
Monofunctional enclosure (industrial and com-mercial buildings, infrastructures, tourist facilities)	**River**
Historical factory enclosure	**Crests**

Map of settlement matrices made for the Susa Valley deepening studies of the Regional Territorial Plan of Piedmont (graphic processing Dipra, Turin Polythecnic, 2005)

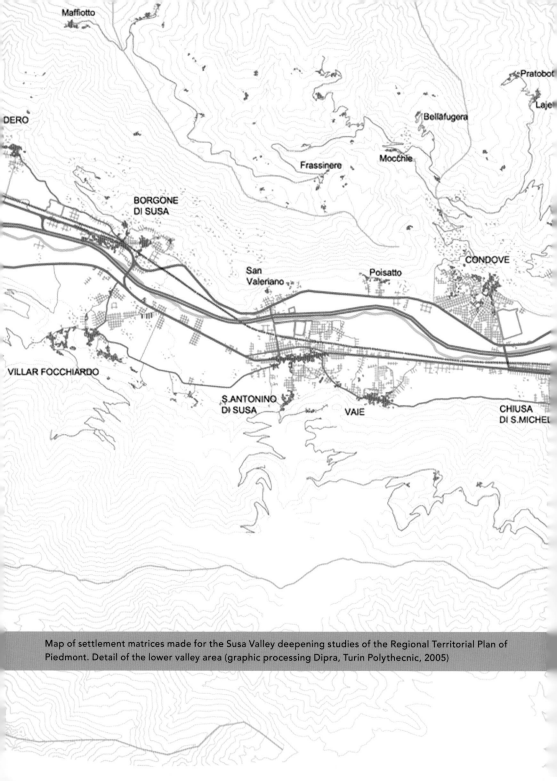

Map of settlement matrices made for the Susa Valley deepening studies of the Regional Territorial Plan of Piedmont. Detail of the lower valley area (graphic processing Dipra, Turin Polythecnic, 2005)

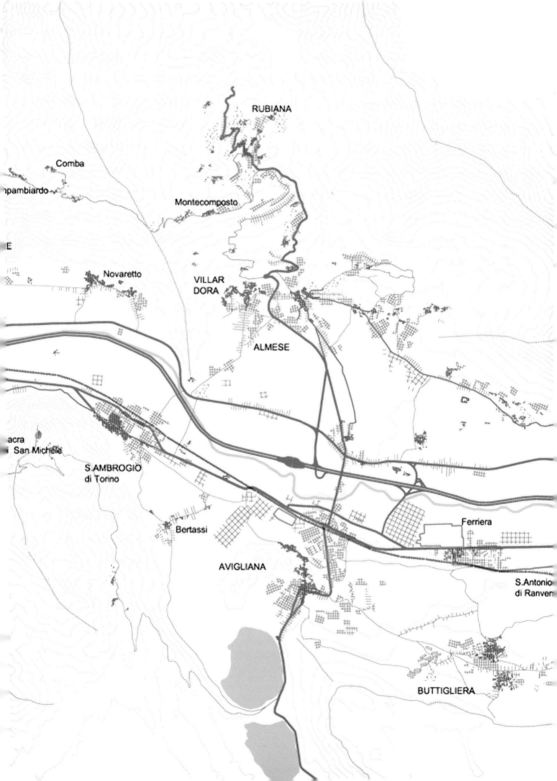

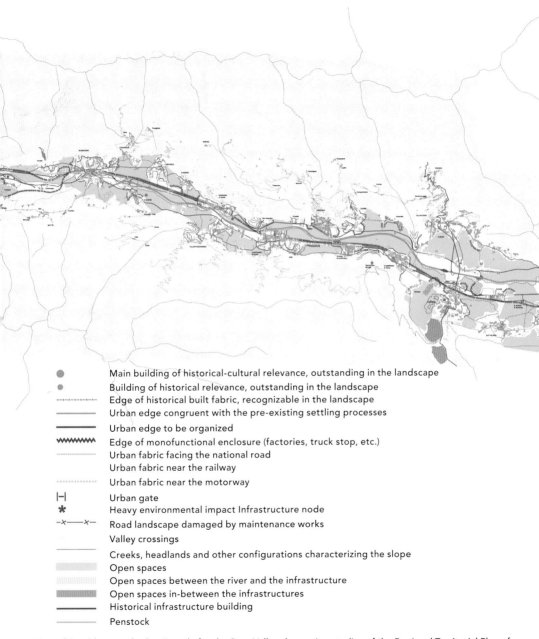

- Main building of historical-cultural relevance, outstanding in the landscape
- Building of historical relevance, outstanding in the landscape
- Edge of historical built fabric, recognizable in the landscape
- Urban edge congruent with the pre-existing settling processes
- Urban edge to be organized
- Edge of monofunctional enclosure (factories, truck stop, etc.)
- Urban fabric facing the national road
- Urban fabric near the railway
- Urban fabric near the motorway
- Urban gate
- Heavy environmental impact Infrastructure node
- Road landscape damaged by maintenance works
- Valley crossings
- Creeks, headlands and other configurations characterizing the slope
- Open spaces
- Open spaces between the river and the infrastructure
- Open spaces in-between the infrastructures
- Historical infrastructure building
- Penstock

Map of "problems and values" made for the Susa Valley deepening studies of the Regional Territorial Plan of Piedmont (graphic processing Dipra, Turin Polythecnic, 2005)

III. New required projects

First of all, in order to open a new, different season of territorial projects, the local communities must abandon the logic of diversified and particularistic compensations, that until now has prevailed as far the big infrastructural projects are concerned; the effects on the quality of the landscape and on the settlement pattern of the valley have been negative (or null). As highlighted by the *Piano Strategico*, this means to concentrate the resources to start a new planning vision of the territory on a supra-local scale, one "that goes beyond the particular visions, and situates the local problems adopting a wide perspective, a territorial framework". A scale that identifies strategic primary topics and interventions to be put into practice in a concentrated effort.

Among the examples of an innovative use of the resources available for complementary infrastructural activities on the territory there are the French experiences, enabled into being by the *1% paysage et developpement* law of 1994. This law covers the 1 per cent of the intervention costs, and an analogous amount is covered by local administrations. These funds are to be invested in studies and actions on the landscape, and in the development of the areas affected by great road and railway projects, which have deep effects on the settlement and environmental context. Something very similar actually happened in the case of the departmental funding for the *Osservatorio* and the *Piano Strategico* after the suspension imposed by the No TAV mobilization. Several are the advantages entailed by the setting up of a dialog with the territory, in parallel with the technical project. A debate translating into a common choice and a factual commitment of all the involved actors, a time reduction of the implementing process, and also an experimental approach that is finally able to interweave infrastructural works and landscape patterns.

Nevertheless, as far as the Susa Valley and the troublesome project of the new Turin-Lyon railway line are concerned, one thing is for sure: the protests of 2005 have opened a season of confrontation and debate. This in turn has watched the development of the project from a technical point of view and, most importantly, has shifted and broadened the look on the territory and its different geographies (physical, social, economic, etc.). The infrastructural project today has the requirements to find a *conceptual space* where the complexity of the topic can unfold on a territorial scale, and a common *political space*, as opposed to sectional and particularistic views. This mirrors in the technical and multi-disciplinary literature on the TAV and its territory of the last few years. In this sense the *Piano Strategico per la Provincia*[7] is a concrete initial point of reference, that can turn into a chance for a functional reorganization of the territory, combined (this is the novelty) with the modeling of the transformations; that is to say, it is an architecture of the territory interweaving ordinary modifications with great infrastructural works.

Therefore the case of high speed in the Susa Valley appears as a paradigmatic example of a topic that has been discussed throughout this volume: the key role of the morphological project as a means of agreement and mediation of the government on the territory. The dramatic -and still ongoing- events of the recent years showed the full potential of resistance and mobilization of the inhabitants of the valley when they are left out from the decision-making process regarding *their* places, in the name of extra-local strategies and rationalities. The project for an infrastructure points out the correspondence between soil patterns and geographies of power, since it concentrates the relationships and the conflicts within a large territory in one continuous construction process. The design of the shape therefore has been generating conflicts because nobody, until now, has accepted to regard it as a political project in the first place.

IV. A territorial action by rooms

The challenge today is to open a new season of projects and actions on the *GrandeScala* for the Susa Valley, especially in the low valley: on the one hand the area between Rivoli, at the western end of Turin metropolitan area, and Avigliana, including the valley plain at the foot of the Abbey of the Sacra di San Michele -where the valley meets the foot of the mountain; on the other hand, the area of Bussoleno and Susa, delimiting the low valley, which is the point of departure of the roads to France. On the north-western side they head towards the Cenischia Valley and the Moncenisio Hill; on the south-western side, towards the high Susa Valley, further branching off between the *Fréjus* tunnel towards the *Maurienne* Valley, and the *Montgenèvre* towards the *Durance* Valley.

All the possible territories between Rivoli, Avigliana, Bussoleno and Susa constitute one of the key landscape areas of western Italy. It is in this dense and structured part of the valley that it is necessary to formulate hypotheses on the territory in the context of the actions and project defined by the *Piano Strategico*. We should start from the perspective of a flying-bird, looking at the landscape through those images

---

[7] Ndt: Strategic Plan for the Province

of the low valley established at the beginning of the century by Mario Gabinio. It could also be very useful to look back at the preliminary papers for the *Piano Paesaggistico della Regione Piemonte* (PPR, 2009)[8], to start over from the interpretations and the planning explorations provided by the *Approfondimento Val di Susa* of the PTR and eventually superpose them to the ones provided by the *Piano Strategico*. The goal is to try to understand and express the reality of the settlements of an extraordinary and diverse landscape, defining topics, places and specificities for the project.

The *acknowledgment* of the logics of consolidation and development of the ground shapes on the built-up area -the so-called "settlement matrix"-, involved in both long-term and recent transformations; the highlighting of the physical form and of the importance of the substratum, which combines the geomorphologic and pedologic nature of the soil with the artificialization generated by a multitude of small and big transformations; the *re-composition* of the critical nodes regarding the landscape, environment, settlements and connections of the transversal and longitudinal sections of the valley; the *representation* of the historical, architectonic, cultural, and landscape values on the territory: these are the essential interpretative practices that must be interwoven with images and visions from below, with three-dimensional project visualizations and transformative explorations that, if combined, could reveal the specificity to be addressed. The goal is to obtain that *territorial quality* which, in the *Piano Strategico* as well, is now being urgently evoked.

Moving from the *guiding vision* to the *strategic lines* on the axis of the *territorial quality*, the *Piano Strategico* also acknowledges the need to "mend the settlements crossed by the linear infrastructure", and "promotes urban reorganization and the design of the landscape" [Provincia di Torino 2008].

Therefore the *Piano Strategico* produces a general hypothesis that does not deny the interconnections within the built-up area, moving transversally with respect to the valley corridor. On the contrary, these incremental activities can merge into an extensive project (not municipality by municipality, or border by border) through the assumption of the conditions of expansion, and the dialog with the local managements of the soils. Until now this has only been wished for (i.e. in the studies of the 2001 PTR), because the decision-makers, at all levels, did not have a reason to adopt these strategies, if not by free will.

---

[8] Landscape Plan for the Regione Piemonte

The *trauma* of the failure of an imposing policy on the TAV represents a constraint and a *pretext* to try to set the agreements and the balances according to the pattern of the soil. Only within this balance an order of *settlement quality* for the Susa Valley will be possible.

One of the main operative topics for the system project concerns the possible laying underground of the "iron plan" when crossing the populated centers, and the subsequent urban re-planning of the cleared areas. The effectiveness of the projects will depend on the ability to extend the interventions beyond the borders of the single centers, merging with the extended and scattered fabric of the settlements through the re-appropriation of the space, the urban reorganization and the creation of a shape, identity and image of the territory.

In the shift from the strategic level to the imminent level of the projects and the interventions (which will hopefully be innovative and effective), it is important to pose the issue of the relationship between settlements and infrastructural patterns, and between geographic and geomorphologic considerations. This means, in the first place, to overcome the self-referential terms of shipment, coherence, and continuity, seen as mechanistic answers to recognized critical points (i.e. to lay the railway underground to increase the availability of *usable* soil): the goal is an improved adaptability of the diversified, interpretative and proponent *planning tactics*, within a common strategy on the *GrandeScala*.

The new geography of the low Susa Valley can move from a principle of territorial reorganization by *rooms*, that is to say by sections of the territory in which the peculiarities of both the construct (the settlement matrix of the residential area, infrastructure pattern, monofunctional fences, historical excellencies, agricultural structure), and the substratum (the geomorphologic structure of the soil, hydrographic network, topography) are clearly recognizable. The next step is to develop the design of territorial images: *ad hoc* landscape figures to be pursued through targeted interventions, but also through the ordinary transformative processes.

In other words, it might be necessary to realize challenging and diverse works, such as the laying underground of railway stretches, but only when this is the only possible solution to a recognized specific problem, not solvable otherwise. An alternative to that vision of territorial topics that preposes *the solution to the problem* (whose paradigm was the idea of the base tunnel for the TAV), is to work on the discontinuity and breaking lines between the *rooms* in the low valley, meant as settling programs on specific geomorphologic environments. Another possibility is to strengthen the existing continuity, which is of an environmental kind: the *natural* or agricultural corridors (take as an example the transversal landscape section of the Abbey of San Antonio di Ranverso or the agricultural remnants of the Susa plain). The territorial project should be built upon the relational spaces, within the built in areas and on the thresholds and the margins by using the soil -the substratum- as a project material (the slopes, the fault lines, the alluvial cones); it should regard infrastructures as a chance of a networking and hierarchic structuring of the paths and the crossings; it should be based on the expansion of the metropolitan railway system connected to the road network, so as to organize and redirect the future settlement processes.

The containment of soil consumption is actually pursued through the densification of the unsettled fabrics and the hierarchic organization of accessibility. On the contrary, the tendency to artificially eliminate the differences within the substratum and the constructions (such as the laying underground of the railway) risks to produce that amorphous and indifferent vision of the soil in which, according to the French landscape architect Michel Corajoud, the project and the modifications do not take into account the *inertia* of nature, the resistance to transformation of the soil that constitute its identity and physical memory.

Bibliography

BOBBIO, L., DANSERO, E., 2008, *La TAV e la valle di Susa Susa Valley*. Geografie in competizione, Allemandi, Torino.

DE ROSSI, A., DURBIANO, G., GOVERNA, F., REINERIO, L., ROBIGLIO, M. (edited by), 1999, *Linee nel paesaggio. Esplorazioni nei territori della trasformazione*, Utet, Torino.

DE ROSSI, A. et al., 2002 (a), *La Valle di Susa Susa Valley, il corridoio infrastrutturale e il sistema insediativo*, in In.fra., Piemonte. Sette luoghi in trasformazione, Quaderni di In.fra Forme insediative e infrastrutture, Otto editore, Torino.

DE ROSSI, A. et al. (b), *Il corridoio della Valle di Susa Susa Valley. Linearità infrastrutturali e palinsesto insediativo*, in: Isola, A. et al., 2002, *In.fra Forme insediative e infrastrutture. Ricerche coordinate da Aimaro Isola in 12 scuole di architettura. Atlante, Venezia, Marsilio.*

CROTTI, M., *Nouveaux regards sur les infrastructures entre recherche, formation et projet*, in : A. Coste (edited by), 2008, *Design et projets d'équipements publics " Infrastructures et paysage " Colloque – atelier international et interdisciplinaire Biennale du Design 2006 – Saint-Étienne*, n. 57, Certu, Lyon.

ISOLA, A. et al., *L'arco del pedemonte e le linee alpine di valle*, in: Isola, A. et al., 2002, *In.fra Forme insediative e infrastrutture. Ricerche coordinate da Aimaro Isola in 12 scuole di architettura. Atlante,* Venezia, Marsilio

ISOLA, A. et al., *Corridoio infrastrutturale e palinsesto insediativo. La Valle di Susa Susa Valley,* in: Isola, A., et al., 2002, *In.fra Forme insediative e infrastrutture. Ricerche coordinate da Aimaro Isola in 12 scuole di architettura. Manuale,* Venezia, Marsilio

ISOLA, A. et al., *L'arco del pedemonte e le linee alpine di valle,* in: Isola, A. et al., 2002, *In.fra Forme insediative e infrastrutture. Ricerche coordinate da Aimaro Isola in 12 scuole di architettura. Atlante,* Venezia, Marsilio

BOBBIO, L., DANSERO, E., 2008, *La TAV e la valle di Susa Susa Valley*. Geografie in competizione, Allemandi, Torino.

PROVINCIA DI TORINO, 2008, *Schema di piano strategico per il territorio interessato dalla direttrice ferroviaria Torino-Lione. Strategie e progetti per lo sviluppo*, Provincia di Torino, Torino.

REGIONE PIEMONTE, 2005, *Piano Territoriale Regionale. Approfondimento della Valle di Susa. Gli studi e gli elaborati preliminari*, Regione Piemonte, Torino.

SERGI, G., 1981, *Potere e territorio lungo la strada di Francia*, Liguori editore, Napoli.

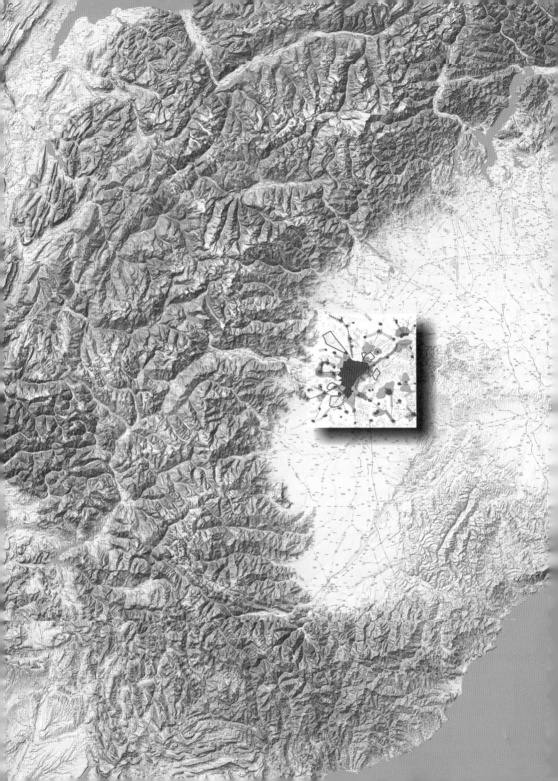

3.5 GRAN TORINO

Paolo Antonelli, Alessandro Armando, Francesca Camorali

I. Metropolitan Territory

A territorial area of about 135 thousand hectares, divided internally in 53 municipalities, and a population, the so called "legal population", amounting to 1 million and 650 thousand people. According to the 2001 ISTAT[1] data, these are the numbers describing the Turin metropolis today. Of course, this is just one of the many possible sets of *variable parameters* defining the aggregation of different municipal units. The Turin metropolis can also be represented through regional demographical limitations, just like through the representations and borders defined by the Territorial Plan for Provincial Coordination (PTCP, 16 Municipalities), by the Metropolitan Conference (38 Municipalities) - subsequently replaced by the Metropolitan Table (17 Municipalities) - by the Agency for metropolitan mobility, by the *Corona Verde* project or by the combination of Integrated Territorial Plans (PTI) which have been extended to cover wider territories like the *Valle di Susa* corridor. This continuous overlapping of places and borders is not unrelated to the way in which projects are set up and built.

In this context, however, it would be more interesting to try to suspend, for one moment, the ordinary and consolidated political and administrative vision behind those projects, in order to try to elaborate interpreting schemes concentrating on the features, as well as on the constraints, of the Turin metropolitan territory, which can indeed contribute to describing its form and orienting its transformation. These include the territorial geomorphology in its orographic, hydrographical and pedological configuration; the event planning schemes; the diachronic evolution of persisting settlement patterns, according to matrixes, directions and expansion tendencies that are the result of substitution or deformation processes involving multiple material deposits; and, finally, the very technical and political nature of

[1] The Italian Institute of Statistics

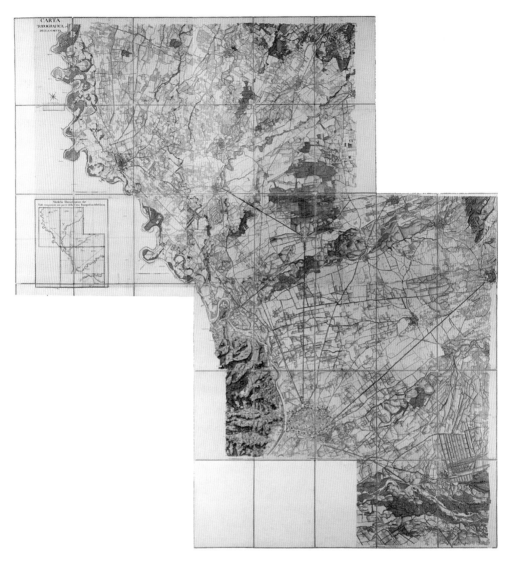

The interweaving of settlement structures, large baroque axes, hydrographic configurations and agriculture of the plains of Turin in the eighteenth-century representations of Savoy. Topographic maps of the Hunt (three designs on thin paper, in ink and watercolor in various colors), Turin, State Archives, Court, secret topographic maps, 15 A 6th red (surveyor Piedmont, c. 1760-1766)

municipal areas and of dominating entities, which are directly linked to territorial segments and are separated by "immaterial" borders around land properties, planning instruments, but also around risk mappings and environmental or hydro-geological constraints. These different but complementary plans constitute together the necessary background for all urban and territorial transformation processes.

On the morphological level, the connecting line between a plurality of perspectives and transformations is that which intertwines the waterways, the alpine features and the hill system with local historical events connected to the structure acquired by the city in the 60s and 70s. The system of Savoy residences connected to the position of rivers, the great baroque axes embedded in the depths of hills and alpine reliefs, the passages opening towards agricultural plains and the valley mouths provide the contemporary urban space with a direction and a character that do not allow for radial development or qualify it for the definition of centralised territory. In the light of the current issues concerning the metropolitan project, this is particularly interesting, since territorial history and geography outline a long-term "metropolitan" vision, with regard to large scale morphological structures, which even anticipates the development of the industrial city.

This is indicative, within the Turin context, of a historically consolidated and stratified "metropolitan culture" which goes even beyond the architectural and urban perspective and sees in the large scale, as well as in the interweaving between *territorial and architectural dimensions*, a fundamental interpreting and operating value. Since the 50s and 60s, when the large scale in urban growth and landscape transformation phenomena became more visible everywhere, this value has somehow tried to guide transformations in Turin and in the surrounding territory. As an example, we could analyse the idea of the "productive strip of the Po Valley", contained in the 1947 Astengo plan; or the "big hand" in the 1956 Rigotti plan, which tries to direct quantitative growth after the war and during the economic boom; or the Turin inter-municipal plan during the 60s; up to the more recent experiences of the Gregotti and Cagnardi Town Planning Scheme (1995) and the first and second Turin Strategic Plans (2000-2006). In their attempt to bravely reinvent models which are also quite distant from each other, these examples could be viewed as a sort of preamble to a contemporary reflection over the *Grand Scale* architecture, by at least taking into consideration the "reverberation" [Cavallari Murat, 1968] between *internal* and *external* events, where the form of the city almost seems to harbour its

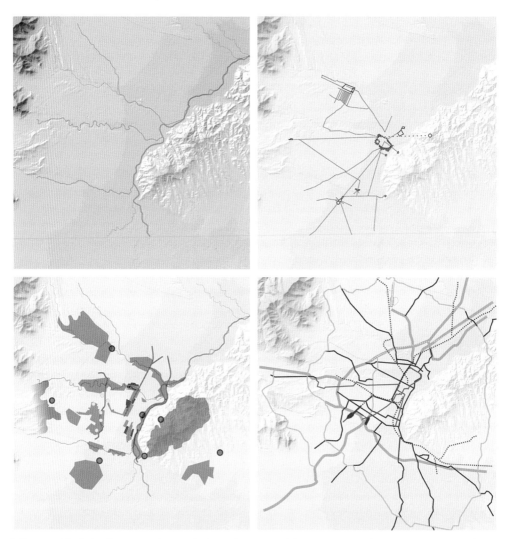

Palimpsest (clockwise from top). The morphology of territory of the Turin metropolitan area: the system of rivers, the hills and the entrances to the valley. The baroque structure of the territory: the system of axes and Savoy residences. The three centralities of the master plan of '95: the river Po, the rail link and the axis of the tracks, and the new Corso Marche. The structuring of the contemporary city: the orthogonal "grid" and radial output into the territory own architectural rules.

A permanently open configuration of the city, the territorial scale as the long-term structural horizon, the *historically metropolitan* dimension that closely interweaves with infrastructural projects (the "frame" concept) are the crucial elements around which different projects aggregate and organise themselves over time. This is maybe, even today, one of the most characterising features of the metropolitan city of Turin. This dimension is certainly *physical*, since it is built around materials and territorial objects that are capable of influencing and orienting space transformation dynamics, but it is also a rhetorical and *narrative* one. As a result, a long-term vision, structured on the basis of permanent elements that could extensively be defined as *morphological-territorial fixed assets,* is added to territorial building practices based on incrementalism and on the juxtaposition of rationales that are both limited, because they are based on simplifications and reductions, and absolute, because they aim at the exclusive control of an area by establishing borders.

If, on the one hand, extending the space-time scale makes it possible to produce territorial descriptions according to values of permanence and continuity, on the other hand, it is also undeniable that the opportunities for contemporary transformation, in their contingent nature, respond to limited and fragmented rationales, whose permeability cannot be neglected. It is indeed the movement between the metropolitan perspective and the tangibility of single opportunities that prompts an attempt to interpret some of the transformation phenomena taking place in the metropolis of Turin.

This movement is not, however, devoid of critical points, fractures and discontinuities. Non-linearity is the key feature of every step along the scale, just like the gap existing between the recognition of geographical identities, of "territorial situations" [Dematteis, 1989], and the various plans and instruments being used for territorial governance. A gap which produces a mismatch between the ways and forms in which cities and territories are built, transformed and "conceived", through their *images* [De Rossi, Durbiano, 2006], and the rules established at different institutional levels to orient transformation. This is not just a technical question, but it is rather related to both political and planning issues. It is directly related to a shifted way of interpreting *borders*, which is made even more apparent by the contemporary territorial "metropolisation", whereby *physical* borders have become increasingly *legal* and *sectoral*. These are the critical spheres where large scale projects, power models and ordinary land construction and transformation processes clash with one another.

This clash, however, highlights the need to outline new territorial images that are capable of shaping coordination opportunities between different levels of local government, starting from a conceptual review of the role of *Grand Scale* projects. It is about elaborating *pertinent descriptions* of the metropolitan dimension, which might become instruments for mediation and argumentative reasoning among the plurality of decision-making and space administration processes. The progressive transformation of urban legislation (i.e. the review of the different regional urban laws in Italy) and also the procedural evolution of implementing instruments, for which the City of Turin is one of the most active laboratories, account for a practically achieved transition towards governance models that can no longer be attributed to linear delegation or hierarchization processes. It is indeed the inefficacy of *top-down* schemes, using non-negotiable procedures, which has increasingly raised the problem of distinguishing between, on the one hand, the degree of agreement on future city scenarios amongst operators, decision-makers and citizens, and, on the other hand, the more traditional formalised procedures for sectoral assignments and delegations. Under this perspective, the representation of large scale transformations will have to be able to orient shared visions by outlining the arguments concerning the physical form in progress, even before prescribing its implementing modalities or defining its scientific and technical terms.

Within transformation contexts characterised by variable parameters, the need for pertinent descriptions becomes even more apparent if we take into consideration the progressive enlargement of the public decision-making sphere, as well as the dialectic dimension associated with every urban project, where every stakeholder, be it public or private, is increasingly called upon to justify and share his decisions. Thus, insofar as the architectural project is primarily intended as a set of describing actions, which represent and simultaneously organise the *physical* transformation of places, the definition of some "geographies" becomes the main referring element. And it does so in a double way.

On the one hand, the objective is to recognise and build the identity of places, which intensively consist in historically embedded events, memories and meanings, but are also extensively characterised by spatial articulations, physical and environmental connotations, as well as morphological settlements. On the other hand, the objective is to represent the conditions under which such settlements take place, by taking stock of the territorial power structure, the vertical divisions - in terms of territorial specialisation according to different functions and dominating entities - as well as the horizontal ones - according to the fragmentation of the political power with regard to transformation. Thus, the *Grand Scale* architecture can try to act on these *physical* and *political* geographies, whose intersection generates the contingent existence of the metropolis, by shaping the form, in its double meaningfulness.

II. Borders
Some of the projects currently at a drafting stage for the metropolitan area of Turin could be used as an example to illustrate the changed conditions under which reductionist territorial interpretations combine with partial rationales of local government actions - although "protected" by *morphological-territorial fixed assets* capable of establishing considerable degrees of settlement consistency and continuity. These are essentially infrastructural projects which force us to reconsider the action perspective, both in political and technical terms, given their intrinsically metropolitan nature (and extension).
Unlike other extensive projects - including redesigning agricultural and water parks, defining coordination rules for settlement developments, landscape planning, etc. - infrastructural projects ensure a certain degree of linearity and control over their implementation development. From their layout, it is possible to infer some constant elements in the works' sections, in the relationship with the flows' networks, thus elaborating, step by step, the final and executive hypotheses leading to the setting up of the building site. It is not a coincidence that infrastructures were indeed one of the major material drivers of the most recent transformations in the Turin metropolis. The development of an infrastructural project is perhaps the only category of large scale transformations that could be dangerously assimilated (for procedural reasons) to an ordinary building transformation, originating from a regulation and then developing into successive and mutually inferable phases of approximation. Nevertheless, this linearity conceals a key issue for the reassessment of the *Grand Scale* architecture: it is precisely through the centrality of the technical rationality in the infrastructural project that the arguments on the plural and conflicting housing dimension can be made more effective, falsifiable and translatable.
In other words, these infrastructural projects make it possible to *recognise* the new and necessary metropolitan dimension, by physically characterising settlement patterns even before any legislative proposal on metropolitan areas. Indeed, the current conditions around the Turin metropolis allow us to discern a set of projects

on what could be defined as a sort of *North-West City*, which will witness some of the main infrastructure and settlement transformations in the coming years. These will include the high speed train and the related logistical system; a metropolitan rail system (SFM); a redesigned infrastructural axis in *corso Marche* with all the related transformation zones - the industrial brownfield sites of *Alenia* and *Fiat Mirafiori* and the project for a new hospital hub in *Città della salute*; its intersection with peri-urban open spaces and waterways; the dismantling of the municipal landfill along the *Stura* river; the transformation areas across the north ring-road close to the *Falchera* neighbourhood; the reconfiguration of big industrial centres between Turin and its neighbouring municipalities; the dismantling of the *Vanchiglia* railway yard for the construction of Underground Line 2 and its connection with the *Passante Ferroviario* and *Spina centrale* (the Underground Railway Link and the Central Backbone Route). A whole set of issues and areas amounting to a few million square meters, following the considerable changes triggered by the Gregotti and Cagnardi Town Planning Scheme in the mid-90s, which are today partially concluded.

All of these issues are in connection and in conflict with each other - be it only for the internal order of priorities - even though there is not a unique place especially provided for their development. A critical element and a constant risk is the inability to seize the territorial potential of infrastructural projects, by limiting them to a restrictively engineering interpretation. The territory is designed and built by lines and infrastructural spaces, even before being defined by the great areal elements of constructions, open spaces and monofunctional fences. This might sound obvious to those who are knowledgeable about history and about contemporary territorial transformation processes. Nonetheless, there continues to be a predominant reductive vision which conceives infrastructures uniquely in terms of flows, movements of goods and people, thus minimising the constructive and morphological value of infrastructures with respect to the physical territory. The burdensome management of transformations in terms of extremely complicated and diversified technical rationales - the aforementioned *disciplinary borders* - runs the risk of overshadowing the need to truly consider the effects of these projects on *living conditions*. The very compensation criteria and impact assessment, in terms of energy but also of land consumption and building density, run the risk of becoming linear and deterministic operations generating self-regarding actions. The mobilisation of various stakeholders involved in a great infrastructural project is often seen as a strongly critical indicator, rather than as an opportunity to reflect

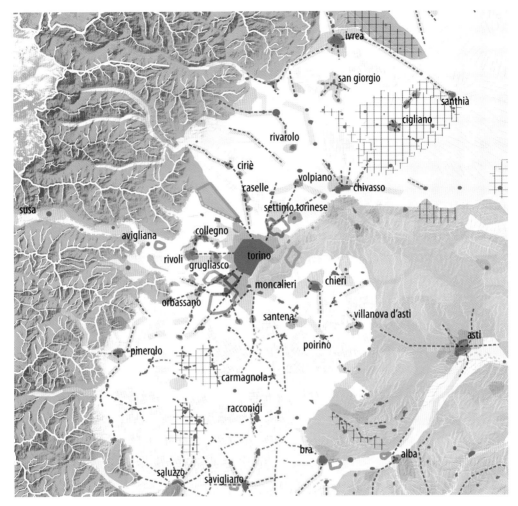

Map of the settlement structure of the Turin Metropolitan Area, designed by Dipradi-Polytechnic of Turin for the Landscape Plan of the Piedmont Region (graphic processing Andrea Delpiano, 2009)

upon and reconsider the territorial scale. Agreement among different stakeholders is reached by apportioning compensation works which, in order to satisfy different specific interests, necessarily acquire a fragmented character. After all, these processes are not capable of producing a real added-value for territorial set-up. However, all of these infrastructural projects have a very interesting potential in "structuring" the transformations that will concern Turin and its metropolitan territory in the near future. Planning an infrastructure can entail, in the first place, working on the morphology of the city and of its territory. If infrastructures can *generate* transformation, they can also potentially *regulate* and *organise* it. The outline of a crossing infrastructure, such as ring roads or clearways, is often capable of showing, already in its preliminary form - even though with a "negative image" - the morphology that will be subsequently acquired by the construction. Providing the outline with an absolute value - i.e. crossing the territory while bumping into as few obstacles as possible - runs the risk of neglecting the specific role played by infrastructures in the Turin area or, more generally, all over Italy, particularly since after the Second World War, where roads have taken up the task of "organising" an incremental model of territorial transformation.

III. North-West City

Out of all the various infrastructural projects that will be concerning the Turin metropolitan territory in the near future, three of them deserve to be pinpointed here for their exemplificative character and for the technical and political actions that they require to be implemented.

The first one is the project for the new *corso Marche*, which is a very interesting example to better understand the possible implications of an often hackneyed word - *governance* - within the ordinary practices of territorial transformation. One just needs to recompose and *assemble* all the "politically consolidated" transformation images, expressed in the town planning schemes, in order to understand that such a new axis will be much more articulated and complex than a "simple" infrastructure, which will be crossing the western part of the Turin metropolis, from north to south. The *corso Marche*, which is the last of three *central linear axes* provided for by the Gregotti and Cagnardi Town Planning scheme - together with the Po river axis and the *Passante Ferroviario* under the *Spina Centrale* - presents itself as an infrastructure which straddles different administrative *borders* and is framed by two historical architectural and environmental cornerstones: the *Palazzina di caccia di Stupinigi*, in

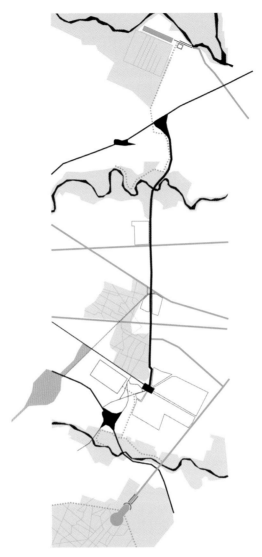

The axis of Corso Marche: the historical and architectural landmarks of the Venaria (north) and hunting lodge of Stupinigi in the (south), the infrastructure system and river environmental related to the courses of the rivers Sangone, Dora and Stura; The main areas of transformation.

the south, and the *Venaria Palace*, in the north. This condition has quickly highlighted the critical absence of "institutionalised" fora dedicated to issues management. Even the in-depth study, commissioned to the *Gregotti Associati* cabinet by the Province of Turin, has sparked considerations which have been dominated by an interpretation of infrastructures as mobility axes, with all its consequences in terms of landscape constraints. At the same time, a series of settlement and environment-related projects have started to come forward and, by leveraging on the new infrastructure, have become increasingly visible, thus becoming a highly critical issue, but one that is full of potential too. As a matter of fact, the short-circuiting between infrastructural and territorial projects has already started in ordinary practices. Thus, different projects, which are administratively governed by fragmented political and technical actions, have begun aggregating around the infrastructure and providing it with a significance that had remained so far implicit. This significance turns the *corso Marche* engineering project into a territorial project which, because of its metropolitan character straddling different borders, must find suitable places and instruments to elaborate open and interpretable designs capable of orienting both political, technical and planning choices.

Moving towards the east, towards the hills and along this potential north-west city, we find other infrastructural opportunities that would be suitable to provide inspiration for larger territorial projects. Here, the roll-out of the high speed train is the main topic, together with a general review of a territory which, at least since the railway was built towards the end of the 80s, has historically functioned as an "infrastructural corridor" providing access to the city for those arriving from Milan or the Po Valley. The territory is structured around a frame whose close texture is rather differentiated in terms of fibre and permeability. It contains wide-spanning ring-road and motorway infrastructures, historical railway lines coupled today with high speed lines, but also local roads around which urban centres have been organised, and "white" roads, which are material deposits of the agricultural landscape that used to characterise the entry to the plain until the second post-war period. As shown in the housing patterns of the area between Turin and *Settimo*, what is missing here is a true hierarchization of such a web, in order to be able to solve critical situations in terms of accessibility and permeability and, at the same time, enhance highly valuable landscapes, starting from the river banks where the *Po* and the *Stura* merge together. Here too, the opportunity is given by the possibility to establish interconnections between territorial *re-structuring* processes and the transformation of some large industrial brownfields. Again, just like for *corso Marche*, administrative borders become blurred when approached by a territorial project that wants to overcome a fragmented and disaggregated rationale, by looking for materials to re-interpret, implement and enhance within long-existing permanent entities. A project that uses materials found on the ground, such as waterlines, geo-morphological features, old frames and textures, as well as recent structures, to create meaningful *images* that can stimulate useful considerations and orientations for the transformation project.

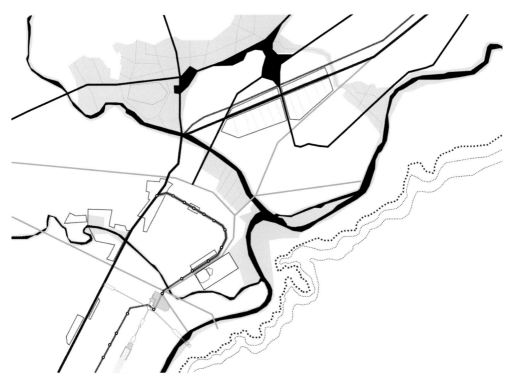

The northern quadrant of the metropolitan area in Turin: the environmental system related to the confluence of the Rivers Po and the Stura, the infrastructure system and rail, the new Metro line 2, the main areas of transformation.

These considerations on the northern part of Turin can also embrace another infrastructural project centred on the issues of public mobility and urban requalification. This is the project concerning the construction of a second Underground line in Turin (Line 2), which will be running across the city from north to south, criss-crossing, right in the historical centre, Underground Line 1, which already connects *Porta Nuova* central station to the western portion of the metropolitan area and which will soon also reach the *Lingotto* station in the south. Line 2 will be organised around two strategic hubs. In the north, it will be organised around the new *Rebaudengo* station, which is the heart of the latest transformation segment in the brownfield sites along the *Passante Ferroviario*, the so-called *"Spina 4"*. In the south, it will be organised around the *Fiat Mirafiori* area and along the new axis in *corso Marche*. Within the whole project for the new underground line, the most favourable opportunities for a rapid initiation of transformation processes are to be found around the northern segment. The key issues revolve around the dismantling of wide portions of railway areas: in the east, the *Vanchiglia* railway yard and, in the west, the *"Spina 4"* along the *Passante Ferroviario*, interconnected by an open-air rail track, the "trincerone", for a total surface of almost one million square meters.

Unlike *corso Marche* and the northern area, the Line 2 project is contained within the limits of the consolidated city. However, its interest does not quite lie in the way borders are worked out and highlighted, but rather in the fact that it is conceived, from a very early stage, with the intention to combine mobility issues with settling and environmental themes. Indeed, the construction of the new public transport line will engender the transformation of brownfield or underutilized areas, which will be followed by a pervading requalification process of the existing city, of the "Milan barrier" which is the historical working class neighbourhood along the north-east border of the city. The incipient Line 2 experience is, at least in its preliminary phase, an opportunity to experience true *integration* between public mobility and settlement projects. And this is an aspect which cannot be taken for granted, at least in Italy. In this context, the technical complexity of an infrastructural project consisting in the construction of a new underground line highlights the need to anticipate the critical hubs, as well as the urban and metropolitan potential triggered by the project. It is a large scale anticipation exercise which tries to veer away from a conformity vision, typical of "quantitative" urban planning in relation to sectoral technical specialities, in order to orient the action towards a more argumentative perspective, capable of *recognising* issues and *representing* the possible scenarios on which the very legitimacy of the project should be founded. All these issues indicate a potential, but at the same time critical dimension to the project, not only in terms of *scale*, but primarily from a conceptual and operating perspective. First of all, this is a political issue, determined by the lack of institutional and negotiation fora, where one could develop a vision capable of seizing the plurality of values enshrined in every project. Secondly, this is also a technical issue, characterised by a tendency to handle complex projects by applying procedural and regulatory conformity criteria, thus leading to partial sectoral responses and scenarios. This problem, however, is mainly internal to the way in which issues are conceived by the very architectural science, which views technical and political data as being "external" to its subject field. By reversing the issue, we could say that indeed the organisation of morphological representations, through the project, would give *visibility* to political and technical issues related to urban and territorial transformation. This would imply "weakening" the traditional status of architecture and is therefore uneasily perceived by the professional and academic world, since the project would use its representation potential to serve external intentions. In so doing, it would become a "deformable" strategic and dialogue-oriented instrument, where the plurality of *interpretations* around it would prevail over the need for the *constructions* that determine it.

Today, even within local government practices, the plurality and vagueness of the processes that set the context for potential physical arrangements in the Turin metropolitan area favour a less stringent use of quantitative-qualitative rules, according to non-negotiable sectoral and specific rationales. This contributes to supporting a "dialectic culture" [Gehtmann, 2001], capable of consolidating "preferable places" [Perelman, 1977] well before planning productive interventions in the construction sector according to conformity procedures.

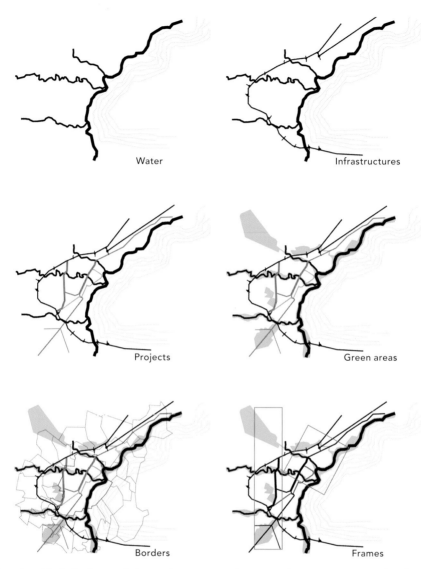

Water   Infrastructures

Projects   Green areas

Borders   Frames

Spatial matrices (clockwise from top): the catchment area and existing infrastructure systems, the planning of infrastructure and the environmental systems, the administrative boundaries, the planning frames the northwest quadrant of Turin metropolitan area

In orange, the main projects of settlement and infrastructure that characterizes the Turin metropolitan area in the near future

Design figure: the new North-Western City

Bibliography
CAVALLARI MURAT, A., 1968, *Forma urbana ed architettura nella Torino barocca*, Torino, Utet
DEMATTEIS, G., 1989, *Contesti e situazioni territoriali in Piemonte. Abbozzo di una geografia regionale dei possibili*, "Urbanistica", n. 96
DEMATTEIS, G., 1991, *Per progettare il territorio*, "Archivio di studi urbani e regionali", n. 42
DE ROSSI, A., DURBIANO, G., 2006, *Torino 1980-2011. La trasformazione e le sue immagini*, Torino, Allemandi
GABETTI, R., ISOLA, A., 1988, *Nuovi valore per l'ambiente*, "Domus", n. 700
GEHTMANN C. F., 2001, *La fondazione ultima versus il fondamento del sapere e dell'agire legato al mondo della vita*, in BORRELLI, M. (edited by), 2001, *Metodologia delle scienze sociali: dissoluzione della filosofia, discorso sulla soggettività, fondazione ultima, razionalismo critico e filosofia politica, valori e valutazioni, ragione trasversale, metafisica e esperienza*, Quaderni interdisciplinari 5, Cosenza, Pellegrini Editore
PERELMAN C., 1981, *Il dominio retorico. Retorica e argomentazione*, Torino, Einaudi (1977)
SECCHI, B., 2001, *Prima lezione di urbanistica*, Bari, Laterza
VIGANÒ, P., 1999, *La città elementare*, Milano, Skira

Part IV Overtures
Edited by Antonio De Rossi

Geography, poetics and architecture in the construction of places

Giuseppe Dematteis

Language of the places: geographical, poetic-literary and architectural
Let us try to imagine architecture and geography as "arts" with a referential relationship to the environment. This certainly does not fulfill their whole essence (even
though someone might think so, as far as geography is concerned) but it is a common ground for all arts; it allows an overall self-confrontation between all the potentially mimetic arts, i.e. poetic-literary description, painting, photography, theater,
music, and dance, to name a few. I am only going to examine the triangle constituted by geography, poetic description and architecture. A dissymmetry is immediately evident: the relationship of geography with places is translated by a discursive
language which is partly figurative; the poetic-literary discourse is expressed through words and the writing process; the language of architecture talks about the places *by means of* the places themselves, attributing forms and functions. At first sight
it might seems that this difference lies essentially in the fact that only architecture
transforms the places. Nonetheless, things are not as simple, because places are not
only what they physically look like, but also entities which are built and experienced
as symbols by theirs inhabitants or visitors: Paris, London, Florence, San Remo etc.
would surely be different without Zola, Dickens, Pratolini, Calvino etc[1] To this symbolic construction we must add the contribution of a few geographical and literary
texts that do not limit themselves to reproducing reality; they prefer to interpret it,
unveiling its unlimited generative possibilities and hidden potentialities. It would be
nonetheless misleading to consider literary texts as only operating on a symbolic level, and works of architecture as only affecting material reality. On the one hand we
must keep in mind that symbolic representations are potentially performative, which
means they can act upon the material form of places. On the other hand everyone
knows that architectural forms provides the places with a strong symbolic charge;
thus it is a manifestation of a geo-poetic.

Metaphor and fiction
The main differences are probably to be found elsewhere. From the perspective of a
geographer observing architecture from the outside, I would like to focus on the use
of metaphor and fiction. Metaphors obviously have a vital role in literary language,
and a significant one in the geographic language as well[2]. In the field of architecture I doubt that metaphors could be dealt with in the same way, given the lack of

---

[1] See F. Moretti, *Atlante del romanzo europeo 1800-1900*, Torino, Einaudi, 1997, and B. Westphal, *Geocritica. Reale
Finzione Spazio*, Roma, Armando, 2009.

[2] I have dealt with the issue in my essay *Le metafore della Terra*, Milano, Feltrinelli, 1985. See also A. Vanolo,
"L'immagine del sistema economico mondiale. Riflessioni sulle metafore geografiche", Rivista Geografica Italiana, 116 (2009), pp. 1-22.

indefiniteness and freedom enjoyed by the work of architecture with respect to the literary text. The architectural work cannot ignore its material and social dimension, even when it is highly emotionally charged and aimed at providing a meaning for the landscapes and the urban context in which it is embedded (the "center", the "door" etc.) I am going to take no notice of the idea that a building can act as a metaphor simply by taking the shape of something else to which it intends to refer (i.e. the profile of a mountain). It actually seems to me the expression of a trivial mimesis, if compared to the power and the immense scope of literary metaphors.

As far as the fictional aspect is concerned, we all know that it has no boundaries within literary discourse. We can discuss whether it has some in its geographical representations, that is to say whether the description of a purely fictional territory could still be considered geography, but this is not our concern. It seems to me that fiction does have limits in the architectural field, since even the Sleeping Beauty's castle in Eurodisney must be built with certain criteria. On the other hand, within these obvious limits, architecture seems to be widely functional, to the extent in which it "derealizes" itself by decontextualizing itself, producing a reality which "imitates fictions"[3]. We could argue that the performative role of literary and geographic imagination can lead us to analogous results, but the difference is that we are dealing with fictions which do not limit themselves to imitating or reproducing imaginary models: they shape themselves using complex interpretative filters, capable of producing different forms and entire contexts that are nor predictable or exactly foreseeable. Take for example some venues in the Alps, modeled on the imagery of Romantic literature; or the reclaimed land, or some urban areas (in the Soviet Union, in Italy and elsewhere) that are utopias materialized in historical-geographical contexts that interact with the models, adapt them and influence their actual shaping.

Responsibility

A different relationship to fiction translates into a different degree of responsibility towards society, with respect to the constructed and lived-in environment. I believe the poet is totally free of responsibility, since his words and images have the power to evoke a countless plurality of worlds. It is up to us to choose what we eventually want to realize. The geographer has a more ambiguous stance, because while describing *this* world he/she has to choose the elements and the underlying connections, according to some implicit criteria of relevance. The geographer cannot but interpret the particular reality that is the object of description; as Gadamer teaches us, the person who interprets always has some project in mind, even when

---

[3] M. Augé, *Disneyland e altri non luoghi*, Torino, Bollati Boringhieri 1999, p. 48.

unconscious of it. Nevertheless the project, in which the geographer plays a part, guiding us toward a certain vision of reality, remains implicit. Should this implicitly suggested reality be catastrophic by disgrace, the geographer would only be a bad teacher, one that no modern court could punish; on the other hand, an engineer whose bridge collapsed for a project failure would definitely be condemned. For example the geographer Walter Christaller surely did not experienced trouble in the aftermath of the Nazi occupation because he had described Bavaria as a system of central places, but because he assumed the role of a planner and used his theory to (explicitly) plan his territorial organization of the territories occupied by Hitler beyond the Oder River.

It seems to me that the architect has quite a different role. His/her fictions are *simulations*; in the words of C. Raffestin, they are the "rational construction of a dream willing to take the place of present reality (...) by means of an invention"[4], of a well-defined project; a project that foresee a definite, specific building. As a consequence, the responsibility of the architect as a designer is much more specific than the poet's and the geographer's. The issue at stake not only concerns the solidity of a building, or the safety of its occupants. The main responsibility concerns the shape of places, and the system of connections in which the work of architecture carves its place; it concerns the symbolic values of the landscape, the ecological-environmental and the socio-economic ones. It regards the chance to improve or deteriorate the territory, seen as a common patrimony, and thus to *determine* the quality of the life of its inhabitants and visitors. No scholar, artist or geographer has this power.

Such a high and complex level of responsibility can only be found in the legislative and executive dimension of the regulations that affect the local quality of the life, both directly (building and urban planning norms, environmental laws and public goods protection) and indirectly (private goods and tax regime, local authorities' duties and powers).

It is nonetheless true that these are binding norms for the architect, but creativity provides a sufficiently wide range of possible options, so that his/her decisions can be determinant for the quality of the lived-in places. Unlike the legislator, in a liberal-democratic society the architect exerts this power beyond any form of control. Not only there is no authority with such a discretional power, there is not even a democratic form of control of his/her work: despite having the powers to decide on existentially significant public goods, the project architect is not elected by the people, and most of the times the quality of the projects is ignored by the discretional evaluation of elected administrators. The other side of this great freedom of deci-

---

[4] C. Raffestin, *Dalla nostalgia del territorio al desiderio di paesaggio*. Firenze, Alinea, p. 15.

sion, which is surely positive, is the big responsibility to the inhabitants of the place. But it would be deeply unfair to leave this entire burden on the back of the architect alone. First of all I would like to point out that, beyond the constraints of the market, there is a shared responsibility between the client and the general feeling and consensus of the place. This would explain the sharp differences in the constructed quality of places that are subject to the same general market and State laws. To the extent that the examples of poor quality are ascribable to a cultural deficit of local (and national) societies, the responsibility for the bad projects includes those whose task is to elaborate and spread a culture of the quality of places.

From knowledge to the politics of place
As far as elaboration is concerned, the disciplines involved are the scientific ones, in particular Environmental and Territory Sciences. Geography, being able to provide connective, synthetic, and implicitly planning visions of places cannot just lie in the background, also because it is widely taught in schools. It can be held responsible not only for the consequences of providing interpretations and descriptions of specific realities, but also for a poor effort to spread a culture of the places that is capable of affecting the collective visions and behavior. Without this effort any planning activity of the territory, the landscape and the environment is doomed to fail.
More in general, the issue is how the knowledge of places is produced by the various disciplines. To put this schematically: at one end we have a type of academic elaboration that is largely self-referential (colloquially called "theoretic") and that does not leave any mark in the collective visions and behavior, even if it can have extremely negative consequences when assessing political decisions. At the other end there is a knowledge which starts from the actions and the "wordless thinking" of the territorial actors, aimed at activating some forms of interaction with both contextual knowledge and more or less implicit planning visions of the local subjects[5]. It does not strive to translate all into just one language or into a harmonic and pacified vision of what a good quality of (living in) the places should be. On the other hand it does accept the mutual irreducibility of these polyphonic visions and the conflicts that they normally produce at the time of shaping a local context[6]. Unfortunately the territory of this geography –like the one of operating architecture– is only one, even though it has to satisfy the diverse and multiple needs of its inhabitants. It also

---

[5] See for example L. Decandia, *Polifonie urbane. Oltre i confini della visione prospettica*, Roma, Meltemi, 2008. In particular chapter 6: "Breaking the window which isolates us from the world in order to return to it".
[6] As for geography, these are also the stance of the followers of Nigel Thrift's *non representational theory*, which in turn refers to the *actor network theory* by sociologist Bruno Latour. For an overall view of these positions, largely present in Anglo Saxon geography, see J. Murdoch, *Post-structuralist Geography*, London, Sage, 2005.

has to be presented in order to fully satisfy these needs in *just one* project, which must be physically realizable. To my perspective this is the central node, hard to be untied, of the relationship between politics and the shape of the places, which is mostly a relationship between presentation and representation, between what is done and what is though (or supposed) to be realizable.

The problem is of a political order, but to treat it adequately we should take a step back, starting on a pre-political ground. In this case, to shift from "many" to "one" does not mean to transform –that is to reduce– diverse visions and languages into a single one. This is what the media do, as instruments of power that are increasingly used to create consensus[7]; therefore they are less oriented to give answers to the specific needs of our relationship to the place and, generally speaking, to deal with the "world of life", which is everyday more disconnected from politics. We should try to foster intercommunication between the different underlying reasons implied by different visions and expressed by different, often wordless, languages. During the cognitive phase, the relation to be built is not many-to-one, but many-to-many, so that cognitive abstraction does not consist in generalizing, but in mediating between different *frames of reference*[8].

I think we should start from this point, and particularly from all the meanings of co-existing, as a practice of living together of all living beings and things themselves, which M. Merleau-Ponty, [9]saw as previous to the meanings produced through reasoning and discourse. This pre-logic and pre-political attitude, open to others and the world, is what allows its diverse potentialities to be enhanced and expanded. We find ourselves compelled to assume the resulting responsibility of a being-in-common which is at the same time ecological, cultural, social, economical and political. I think that a common project meant to shape places can only be built on these bases. It does not need to be harmonic, nor homogeneous or solidified, but it ought to pave the way for a mutual recognition of differences, disharmonies and conflicts. It is not just a matter of mutual tolerance; it is the need to foster a fruitful interchange between co-inhabitants, with different needs and values, in the building process of the territory, seen as a common good.

---

[7] M. Castells, *Potere e comunicazione*, Milano, Univesità Bocconi ed., 2009.

[8] N. Bingham e N. Thrift, "Some new instructions for travellers. The geography of Bruno Latour and Michel Serres", in M. Crang e N. Thrift (eds), *Thinking space*, London-New York, Routledge, 2000, pp. 281-301, v. p. 286. I am using the term "frames of reference" in reference to everyday life, as does L. Gallino (*La sociologia. Concetti fondamentali*, Torino, Utet Libreria, 1989, pp. 233-234).

[9] In *Il visibile e l'invisibile*, Milano, Bompiani, 1993, pp. 39-40.

[10] From the above mentioned *Le metafore della Terra*.

Heuristic and poetic metaphors

In the introduction to this volume, Antonio De Rossi -if I properly read his words- not only takes a stance in this sense, but also assigns an important, interpretative and constructive role to geography. I will try to focus on this aspect, keeping in mind the aforementioned connections between geography, poetry and architecture. Situating poetry (and fictional literature in general) within this triad cannot be a random operation: it has to be regarded as a bridge, whose absence would mean limiting geography to a "scientific" interpretation of the places, only pursuing effective interventions. It is nonetheless true that geography can give an essential contribution in this respect because, as I have been long saying, [10] it is a discipline that makes a systematic use of metaphors as a heuristic instrument. This relates geography to "hard sciences", where metaphors create an "inductive openness" and a "non defining determination of references"[11] with the goal of talking about things that are not well defined yet, in order to provide them with a more precise definition. Since geographical representations are highly connective, they provide a comprehensive vision of places, which normally suggests new interpretative and implicitly planning hypothesis. These hypotheses will be eventually verified by disciplines that are less connective, but more analytically prepared, and these projects will be built into a definite shape by engineers, architects, planners and economists. In this manner geography can play a part in the sustainability of our relationship with ecosystems, in protecting biodiversity and cultural diversity, in economic development, and in providing *spatial equity* of access to common goods, services and the likes.

These are undoubtedly important aspects, but they are nonetheless insufficient to satisfy the need of a polyphonic and shared interpretation and construction of places. Insufficient at least to my opinion, because they reduce the poetic liaison with architecture to a mere instrumental factor. This type of geography, serving a rationality which is targeted to be effective, uses a metaphor that, despite starting at the same point, goes the opposite direction with respect to poetry. The latter pursues an endless dilation of meanings, whereas geography (the effectiveness-oriented one) limits its own imagination to formulating connecting and explicative hypothesis. These in turn must be transmitted to disciplines and techniques capable of reducing their ambiguity, so that they fit in an unambiguous definition, codification, and calculation. While poetry keeps opening, architecture helps closing what it has opened before. One creates the possibility, the other one satisfy the need. It is surely worthy, but limited. Can we ask for something else?

---

[11] R. Byd e T. Khun, *La metafora nella scienza*, Feltrinelli, Milano, 1983, p. 23.

[12] In: " Dans la tête de Janus. Réflexions sur le coté poétique de la Géographie ", in: C. Raffestin e J.B. Racine eds, *Géotopiques. L'imagination géographique*, Universités de Genève et Lausanne, 1985, pp. 109- 125. A good part of it is translated in "Nella testa di Giano. Riflessioni sulla geografia poetica", *Urbanistica urban planning* 82, 1986, pp. 100-107.

A few years ago[12] I tried to imagine a poetic geography in which metaphors helped us to overcome what appears as "real", that is ideologies, stereotypes and common places, for they have influence on our way to see, think and practice space. In other words: a geography that is open to new possible world rather than using spatial representation to underline this particular need, and at the same time can prove their contingency. On the other hand I used to think that geography, as a science, should play a "public" role, which entailed a limited affinity to poetry. Now I am changing my mind, because I regard the "public" role of geography as a far more complex aspect. I do not think it only produces representations whose inner metaphoric ambiguity necessarily has to be unveiled in order to meet the needs of rational discourse –be it directed to technical applications or to the creation of a real contrastive dialog in the agora. If we regard this *reductio ad unum* as unfair and unviable at the time of discussing the shape and quality of the single places, the ambiguous geographic metaphors become totally compatible, and even valuable, in the dialogic practices that use non-discursive forms of language as well. Therefore the objects and the subjects can present themselves, instead of just representing, or representing themselves.[13] The implicit knowledge thus reveals itself in the practice ("thinking with one's hands", in the word of S. Weil), and the implicit desires and projects can come to light. In this way geography can restart its journey (which has never really interrupted)[14] hand in hand with poetry, regaining that emotive and emotional charge that is vital to establish a proper connection with the places and their inhabitants.[15] I believe that only a poetic imagination that draws freely on the dark and swarming well of life can bridge the gap between geography and architecture. It will be able to suggest to architecture, urban, and landscape projects the specific modes of co-inhabiting of the different places, the multiple needs and desires that contribute -sometimes in a conflictive manner- to the shaping of a territory meant as a common good, and, ultimately, the possible alternatives that lie in the shadow of the false needs.

---

[13] See the issue no. 33 (2002) of *Geoforum*, dedicated to the Enacting geographies and especially the introduction by J.D. Dewesbury et al. (pp. 437-440).

[14] From Homer, who in ancient times was considered the first geographer, to the Eindruck, practiced and theorized by A. Humboldt in his description of the landscape, to Eric Dardel's (1899-1967) poetic geography, to the recent works of a few Italian authors, such as Eugenio Turri.

[15] See B. Bochet e J-B. Racine, "Connaître et penser la ville: des formes aux affects et aux emotions, explorer ce qu'il nous reste à trouver. Manifeste pour une géographie sensible autant que rigoureuse ", *Geocarrefour*, 27 (2002), no. 2, pp. 117-132.

A few methodological issues, drawing on the gained experience[1]

Arnaldo Bagnasco

[1] This essay was presented during the congress organised by the *Associazione Torino Internazionale*, entitled *"The North-West City, the Northern Triangle"*, held on 28th November 2008, in Turin.

I have been entrusted with the task of providing some notes in order to kick off this day, during which we will try to reflect upon a new phase in the life of a city, in a world which has changed rapidly, perhaps more rapidly than we expected. I will do so by drawing on some suggestions which seem to stem from the experience gained over the past few years. These will be somehow background or methodological issues, which it would be useful to bear in mind for future discussions.

1. Turin: what are we talking about?

The first issue concerns the following question: what are we talking about when we mention Turin? This is not a trivial question and goes well back in time. When we think of Turin as a society whose borders are defined by the municipality bearing this name, in fact, we only carve out part of the "true" Turin, both in economical and sociological terms.

The real topic of our discussion is not a society consisting in around nine hundred thousand inhabitants, but rather a society made up of slightly less than two million people who are interconnected in a complex network of relationships. This is the local society that we should focus on, with all its problems, opportunities and potential strategies. A local society is organised according to a multi-level governance, with different competences and limits. Of course, it is not my task here to decide which institutional set-up would be best suited to our case: it is a political issue, not a technical one. It is clear, however, that we need a set-up which enables us to conceive and organise Turin in its enlarged wholeness. Over the past few years, we have made considerable steps forward, but in my opinion, this issue has now become very urgent. In times of crisis, it is necessary to be able to easily govern the whole metropolitan area. The key concept of metropolitan area is enshrined in principles, but also enforced, for instance, in the organisation of services covering large areas. However, we are often constrained by limited conceptual schemes, when it comes to assessing problems, presenting issues, budgeting the available resources or identifying and empowering stakeholders capable of promoting innovation. This is tantamount to shooting oneself in the foot, because we do not maximise opportunities and resources at a time when we most need them. This is somehow paradoxical, if we consider that Turin was quick to understand that strong cities would become the new economic stakeholders, as a result of globalisation and the opening up of markets.

2. Cities at a time of economic changes

This is the second issue that we should take into consideration, which was important yesterday, and is all the more important today. As a starting point, we ought to use the basic assumption that capital, enterprises and people are now moving around markets and places, in search of favourable conditions. If there are good reasons, under certain conditions, to decide to move elsewhere or reorient one's relationships towards the outside, indeed there are also good reasons to stay and grow where we are settled or to reach this space from the outside. The point is that, although they are numerous, the conditions that would make us stay, because they favour economic efficiency rather than inappropriate and therefore unnecessary advantages, have become less constraining than in the past and, what is more, need to be better constructed and continuously reproduced. There are many good reasons for which efficient enterprises and people should concentrate in a given area. Globalisation goes hand in hand with a visible regionalisation of the economic structure. On the plan, we can observe different types of local systems, with varying sizes and specialisations, which have become new or renewed economic stakeholders. There are several reasons to support proximity work, such as the possibility to rely on suitable industrial partners, a financial system capable of supporting new initiatives, an efficient administration, schools and research institutes geared towards economic specialisations, fast communication systems and properly equipped environments for everyday life, just to mention a few. I do not deem it necessary to provide here a full list.

In the light of such parameters, many European cities have adopted measures, over the past few decades, in order to keep pace with globalisation. In a rather generalised manner, we observed cities becoming aware of the resources they could invest in the new context to make them thrive.

Following the end of *Fordism*, while people were trying to understand where urban growth should be oriented, analysts and attentive policymakers showed interest in Turin and in its urban innovation patterns. As a result, ideas began to move around, just like the various European key players in that growth process. The most favourable conditions emerged in those places where processes of competence and resource decentralisation had been initiated, so as to enable cities to act freely in a context, however, characterised by large scale modernised country infrastructures, and national and regional rules organising the wide "game field" where cities and enterprises moved around. I have used this metaphor on purpose. I think that it would be useful to imagine the national State and regional Governments as being the organisers of wide "game fields", and cities and enterprises as being their players. You cannot play a good game without good cities and enterprises or, more generally, good local systems. In this respect, we can also imagine cities and enterprises as being together the stakeholders of the new economy.

Over the years, the acceleration and intensification of context-setting processes has had an impact on cities. Today, in order to be able to stay afloat in a society of fluxes and networks, without being swept away by it, cities must take action by profiting from what they have learnt over the years on their functioning and existence.

3. A new political task
We have thus managed to elucidate another important methodological issue concerning the necessary political action observed in the most active cities over the past decades. Together with their political leaders and key civil society representatives, they clearly understood the necessity of digging out, mobilising and, insofar as possible, shaping all the available resources within a comprehensive plan, while constantly replicating the conditions capable of supporting growth. This was a political task in a wider sense, since it did not only concern the activity of public institutions, but it also involved, within European cities, policymakers and public authority representatives, category associations, chambers of commerce, universities and research centres, banks and foundations, individuals in touch with the public or involved in specific forms of cooperation on specific occasions.
In this context, the decisive role of politics, in the strict sense of the word, was the following: convincing different stakeholders, who can often suddenly decide to move elsewhere or re-orient their relationships, to carry out crossed investments, by simultaneously jumping at opportunities and setting the conditions for a long-lasting collaboration. This task, performed to increase efficiency rather than reproduce locally inefficient relationships, is by no means an easy one. Indeed, it must respect the autonomy of those enterprises operating on the market, as well as market audits, while recognising that no local system can shut itself from the rest of the world, but has to be necessarily involved in relationships and external networks. It is a task that requires new skills and an adequate leadership. The general impression is that success stories have always required a decisive and realistic political leadership over processes. "We have acted as a team", this is what we hear say when a city has achieved a certain result by coordinating different stakeholders. But what are the rules for a good team game? How can we ensure that different interests find their place in the game? How can we consolidate and make the game systematic over time, even when the stakeholders change? How can we enable the comparison and confrontation of different perspectives? These are the types of questions that need to find an answer, if the perspectives are to be consolidated. These are the types of questions that innovative cities asked themselves and replied to, in a way that was suited to their history and peculiarities, without losing sight

of an established principle: today public and private stakeholders contribute to shaping public policies by cooperating with each other in order to design decisions that can be easily implemented once they have been adopted.

One could argue that it all sounds slightly complicated or simply based on individual will. But we could react by saying that, all over Europe, many cities tried to consolidate similar methodologies and obtained excellent results. Such a successful and consolidated experience constitutes a resource for the local government tasked with political harmonisation, since it allows for the coordination of stakeholders and action perspectives that the market alone cannot conciliate, and that politics, for their part, have difficulties accommodating. Furthermore, there is an implication that should not be underestimated: if properly understood, it tends to widen the public sphere, because it draws together different stakeholders who are called upon to publicly defend an opinion or an action in the name of the common interest. And this is somehow what we are doing here today. Let us get back to Turin, then, for some brief remarks. At least since the mid-eighties, but in fact even before, it was possible to see that Turin had changed forever, for the essential reason that the industrial society, as we had known it in advanced countries, had disappeared. Turin was lagging behind and it was probably going to have more difficulties finding its own way than other cities, since it had been a true example of industrial society and had a lot of economic and social issues weighing heavily on its shoulders. But it had an asset. Before becoming the city-factory, it had been one of the regional capitals of European modernisation. In so doing, it had forged an important material, cultural and professional heritage that had remained hidden, but was far from being erased. During the years of transition, in the early phase of conflicts and endurance tests, new ideas made progressively their way on how to find opportunities and ways to trace a new path. This was possible thanks to the contribution of many stakeholders, proceeding by trial and error, and building experience, with new opportunities opening up along the way as a result, for instance, of the new rules for the direct election of mayors, or the new contracting opportunities laid down by the national government.

Despite the existing weaknesses and limitations, in my opinion, even an external observer would be able to acknowledge that, over the years, we have developed the ability, or the culture I dare say, of strategic actions capable of focusing on different problems. This includes the spreading of a common vocabulary to communicate with each other; a relatively shared image of the city and of its opportunities and major criticalities; moments for public policy evaluation; the outlining of action guidelines and combined actions that have continued over time and have thus contributed, insofar as possible, to a coordinated and comprehensive picture of what was going on in the local economy and society. In reflecting upon the heritage of these years of transformation, we should also bear in mind the generation of "social capital", an expression used by economists and sociologists to designate the widespread capacity to create contexts endowed with a spirit of cooperation, and which has been recognised as being a key ingredient to development, together with economic and cultural capital, i.e. people's skills and abilities.

I will only recall two episodes in which this capacity became apparent. The first is the awarding of the Olympic Games, obtained thanks to the submission of a reliable dossier, followed by the management of the games themselves, where the whole city can be said to have mobilised. The second episode is the setting-up of *Torino Internazionale*, the association which started a pioneer process in Italy for the elaboration of a strategic plan using methods that are similar to the ones used at international level. Today, we are able to assess past experiences, appreciating the positive results while recognising the limits and missed opportunities, as well as persisting criticalities. Armed with all the economic, cultural and social capital that we have built over time, we are now faced with the challenge of the global crisis. We have to reassess the situation, cope with emergencies without undermining a more comprehensive and far-sighted vision. For instance, we will have to assess whether the policies implemented to coordinate resources, transfer technologies over to businesses and attract foreign partners need to be fine-tuned in order to support innovative sectors with guaranteed potential - such as mechanics, ICTs, biotechnologies. We will have to assess if and how the modernisation of our universities can be intensified more quickly, once it will be undisputedly acknowledged that these institutions offer the best parameters countrywide. We will have to understand why, even in favourable years, few enterprises have been started or developed further. We will have to see how we can update the context for interest representation in order to better reflect a changing environment.

We will also discuss these issues in the forthcoming roundtable. Here, I would only like to reiterate a consolidated point on which we agreed during the previous phase, and which should not be forgotten, because it has been an epoch-making feature in Turin's history: the need for a more differentiated economy, implying a more differentiated industry and an economy that is not solely industry-based but expands in the service sector. Nobody, in my opinion, nobody has ever thought that industry would stop being a fundamental resource for Turin, and that we should cease enhancing it. On this point, let us clear the ground of possible misunderstandings, which have in the past aroused unproductive disputes. Industry and the activities in related innovative sectors, mainly research and training, must continue to be supported during the crisis. However, industry alone will not suffice a great city in a post-industrial era, both for strictly economic reasons, for the organisation of urban quality life and for its social and cultural style. It is true that, in times of crisis, building an extra nursery school would be preferred to organising an event, but it would not be wise to dissipate all the results achieved, so far, as a lively and reliable cultural city, which have changed the international image of Turin in a few years. Otherwise, we would have to restart everything from scratch, because - and I underline it again - industry alone will not suffice a great city in a post-industrial era.

4. The North-West city

A difference exists between the way we used to see Turin in the past and the way we see it today, with all its strategies finding their place in a framework of macro-regional cooperation initiatives. This is not to say that this aspect was absent in the past, but the perspective is widening through a series of different initiatives, and not only as a consequence of the pressing crisis. It was already happening before, as a result of the economic and social set-up evolution in the North-West. It is likely that the new elements introduced with the federalist projects will contribute to reinforcing this trend. Rather than talk about past experiences, which could also be seen as a progressive advancement process, I can also introduce here the experience gained from observing what happens elsewhere, and which has recently become the object of many studies. It turns out that extending and integrating macro-regional frameworks for strategic actions is indeed a currently widespread tendency. A new concept has recently been introduced: the world city-region. This concept designates regional contexts, with varying sizes but always sub-national, sometimes cross-border, where economic activities and people concentrate massively and which, viewed as a whole, appear to be the economic engine of the new globalised economy. Allen J. Scott, the American geographer who has introduced this term, claims that this is necessary in order to seize new "processes of territorial and political amalgamation".

The word "amalgamation" conjures up the idea of more or less spontaneous processes involved in the adjustment of economies and societies that were relatively compatible with each other. The reference to the political sphere entails the process of shaping the amalgam, providing it with an internal organisation, with a view to presenting it as a united whole to the external world. Once again, this process does not only concern political actions in the strict sense of the word, but it involves the contribution of public and private stakeholders searching for strategic actions and structures. Another clear feature is that cities-regions are becoming increasingly polycentric conglomerates with different specialisations. It is clear to me that those who enquire about the "North-West City" have already discovered that the creation of a city-region is under way. This is an amalgamation of economies and societies waiting to be politically represented, in other words, to find suitable means of representation both internally and externally. Moreover, the tendency towards a polycentric set-up for the cities-regions reasserts the meaningfulness and the autonomy of cities throughout their creation processes. In a nutshell, I believe we are on the right path and that we should watch carefully what happens elsewhere, paying attention to the good practices for a city-region, among central governments, regional governments and cities. We have already embarked on this journey: banks, infrastructures and enterprises operating in the major utilities sectors are right at the heart of today's political debate in the North-West, and it is not a coincidence they will also dominate all forthcoming discussions.

5. Two final remarks

I would like to make two concluding remarks. As I said before, in order to play a good team game, it is important to define good rules and accommodate different interests, some of which might be less visible. It is also important to consolidate and make the game systematic over time, even if the players change, and enable the exchange and confrontation of different perspectives, without losing sight of the fact that effective public policies can be defined with the input of public and private stakeholders contributing to decisions that can be easily implemented after they have been adopted. In all this, a key element consists in accommodating different interests and consolidating the game over time, even if the players change. This implies a risk: consolidated social networks might become rusty, in other words, they might end up establishing income systems revolving around strong and consolidated economic and political interests that hinder innovation. To contrast this tendency, a recognised antidote, which is also suited to Turin's specific case, was made up of two ingredients. The first was acknowledging the importance of the market, in a city that had seen very little of it, until not long ago. The second was creating a platform where decisions could be publicly compared and argued in terms of their future and wider-ranging consequences, by using consultation practices that avoided overpowering ambitions and were so different from more ancient suffocating planning processes. In so doing, it was also possible to support specific political actions. But have these antidotes been applied and have they worked? I believe they have done it only partially, or at least, they should be replicated with greater attention to the transition we are going through. If, as I said before, it makes sense to assert that both cities and enterprises are important stakeholders in today's economy, on the other hand we cannot obviously assimilate a city to a company. This is the second issue which I would like to indulge upon and which has become more pressing in the face of a potential social crisis. Turin has developed considerable political experience and considerable sensitivity towards identifying and tackling social problems. In taking concrete steps, local councils, service sector associations and organisations, Church institutions and foundations have often tried to better coordinate their actions and set up cooperation networks through procedures that can somehow be likened to development-oriented approaches. Generally speaking, political attention has been kept on the balance between development and fairness, and an integrated vision of these two aspects has been applied to the plurality of projects emerging from within the society. Perhaps, we did and obtained less than what could have been achieved, but it would be a mistake to underestimate the attained goals and the spreading of a political culture that combines both economic efficiency and social fairness.

Although we are faced with considerable general problems, there is at least one favourable condition to take them on board. Gone is the idea that an unregulated market led by its own forces is the best solution for the economy and a consumer-based society. We know today that the society was indeed on the verge of collapse and that the economy was not reaching efficiency. Cities became soon aware of this, and this is why they reacted with strategies intended to mobilise and synchronise public and private resources, while anticipating that social problems would be unloaded on them and that societies would become more and more polarised. This is why the experience accumulated by Turin over time is a cultural resource that should not be dissipated, even if it should result in different practices, and regardless of future stakeholders and political or economic events.

Boundaries, values, and impartiality beyond the Village of Euclid[1]

Carlo Olmo

[1] An earlier version of this essay was presented at the convention "Regioni Globali e Fondazioni Bancarie. Priorità e prospettive" promoted by the Compagnia di San Paolo, which took place in Alba (Cuneo) January 31, 2009.

Working on the limits

Between 1724 and 1728 an elaborated system of organizational criteria introduce one of the most complex operation concerning the boundaries of a city: Paris. In five years 294 new *bornes*, 188 road paths and 1417 buildings[2] see the light. A work, started in 1682 by a pastoral letter of the Archbishop of the French capital[3], whose aim was to put an end to the uncontrolled growth of a city which already defined itself a metropolis: an interdiction that aspired to base the limit (and the norm) on knowledge. This work, which at concerned at the same time the knowledge and the organization of rights and duties, is called *Travail des Limites*[4]. Nonetheless at present day the legitimacy of boundaries can hardly be related and depending upon knowledge alone (despite a scientific literature which, from Von Humboldt's travels on, explored thoroughly all the known territory of description: literary, botanic, geological, anthropological and economical.) To define the borders of a territory is a very sophisticated exercise, which seemed, during the 18th century[5], a constitutive and constitutional prerogative of some kind of power (public or private, juridical or cultural). A key feature of the democratic public power is its uniform organization in electoral districts: the "people" (like in the first French departments during the Revolution) exercise its power because it is made politically homogeneous through the space. The debate on the limits of the departments during the Constituent Assembly preceded a number of discussions on the authorities (at least formally scientific) which are entitled to trace a border[6]. An authority (the Bench and the local Superintendences) is legitimated by a right which is based on and springs from a border. But there is nothing which divide more than a border, even when it is not man-made[7].The attempt, in 1926 in the United States, to introduce a division of the space based on its use (*zoning*) opened a famous judicial case –the *Village of Euclid*[8]. The case originated from the conflictive zoning ordinance: a debate of constitutional rights, because they affect the rights in the materiality of their boundaries. It is a clash between the Common Law (the *police*

---

[2]Jean Pronteau, *Le travail des limites de la ville et faubourgs de Paris*, in <<Annuaire de l'Ecole Pratique des Hautes Etudes>>, IV, septembre 1977-78, p.707-8.

[3]A. Lemaitre, *La Mètropolitée ou l'établissement des villes capitales*, Paris 1682.

[4]J. Pronteau, op.cit. p. 725.

[5]The contemporary reflections on boundaries seems almost overwhelmed by the rhetoric of globalization. Not only there are quite a few walls which were recently built (between Israel and Palestine, between two blocks in Padua, in a square in Turin...), it is also the prevailing judicial dimension of the space that aims at radicalizing borders, which are virtually imperceptible, yet radical in creating exclusion and inequality.

[6]A,N. AD IV bis, *Tableau général de la nouvelle division de la France en départements, arrondissements, communes et justice de paix*, d'après les lois des 28 pluviose an VIII et 8 pluviose an IX.

[7]M. Quaini, *Poiché nulla di quello che la storia sedimenta va perduto*, in <<Quaderni Storici>>, 127, 2008, pp. 55 ff.

[8]J.B. Cullingworth, *The Political Culture of Planning*, Routledge London 1993, p.29-30.

power is a part of it, like zoning was) and the basis of the right of private property; a clash where the organizational power of federal and local authorities' spaces and functions are at stake, and so is their relationship to the individual, hidden in the shade of the property of the land[9].

It may be worth to point out how during the 20th century the border turns from a physical into a judicial element. The two aspects rarely coincide, which helps explaining the poor understanding of the space even among the authorities. When it happens to be the case, (i.e. the wall of the *Fermiers Généraux* shortly before the French Revolution[10], or the Berlin Wall) to build or tear down a wall means to mark a time in History. It also means to attribute new semantic value to a debate, dealt with in the Thorà, on the reconstruction of a physical manufactured entity. It is also through its boundaries that a city reveals its substantial incompatibility with being reduced to a single measure.

The difficult squaring of the grid.

To order the set of values of a space is an instrument of power, as it is clear from Aristotle's *Politics*, where Hippodamus from Miletus (and the well-known grid, named after him, that divides in homologous layouts the space of the city) becomes a political scientist[11].

For the first seventy years of 19th century urban planning, and not the grid, which is one of its possible technical forms, went hand in hand with a city growth that seemed to disregard the spatial values. The endless debate on the relationship between city and countryside; the attempt to formalizing the areas of influence of the city; the bias on those who oppose urban planning, seen as enemies of allegedly universal interests; the misunderstanding between the political action of building a right and the technical action of distributing functions in the space –take for instance city planning and political geography; the illusion that social behaviors can be typified in order to formulate

---

[9]William A. Fischel, *The Economics of Zoning Laws: A Property Rights Approach to American Land Use Control,* John Hopkins University Baltimore 1987, p.46-7.

[10]On the issue of the *Enceinte, cf.* C.Olmo, "La costruzione della città", in R. Gabetti e C.Olmo, *Alle radici dell'architettura contemporanea,* Einaudi Torino 1989, pp. 34-35.

[11]Aristotle, in περι πολιτεια (*Politics* II, and XII 11, 1110b, p.24) referring to Hippodamian plan, identify in the social division of space one of the key instruments of politics. The apparent symmetry between the three classes (craftsmen, workers, warriors) and the three areas of the city constitutes a point of departure, not a constraint, to think about a possible urban governance. Plato, in his πολιτεια (whose subtitle is even more interesting, περι δικαιου πολιτικοσ, on justice, political dialogue) reflects on Hippodamus and his grid, juxtaposing a conservative representation to that division of space, a constitutive element of good governance, rooted in social conservation (*Politics*, vol II, XI. A,b,c).

I owe this idea for this reflection to Luigi Mazza: L. Mazza, *Ippodamo e il piano,* going to press.

predictions and plans: all these aspects do nothing but radicalize a formalist and economicist reductionism of space, especially from 1960s.

The destination and use of the land rarely respect the scheduled timing and form, and in the last decade of the 20th century they produced the collision of two categories of space: risk and prediction. The paradox of a century that opened with an exaltation of risk (of the investment and the investor, its ethic and, later, its esthetic), and which ended – including the first decade of the 21th century- pointing out the consequences of risk (in the financial world) goes hand in hand with the parabola of an *avatar* prediction that is losing its credibility. The unintended oxymoron of an extended city taken as a model for a new historical phase of contemporary cities, best explains the metamorphosis of the city planner, from an intellectual providing norms to a narrator providing interpretations.

The forms of resistance of the space to homologation lies in its relation to some values. It can be an asset value for a citizen who sees the traditional instruments of social mobility (education and work) lose their strength, or for an enterprise whose increasing land income guarantees its own technological development[12]. It can be hereditary, for a family that has to guarantee its children a long-term security[13]; it can be cultural, for a society which learnt to regard its memory (archeological, then historical, and finally the memory of the 20th century) as a vital value[14]; it can be environmental, for a society that discovers (and subsequently tends to turn it into a fetish) the need for every project to be sustainable, and not to be confined to industry, real estate, and tourism. All of the above values keep overlaying, and can help us understand the roots of previous failures and crisis.

In august of 1944 the last owner of the Lingotto dies, and he is not Senator Agnelli. Two thousands squared meters of a plant –the Portolongone for the factory workers of 1921- were never sold by an owner who, defying an executive order/decree law of 1919[15] that was transforming a private factory into a public utility good. That extreme resistance was the umpteenth example of state acquisition of land, back in 1914-1919,which in times of war affected even a company like FIAT. Equal lots of land, evaluated by implacable engineers such as Eugenio Molino, were sold at different prices, depending on the relationship between the seller and the buyer when it came to determine the price. But the list of examples is really endless. Together with the boundaries, it is the

---

[12]In today's paradoxical situation of economic crisis is that banks and companies fight for real estate assets, because they both need property to grant and obtain loans

[13]Osvaldo Raggio, "Costruzione delle fonti e prova: testimoniali, possesso e giurisdizione", in *Quaderni Storici,* 91, 1996, p.136 ff.

[14]C. Olmo, "Una modernità sotto tutela", in *Architettura e Novecento,* going to press.

[15]C. Olmo, "Un teatro di ombre", in (edited by) C. Olmo, *Il Lingotto, 1915-1939,* Allemandi Torino 1994, p.19.

values that stratify the space, that highlight the vital need for a connection between those who "constitute" as an authority a land in a place, and those who define the distribution of the functions in a space that becomes delimited and concrete.

The need for a model to understand the challenge of deciding without an imaginary.
In the era of satellite maps the practice of describing might appear obvious if not idle; nonetheless, few other human activities reveal in such a sharp manner the culture or profession of a citizen or an institution.

The end of the Seventies and the beginning of the Eighties produce a number of description, through the opaque and partial lens of city plans accompanying documents, which superpose on the same cartography up to twenty-five, thirty different patterns. The result is ambiguous: the growing gap between the word (space) and what is meant to be presented as a fact[16] (a territory, a city, a block), and the progressive silence of any form of planning. As a consequence, the future of planning is to become a cognitive, then narrative, even fictionalized activity.

The gradual but steady silence of the vital instrument to affirm a *police power* thus becomes deafening, together with an explosion of "imaginaries" are increasingly produced by descriptions of space which are evocative, but not necessarily reasonable. The use and abuse of the "non-places" –not incidentally, a part of the title of the famous book by Marc Augié- is probably its best-known example, and it might also be the expression of two contrasting needs.

The first may be positive: without imaginaries it is difficult not only to describe but also to create a consensus around a urban or territorial program. Even in our cities, usually it is the imaginaries that take the place of what historians are timidly calling, once again, facts[17].

The problematic aspect, on the other hand, is that the imaginary cannot hide the relentless structuring of functions which takes place in a constructed space: the epistemic root of architecture is to order values (it is not a coincidence that the imaginary is seen as a metaphor –which is all but banal- in those disciplines which connect knowledge[18], and organize it into a hierarchy: IT, biology, music).

---

[16]Bernard Lepetit, "In presenza del luogo stesso… Pratiche dotte e identificazione degli spazi alla fine del XVIII secolo", in *Quaderni Storici*, 90, 1995, p. 657.
[17]Simona Cerutti e Gianna Pomata,"Premessa a Fatti: storia dell'evidenza empirica", in *Quaderni Storici*, 3, 2001, p.647ff.
[18]The delicate shift from the imaginaries as a vision to the metaphor as an utterance, and to the interaction (not the substitution) of facts, are the core of Paul Ricoeur's reflection between 1961 and 1975 (cf. Elena Bugaite, *Linguaggio e azione nelle opere di Paul Ricoeur tra 1961 e 1975*, Pontificia Università Gregoriana 2002.
[19]The most interesting source is the "Extramuros" program, coordinated by Annie Fourcat, Emmanuel Belanger and Mathieu Flonneau: *Une histoire croisée de Paris et des banlieues à l'époque contempiranine*s, from September 2005, then *Paris/Banlieus, Conflicts et solidarietétés*, Creaphis Editions, Paris 2007.

The ordering and, especially, hierarchy process between functions and spaces takes place even spontaneously: the recurring metaphor of the explosion to describe the social hardship and exclusion of the *banlieues* in Paris[19] might reflects the poverty of today's imaginaries, and their unavoidable ideological roots.

A society keeps evolving even without descriptions and explicit imaginaries, consolidating implicit geographies and pre-existent social orders. To have a physical evidence of it, it is enough to drive along the state highways between alba and Bra, or Verona and Mantua, or take the mountain highway between Biella and Romagnano Sesia. A landscape with its own icon, even though it is not a fancy one: the industrial plant. The symbol of the indifference to architecture and the place owned by the investor (essentially not interested in the context, and only looking at an indifferent space that can perform productive as well as tertiary activities, and most of all that represents a real estate asset).

This idea of the territory as a "receptacle" clashes almost immediately with the limited nature of the space, originating conflicts (between functions, actors, and values) and bring about nostalgias: to use the image of the traveler, lifting the gaze to admire the historical settlement of Santa Vittoria d'Alba, the Sacro Monte of Varallo, the... *Virgilian* confluence between the Po and Mincio rivers. Today's architecture and urban planning are facing a very delicate epistemic situation. The poor representation of urban facts produce a singular paradox: codification (that is the final result of the process leading from the rite to the norm) becomes a point of departure of several social actions. First there is the codification, then the recognition of a code which is supposed to order the relationship between the facts, and finally the creation of a rite (it does not matter whether it persuades or strengthen social roles). It is a process that must be thoroughly discussed, and not only at a political level.

In form of possible conclusions.

If the borders, the values, the imaginaries stratify spaces which are possibly made invisible -yet not less real- by the law, how can we not cry for, or hide into, relativistic imaginaries and strict economic and social hierarchies?

I would like to present three key points of a necessarily provisional debate.

The first is the relationship between morphology and architectural figures. The place of a possible reunion between different actors, bearers of different rights and interests, in the presence of a limited good such as space, can still be found in morphology. By this term I mean not only a design that takes the context into account, but one that first of

---

[20] Another term which we could borrow from anthropology is *kinship*. A morphology that is reduced to a mere interpreting of facts would entirely lose its meaning, even its persuasive rhetorical nature.

all makes hypothesis, and then defines the relationships between diverse architectures, and between architecture and space (be it public or private). A previous clarification: morphology cannot really be seen as an result[20]: the responsibility for the shape is, not only formally, of the person who sign the project.

Can morphology constitute a chain of facts, without falling in linguistic *glissements*? Can it highlight and make the connections between values, interests, and actors transparent, can it restore legitimacy to the decision, making it less arbitrary, without stumbling on the exclusively functional principle of equilibrium[21]? Architecture is a unique database of collective representations and of the equilibrium in the time of the construction of use. But even these collective representations seem to be affected by the crisis of empirical evidence of the facts, and dissolve the space in procedures, images, productions of norms[22]. Morphology then is reduced to a sharing of norms and procedures, but by doing so it loses meaning and denies the *enchassment gérarchique* which is always established by a constructed architecture[23].

The real problem is that almost every actor of today's culture is the most distant from the morphologic culture in, basically because they think in terms of fences, also spatial ones: they are subjects mainly interested in a symbolic architecture, a monument to be preserved, a heritage to be promoted in other ways. Therefore we can design (or just think of designing) a morphology only if we accept its dynamic nature: a *jeu d'échelles* which refuses to determine a partition between negotiation and construction[24], but also a *jeu de possibiles*[25], generated by the social production of the space. Unbalanced systems, which focus on models rather than on cynical agreements between actors. Between a social... thermostatics and the absolute relativization of values, an idea of morphology as the acknowledgment of a public interest not abandoned to different and separated spaces might at least be experimented.

Impartiality. If we want this concept to emerge, it is vital to foster associations and institutions which are not based on authority (applying a rule or deciding a destination). An unbiased view in politics is a rare jewel: and it is not a coincidence. This process might be facilitated by a perception of the risk entailed by a development without spaces of confrontation (and a space where the processes and results can be simulated

---

[21]The most intelligent critic of this type of reductionsim is still Gorge Dumézil, *Mythe et épopée. L'idéologie des trois fonctions dans les épopées des peuples indo-européens.*
[22]Gallimard Paris 1968, Einaudi Torino 1982.
[23]An example of this vision is Angelo Torre, "La genesi dello spazio: il miracolo dell'Ostia (24Asti 10 maggio 1718)", in *Quaderni Storici*, 125, p. 355 ff.
[25]C. Olmo, Introduction of "Morfologie urbane", *Quaderni Storici* n.125, p.344.
(Edited by) Jacques Revel, *Jeux d'échelles*, EHESS Paris 1996.
Francio Jacob, *Le jeu des possibles*, Fayard Paris 1981.

and compared). Impartiality definitely risks to be affected by the interruption of the convergence, but the contemporary erosion of limited resources, such as the soil, is questioning the very model of development.

Assistance. An impartial view is not accomplished by replacing the actors (institutions, businesses, policies). This must remain an insurmountable limit, if we wish to be ironic, in the culture of the rule and its application, of sanction and remission, produced the territory –or the landscape- of the anthropized countryside and the extended city. If we want to invert the trend of isolated objects (the concepts of good or bad looking then become mere aesthetic categories) or artificial barriers (carrier of inequality at all levels, from neglected and uneven sidewalks to infrastructures conceived as if they were mere connections between two points) we have to focus on the decisive process of design and evaluation/ of a sustainability which is not only environmental, but also spatial. To be more precise, the key issue is a different use of space, that has to be recognized as a non reproducible good. To assist is an ancient verb. The most beautiful discussion on its meaning is probably Karl Barth's comment to Saint Paul's Epistle to the Romans: "Did we say too much? Yes, and too little indeed! How could it be possible not to say too much when we talk about our hope, and too little when we talk about its fulfillment?... Let us assist the new-made man so that he can be, or it will be chaos and disorder"[26].

Assistance is a also close to terms –tolerance and mildness- widely used by Norberto Bobbio in its *Filosofia Politica,* and it designs a path which is rooted in dialectics, even when contrasting. At the same time it excludes any possible tyranny of the values (and their bearers): be they economic and cultural, aimed at preserving or enhancing a space.

In order to go beyond a subjective theory of values, it is not enough to hide the bearers of a value, whose interests provide the points of view and the point of connection of the evaluating activity. No one can evaluate without devaluating, revaluating, and enhancing the value of something. The intense desire for exclusivity is almost implicit in the same argumentations given to support a value. Only a process which provide tolerance, and at the same time an authority not legitimated by a "norm", can lead to a fulfillment, in Barth's words (and architecture is one of the most definitive forms of fulfillment), which is really mild, but really strong, precisely because it is open and capable of adapting.

There is an ongoing debate on the quality of the constructed environment, seen as a vital resource for the identity of a place and the success of a policy. If the quality of a single architecture is the crossroad of a collective process (made of imaginaries,

---

[26]Karl Barth, *L'Epistola ai Romani* (1954), Feltrinelli Milano 2006, p. 370-1.

norms, economies) and an individual action, then the quality of a constructed environment can be dealt with only in two ways. First of all the slow historical stratification of the signs, and a process of convergence on common goals, and secondly accompanying the process which leads the projects into becoming works, along an *iter* where the only non-negotiable things are the involvement of the actors and the contextual nature of any architecture (be it a museum, an infrastructure or a hospital).

Morphology, impartiality, assistance might all give –and it is not a marginal added value- a deeper meaning to the concept of *utilitas*, that, from Vitruvius on, goes hand in hand with every reflection on what the Res Aedificatoria must be. Maybe even more for those who manipulate a public good such as space, and for all of us, who hope to live, study, be treated, have fun in designed and constructed spaces, accessible and comfortable.

AUTHOR BIOGRAPHIES

Gustavo AMBROSINI (1965), has a degree and PhD at the Faculty of Architecture at Turin Polytechnic, where he now works as a university researcher and professor of architectural design.
He taught at Graduat Superior en Paisatgisme, ETSAB Barcelona (2006) and coordinated international workshops (with Tsinghua University, Beijing and Konkuk University, Seoul, 2008). He carries out research on issues of landscape and urban design. He is founder and partner of Negozio Blu Associates Architects.

Paolo ANTONELLI (1978), architect and PhD in architecture and building design at the Turin Polytechnic with a thesis that investigates the relationship between the economy and form in contemporary practices of transformation. Since 2001 working with various firms in Turin, and since 2003 has held teaching and research positions at the Turin Polytechnic. Since 2007, he has been a consultant in projects for the Metropolitan Urban Center.

Alessandro ARMANDO (1974), architect, conducts research at the Department of Architectural and Industrial Design of Turin Polytechnic. As a lecturer, he teaches architectural design at the Faculty of Architecture at the same university. He received his doctorate in architecture and building design in 2005 and since the same year he has been a consultant in projects for the Metropolitan Urban Center in Turin. He has just published *La Soglia dell'arte* [The threshold of art] (Seb 27, 2009).

Marco BARBIERI (1981), architect, is doing a PhD in Environment and Territory (Planning and Local Development) at the Inter-university Department of Territorial Studies and Planning at the Turin Polytechnic. His research is in relation to polycentric territorial forms of organization found in the Italian sub-regional scales, working with educational activities concerning the processes of transformation in the landscapes of Piedmont. He performs professional work in Cuneo.

Liliana BAZZANELLA (1944), is a Professor of Architectural Technology and Director of the Department of Architectural and Industrial Design at the Turin Polytechnic. She served on numerous governing bodies of the University, including supervision and management boards. She acted as head of the management for building projects of the University. She has conducted funded research at national and European levels, commissioned and coordinated by local and regional authorities, exploring areas of interdisciplinary dialogue on issues of sustainability and built landscapes that have always been reflected in educational level, in inter-project workshops and experiences.

Mauro BERTA (1972), architect and PhD in architecture and building design, teaches architectural design at the Turin Polytechnic where he also researches. He has published essays and articles on numerous books and magazines, at national and international levels and has co-edited with Gustavo Ambrosini *Paesaggi a molte velocità* [Landscapes at Varying Speed] (Meltemi, 2004). He performs professional work as a designer, working both public spaces and housing, and as a consultant to carry out feasibility studies and to write documents that support decision making processes.

Francesca CAMORALI (1978), architect and PhD in architecture and building design at the Turin Polytechnic, where she runs from 2003 teaching and research. Since 2005 she has been a consultant in projects for the Metropolitan Urban Center, where she works on issues of contemporary urban and territorial transformations. Among the publications are *Appunti per una metodologia di ricerca* [Notes for a Research Method] (Meltemi 2004), *Tra "gronda" e autostrada. Il progetto Tangenziale est* [Between the "Gutter" and the Highway. Ring road project](Marsilio 2004), *Mirafiori. Dalla disintegrazione della fabbrica all'integrazione nella città* [Mirafiori. From the disintegration of the factory to integration in the city] (Electa 2008).

Massimo CROTTI (1963), is an architect and researcher in urban and architectural design at the Turin Polytechnic, where he teaches at the Faculty of Architecture and conducts research at the Department of Architectural and Industrial Design. He was adjunct professor at the Ecole Nationale Superieure d'Architecture de Lyon. With the studio crotti + forsans architects, he works in Italy and France, mainly dealing with themes of urban regeneration and landscape, architecture and restoration of heritage buildings (square and parking in Valdo Fusi, restructuring of the downtown district in Cascina Roccafranca in Turin, redevelopment of the railway in Caselle Torinese, City University of Reconciliation in Grugliasco).

Antonio DE ROSSI (1965), is professor of architectural and urban design at the Turin Polytechnic and deputy director of the Metropolitan Urban Center. He deals with transformations of the territory and of the contemporary landscape and urban design. The various publications include the books *Linee nel paesaggio* [Lines in the Landscape] (Utet 1999), *Atlante dei paesaggi costruiti* [Atlas of constructed landscapes] (Blu ed. 2002), *Architettura alpina moderna in Piemonte e Valle d'Aosta* [Modern Architecture in Piedmont and Alpine Valle d'Aosta] (Allemandi 2005), *Turin 1980-2011, The transformation and its images* (Allemandi 2006).

Andrea DELPIANO (1977), architect and PhD in architecture and building design. He teaches architectural design at the Faculty of Architecture of the Turin Polytechnic. He studies the transformation in settlement for the Department of Architectural and Industrial Design. Performs professional work with Enrico Boffa, mainly dealing with regeneration projects in the agricultural landscape.

Roberto DINI (1977), architect and PhD in architecture and building design at the Politecnico di Torino, where since 2007 he is a Research Fellow. For the same university he participated in several research agreements with local government on issues of territory on a large scale. He also deals with research on the topics of recent transformations of land and mountain scenery within the IAM (Institute of Mountain Architecture) of the Turin Polytechnic.

Giovanni DURBIANO (1966), is associate professor of architectural design at the Politecnico di Torino. His publications include: *I "Nuovi Maestri". Architetti tra politica e cultura nell'Italia del dopoguerra* [The "New Masters". Architects of politics and culture in postwar Italy] (Marsilio 2000), *Paesaggio e architettura nell'Italia contemporanea* [Landscape in contemporary architecture] (Donzelli 2003), *Turin 1980-2011, The transformation and its images* (Allemandi 2006).

Carlo GIAMMARCO (1940), is professor of architectural design and urban planning at the Turin Polytechnic. He has directed for four years the Department of Architecture and coordinated the Ph.D. in Architecture and Building Design. He has been a member of the governing bodies of the university and various national and international scientific committees. He has conducted research funded by national and local institutions, developing methodological contributions of reflection and experimentation in project on the innovative roles of architectural design in urban and territorial transformation processes.

Mattia GIUSIANO (1981), graduated with honors from the Turin Polytechnic in 2006. In the same year he began a PhD at the Department of Architectural and Industrial Design, where he conducts research on recent transformations in Piedmont investigating in particular the relationship between settlements, environment and infrastructure. Since 2006, he performs professional work in collaboration with various firms dealing mainly with architecture and urban transformations.

Davide ROLFO (1969), conducts research in the fields of design for large areas and takes the course "Architecture and settled landscapes" at the Turin Polytechnic. He has published essays and articles in Italy and abroad and is secretary of the Editorial Office of the magazine "Atti e Rassegna Tecnica della Società degli Ingegneri e degli Architetti in Torino" [Technical Acts and Reviews of the Society of Engineers and Architects in Turin] He performs design activities in Turin.

Pubblished by
LISt Lab Laboratorio
Internazionale editoriale
SPAIN
Calle Ferlandina,53
08001-E, Barcelona
ITALY
Piazza Lodron, 9
38100-IT, Trento
info@listlab.eu
www.listlab.eu
www.momboo.net

Edited by
Antonio De Rossi

Editing supervisor
Alessandro Armando

Editorial Coordination
Pino Scaglione

Translation
Stefania Contarino
Giulia Canestrari

Art Director
Massimiliano Scaglione

Graphic Design
Harry Scheihing

Printing
Printer Trento

ISBN 978-88-95623-29-0

Printed and bounded in European Union,
October 2009

The cartographic images and the diagrams of the
Part III, "Geographies", have been designed by the
authors of the related essays, except for different
indications. The coordination and recollection
of the iconographic materials are by Alessandro
Armando and Francesca Camorali. Special thanks
to: Arnaldo Bagnasco, Giuseppe Dematteis, Carlo
Olmo, Bernardo Secchi and Martins Rudzitis author
of Portishead Dummy Font (part II and III)

The book was made possible by funds MIUR
Program (national interest) year 2006 "Mobility
infrastructures and construction of the metropolitan
land: guidelines for the integrated project"
(National Coordinator Bernardo Secchi)

International Sales and Promotion
ACTAR D
Roca i Batlle, 2
08023-E Barcelona
T: +34 934174993
F: +34 934186707
office@actar-d.com
www.actar-d.com

ACTAR D USA
158 Lafayette Street 5th Fl.
New York, NY 10013 (USA)
officeusa@actar-d.com
www.actar-d.com

LISt Lab is an editorial workshop, set in Barcelona,
works on the contemporary issues.
List not only publishes, but also researches,
proposes, endeawour, promotes, produces,
creates networks